Uncivil Wars

Uncivil

JOE R. AND TERESA LOZANO LONG SERIES IN
LATIN AMERICAN AND LATINO ART AND CULTURE

Wars

ELENA GARRO, OCTAVIO PAZ, AND THE
BATTLE FOR CULTURAL MEMORY

Sandra Messinger Cypess

UNIVERSITY OF TEXAS PRESS AUSTIN

Requests for permission to reproduce material
from this work should be sent to:
Permissions
University of Texas Press
P.O. Box 7819
Austin, TX 78713-7819
utpress.utexas.edu/about/book-permissions

The paper used in this book meets the minimum requirements
of ANSI/NISO Z39.48-1992 (R1997) (Permanence of Paper). ∞

Library of Congress Cataloging-in-Publication Data

Cypess, Sandra Messinger.
    Uncivil wars : Elena Garro, Octavio Paz, and the battle for
cultural memory / by Sandra Messinger Cypess. — 1st ed.
            p.   cm. — (Joe R. and Teresa Lozano Long series
in Latin American and Latino art and culture)
    Includes bibliographical references and index.
    ISBN 978-0-292-75428-7

    1. Garro, Elena—Criticism and interpretation. 2. Paz, Octavio,
1914–1998—Criticism and interpretation. 3. National characteristics,
Mexican, in literature. 4. Collective memory—Mexico. I. Title.
    PQ7297.G3585Z64   2012
    868'.6409—dc23   2012010950

First paperback printing, 2013

DEDICATED TO

Raymond (everyone knows why)
and to Aaron and Leah, Josh and Rebecca, and their
wonderful contributions to our happiness:

Benjamin
Joey
Shoshana
Sally
Hadassah
David

CONTENTS

"The difficult part is taking the first step."
ELENA GARRO
Reencuentro de personajes (Reunion of Characters)

"I am the shadow my words cast."
OCTAVIO PAZ
"A Draft of Shadows" (*The Collected Poems of
Octavio Paz, 1957–1987*, trans. Eliot Weinberger)

PREFACE

FOR MANY YEARS I CONSIDERED EXPLORING the roles of Elena Garro and Octavio Paz in formulating and transmitting the cultural memory of Mexico during the second part of the twentieth century. The inspiration derived in part from my earlier study of the historical figure of the indigenous woman, La Malinche, and how she was portrayed in Mexican literature and culture through the ages, from the initial chronicles to contemporary literary expressions. It seemed to me that everyone—or perhaps almost everyone—dealing with the topic quoted Octavio Paz's influential essay "Los hijos de la Malinche" (The Sons of Malinche) to discuss the impact and relevance of that historical figure for Mexican ethnic identity. Most readers and critics, however, ignored the subtle commentary of Elena Garro on the same topic (if they even knew that she had attempted such a response). By contrast, my reading suggests that Garro was actually in debate with Paz when she wrote her now canonical short story "La culpa es de los tlaxcaltecas" (It's the Fault of the Tlaxcaltecas). It offers a commentary not only on Mexican ethnic identity but also on gender relationships, an issue that Paz often neglected.

The ideas and esthetic expressions of Garro and Paz project varying perspectives on Mexican cultural memory—both what is recalled and "memorialized" and what is ignored and forgotten. What is poignant and yet paradoxical in the "Garro and Paz story" is that they each had so much to offer to Mexican culture, yet their personal and professional trajectories were so divergent. A case in point: after the traumatic Tlatelelolco Massacre of 1968, Paz became a figurehead for the protesting Mexican students, who called him "El padrino" (the godfather), while Garro was marginalized and forced into exile by both governmental and literary communities for her supposedly inappropriate actions. In this book I document the two writers' war of words, in which they explore in different ways similar themes that cover esthetic, erotic, and ethical questions as well as issues of individual and national identity. Paz was certainly the "go-to" intellectual for any number of esthetic, philosophical, political, and poetic topics in the twentieth century, while Garro's voice was muted, overshadowed by recurring personal issues. Her difficult personal life, spent in exile and marked by financial and psychological stresses, often clouded the vibrant and coherent literary texts that she created. Despite the obstacles, Garro contributed to the Latin American canon three virtuoso texts in three different genres: *Los recuerdos del porvenir* (translated as *Recollections of Things to Come*), "La culpa es de los tlaxcaltecas," and *Un hogar sólido* (A Solid Home). Despite such evaluations by scholars, many of her works have yet to be translated and thus are unknown to an international public.

Paz, in contrast, was lionized, interviewed, translated, and showered with prestigious awards, including the Nobel Prize in 1990. He was recognized early as one of the outstanding poets and essayists of the twentieth century. When he died in April 1998, his funeral justifiably was an event of national import. It was attended by thousands, including Mexican president Ernesto Zedillo, who called him a "universal Mexican" (*New York Times*, April 21, 1998). Paz was mourned by the intellectual elite as well as by average citizens. When Garro died a few months later, in August 1998, her funeral understandably did not occasion the same highly publicized national state of grief caused by Paz's death, although a leader did comment on the meaning of her loss to the world of letters. As reported by the *New York Times* on August 25, 1998, the president of the National Council for Culture and the Arts in Mexico, Rafael Tovar y de Teresa, singled out Garro as one of the three most important female writers of Mexican letters, along with the seventeenth-century nun and poet Sor Juana Inés de la Cruz and Rosario Castellanos (1925–1974), a contemporary of Paz and Garro.

Garro's contributions to cultural memory provide a reckoning of the terrible impact of machismo in Mexican society. She critiqued the negativities of a patriarchal culture throughout her writings, especially in a number of novels published after 1980: *Testimonios sobre Mariana* (Testimonies about Mariana, 1981) and *Mi hermanita Magdalena* (My Little Sister Magdalena, 1998). Although it is easy to read these novels as romans à clef within the genre of autobiography, I suggest that they are more like political statements symptomatic of the troubled connection that Garro felt with the realities of Mexican culture than a vengeful attempt to discredit Paz. Garro is not so much expending her literary energies out of a personal need for retribution as articulating in her own work the complaints and resentments of Mexican women in general. She had dealt with these issues as far back as her initial writings of the 1950s and 1960s, which were created while she was still married to Paz and were encouraged by him, like her early plays and *Los recuerdos del porvenir*. As is clearly evident in the feminist readings of those early works, Garro presents a picture of Mexican womanhood within the context of the patriarchy. It was not her bitter divorce from Paz that brought her to feminism and to harsh criticism of one male member of this society. On the contrary, her works have always explored gender relations and the unequal power relations that characterize Mexican society. Consequently, in a subversion of the traditional use of the muse figure as a "female" who inspires a male writer, Paz instead became the "muse" for Garro: the object of *her* artistic gaze.

Although most of the creative production of Octavio Paz can be found in English versions, many of the works of Elena Garro have not yet been translated. At the first mention of each work I give the Spanish title and its English translation (italicized only if the translation has been published). Thereafter I refer to works in translation by their English titles. All translations of citations from untranslated works by Garro and Paz as well as from other sources are my own.

Working on this research project and completing the manuscript led me to explore many books and essays. More importantly, I enjoyed and benefited from conversations and correspondence with numerous colleagues with similar interests. If I have forgotten anyone or committed other acts of omission throughout the text, I ask for understanding and pardon. I have to thank so many people for their generosity in sharing their thoughts and comments with me—Tanya Huntington Hyde, Carola Marx Kaplan, Joan Korenman, José María Naharro-Calderón, Enrico Mario Santí, Rita Sparrow Mall, Anthony Stanton, Vicky Unruh, and Mary Kay Vaughan. Pat Herron of the University of Maryland Library and the entire staff of the Interlibrary Loan Department, especially Charles Wright, helped me to find many of the resources that enriched my understanding of Garro, Paz, and Mexican culture. Conversations with Regina Harrison, Roberta Lavine, Eyda Merediz, Ana Patricia Rodríguez, and Rochelle Messinger Strauss enabled me to clarify the points I hoped to communicate. Lucía Melgar's own written work on Elena Garro and our personal conversations have also been invaluable. Rebecca Schaefer Cypess applied her excellent editorial skills to key chapters. A few treasured friends read every word. A historian and educator by training, Paul Flaum examined the chapters to make sure that what I was saying would be clear and jargon-free. Elisabeth Guerrero read chapters at different stages of development and was always supportive, offering perceptive and useful observations. My deep appreciation also goes to a dear long-time colleague, Priscilla Meléndez, whose careful evaluation of the manuscript helped me to improve it in so many ways. I also appreciate the long-standing support of Theresa May of the University of Texas Press, whose encouragement of my work goes back a long way. Many thanks go to Kathy Lewis for her painstaking editing of the manuscript; she worked assiduously to maintain clarity and coherence. Don Luis Leal, a mentor from the time I met him in 1964 until his death in 2010, listened carefully when I first outlined my project to him during my 2000 sabbatical and gave constant encouragement and advice, as did a valued colleague and greatly admired writer, José Emilio Pacheco. And as always, above all, my husband, Raymond Cypess, pored over every word more than once, urging me continuously to tell this story of another couple whose lives in no way reflect our own companionship and enduring alliance.

Uncivil Wars

"I am and I was in many eyes. I am only memory
and the memory that one has of me."

ELENA GARRO
Recollections of Things to Come

INTRODUCTION

THIS BOOK DEVELOPED FROM MY ONGOING study of the texts of Elena Garro
(1916–1998), which began at a time when she was still considered a persona
non grata in Latin American studies. Garro was not yet acknowledged as an
author of status in Latin America; she had received no international prizes,
and her works were certainly not canonical within Latin American literary
circles. I don't recall when I first read her narrative, but I know it was not in
a formal setting such as graduate school. It was after reading *Los recuerdos del
porvenir* (published in 1963 and translated in 1969 as *Recollections of Things to
Come*) and then the short story "La culpa es de los tlaxcaltecas" (It's the Fault
of the Tlaxcaltecas) from the collection *La semana de colores* (The Week of
Colors, 1964) that I began to formulate my ideas about the Malinche paradigm in general and Garro's contributions in particular.[1] Garro's many novels,
short stories, and plays were and continue to be an important guide for me in
exploring ideas about gender, ethnicity, and cultural memory. She offered an
alternative vision of the official narrative of her national history and what it
meant to be "Mexican."

In contrast to Garro's omission from the literary canon, I can remember
clearly the class with Don Luis Leal (1907–2010) at the University of Illi-
nois in which I first read the essays of Octavio Paz (1914–1998). Despite the
difficulties of dealing with the infamous word *chingada* (a term with many

meanings, including "the raped one") that was so daringly discussed in the chapter "The Sons of Malinche" from *The Labyrinth of Solitude*, Don Luis conveyed the widely held view that Paz was the literary successor of Alfonso Reyes (1889–1959), the great Mexican intellectual of the first half of the twentieth century. By the late sixties, Paz was being widely read in universities and was admired for his poetry and essays. Today he is internationally recognized as one of the major figures in the rich tradition of Latin American writers—a great poet in the pantheon that includes Pablo Neruda and César Vallejo; a consummate essayist in the tradition of Reyes and the Spaniard José Ortega y Gasset (1883–1955); and a diplomat as well. By the time of his death in 1998, Paz was the most dominant cultural voice in Mexico, winner in 1990 of the only Nobel Prize in Literature (and only the third Nobel Prize of any kind) awarded to a Mexican.

Critical references to Paz's work consistently have used the superlative. George Gordon Wing wrote in *Books Abroad* in 1973: that "[n]o living essayist in the Hispanic world can match the richness and variety of Octavio Paz's thought nor the encyclopedic range of his erudition. Not only has he made original contributions in the fields of esthetics, anthropology and comparative religion, but also in his critical essays on literature, art, and the film he has drawn on these fields and a dozen more" (41). Commenting after Paz's death, Enrique Krauze, a member of the *Vuelta* group and therefore part of Paz's inner circle, ventured that Paz "was the greatest and most generous of Mexican writers. No one wrote as much as Octavio Paz about Mexico's writers and artists" ("The Sun," 99). The influence of Paz on writers is still evident today, and he is considered to be the literary antecedent of such prominent Mexican authors as Carlos Fuentes, Gabriel Zaid, Carlos Monsiváis, Homero Aridjis, and José Emilio Pacheco (Krauze, "The Sun," 99). Besides Paz's influence on writers, his position as editor-in-chief of the literary journal *Plural* (1971–1976) and then as founder and director of its successor, *Vuelta*, led to his reputation as "el último 'cacique cultural'" (the last cultural boss) of the twentieth century (Martínez, "Los caciques culturales," 29). "Cacique"—a word far more powerful than "boss"—implies the ability to make decisions about who will be published and who will be read. Paz certainly is ascribed that power. Elena Garro, his first wife, often found it difficult to publish after their divorce; she and others attributed those problems to Paz and his circle.[2] Whether Paz directly or indirectly interceded against her is difficult to prove. Nevertheless, it is conceivable that members of the Mexican intelligentsia might wish to avoid offending him and therefore rejected the work of his ex-wife.

Paz and Garro had been married in 1937; had a daughter, Helena, in 1939; and were divorced in 1959.[3] Their married life was conflictive and marked by numerous liaisons that generated not only gossip but also literary works in which they and their lovers appear as characters. The novels of the Argentines José Bianco and Adolfo Bioy Casares, who met the couple in Paris in the forties, portray characters who are identified with Garro and Paz.[4] Initially Paz was quite the conventional Mexican husband, expecting his wife to play the role of a traditional housewife within the private sphere of the home, as documented in his letters to Garro archived in the Princeton Library. He later encouraged her to participate in his experimental troupe Poesía en Voz Alta.[5] Paz praised her first novel, *Los recuerdos del porvenir*, calling it one of the best novels of the time.[6] Soon after that brief pacific interlude of mutual recognition, their relationship became increasingly uncivil. They followed very different paths, geographically, politically, and literarily.

As a member of the diplomatic corps of Mexico, Paz was sent to a number of European and Asian venues. During his assignment in India, which began in 1962, he met and married his second wife, Marie José Tramini, who could be seen as a contrast to the volatile and challenging Elena Garro. Garro never remarried, but she and her daughter were constantly together in their travails and travels. She suffered an unofficial exile, living outside of Mexico from 1972 until 1993, in fear of retribution for her conflictive role in the student uprisings of 1968, which culminated in many deaths at the Plaza de Tlatelolco.[7]

In 1968 Paz returned home from his "official exile" as a diplomat in India, having renounced his position in protest against the government's role in the 1968 Tlatelolco Massacre. He became a formidable figure in Mexican cultural life, an icon whose ideas and observations on all aspects of political and esthetic topics were published in his own journals and in the essays that he wrote for other Mexican and international venues. In 1990 he was awarded the Nobel Prize, the ultimate recognition of his significance in international circles.

In contrast to the superlatives and literary accolades heaped upon Octavio Paz, Elena Garro has suffered from what Lucía Melgar has called a "black legend" (*Writing Dark Times*, 2). Even Garro's most ardent supporters—writers like Emilio Carballido and Christopher Domínguez and friendly critics like Melgar and Gabriela Mora—acknowledged that she was a difficult person with whom to interact and that she had offended members of both the political and intellectual elite of Mexico with her outspoken ideas about the treatment of Indians and the interference of intellectuals in the student uprising of 1968. Her stormy relationship with Paz and her flouting of social conventions also compromised her literary recognition. Because of these extraliterary factors that hampered the acceptance of her work for publication and translation, Garro is not well known beyond the borders of Mexico, except in some U.S. academic communities. A review of the bibliographic database of the Modern Language Association reveals that 286 studies of her work had appeared in print by 2009. Most of the critical material focusing on Garro has emerged because of the increased involvement of feminist literary critics, a situation with parallels to other female writers of her generation. Argentina's Silvina Ocampo and Griselda Gambaro, Uruguay's Armonía Somers, and Mexico's Rosario Castellanos are prime examples. Not unexpectedly, Paz is the subject of 1,014 entries, reflecting his stature in the academic world.

As an essayist, Paz dealt with such diverse issues as Aztec art, Tantric Buddhism, Mexican politics, neo-Platonic philosophy, economic reform, avant-garde poetry, structuralist anthropology, utopian socialism, the dissident movement in the Soviet Union, sexuality, and eroticism. *El laberinto de la soledad* (translated as *The Labyrinth of Solitude*) is considered one of the most influential studies of Mexican character and thought and is still his most famous essay, translated into numerous languages. Also translated and widely read are his politically oriented essays—*Posdata* (translated as *The Other Mexico: Critique of the Pyramid*, 1970), *Corriente alterna* (Alternating Current, 1967), and *El ogro filantrópico* (The Philanthropic Ogre, 1979)—as well as those dealing with esthetic issues, such as *El arco y la lira* (1956; translated as *The Bow and the Lyre*, 1973) and *Los hijos del limo: Del romanticismo a la vanguardia* (Children of the Mire, 1974), which explores the history of modern poetry from German Romanticism to the avant-garde movements of the 1960s. His critical study is also significant for its erudition; *Sor Juana Inés de la Cruz o las trampas de la fe* (translated as *Sor Juana or the Traps of Faith*, 1982), which focuses on the Tenth Muse of Mexican letters, is considered a tour de force. His poetry has also found excellent translators, including one of his most important poems, "Piedra de sol" (*Sunstone*, 1957), which blends Aztec and classical European mythologies within the circular form that recalls the famous Aztec calendar stone. English readers may also find *¿Águila o sol?* (*Eagle or Sun?* 1951) as well as *The Collected Poems of Octavio Paz, 1957–1987* in a bilingual edition with translations by respected translators Eliot Weinberger, Elizabeth Bishop, and Paul Blackburn.

Whereas Paz's poetry and essay collections are available in most languages of the world, few texts by Garro's have been translated into English: of her ten novels only *Recollections of Things to Come* is available in a translation from 1969, along with *First Love & Look for My Obituary: Two Novellas*, the short stories "It's the Fault of the Tlaxcaltecas" and "The Day We Were Dogs" from *La semana de colores* (1964), and three plays: *A Solid Home*, *The Dogs*, and *The Tree*.[8] Thus one of my goals is to introduce the work of Elena Garro to a greater audience that cannot easily access her work in Spanish.[9] Although both Garro and Paz explored the role of time and indigenous myth in Mexican life as well as the impact of historical events on the lives of Mexicans, her themes are primarily centered on power and gender relations within the context of the patriarchy and machismo.

Like many Mexican women in real life and in her own texts, Garro considered herself a victim of the patriarchy. Her work was a way to document and criticize the inequalities and obstacles that she suffered as a woman. Her identity as the wife of Paz at first was a difficult role to accept, as she reveals in her memoir about the first year of their married life, *Memorias de España 1937* (Memoirs of Spain 1937). Their ideological differences became acute in that first year of marriage, which was spent in the war zone of the Spanish Civil War. How ironic it was to start their life as newlyweds while all around them were scenes of battles, destruction, violence, and death. Paz had been invited to Spain as one of the delegates to the Second International Congress of Antifascist Writers for the Defense of Culture and was touted as one of the up-and-coming writers of Latin America. Garro was there only because she was the wife of the young poet and was often an embarrassment to Paz because she did not follow the script of the silent and obedient wife. Although their marriage continued for decades after their return from Spain, they would never seem to be on the same page regarding the political and personal issues of importance to the Mexican people. After their divorce, Garro's identity was still tied to Paz in many references to her: she was now his ex-wife.

I realize that in bringing Paz and Garro together within a single critical work I may be accused of substantiating what Elena Poniatowska complained about in *Las siete cabritas*: "Elena Garro has remained so intertwined with Octavio Paz that many times it is difficult to separate her work and life from the name of the poet. 'Ah, the one who was the wife of Paz' is a phrase that seems to form part of her identity" (111).[10]

In presenting a book on both Paz and Garro, I wish to challenge the stereotype implied in that comment. I suggest that Garro's role as an intellectual and as a creative influence on Mexican culture should be acknowledged and reevaluated independently of her difficult relationship with Paz and her erratic personality. My analytical study of their work on similar themes will allow the reader to determine whether she was really just the "wife of Paz" or worthy of being considered one of the important independent agents of cultural memory in Mexico, offering unorthodox readings of the past and of contemporary political and intellectual positions on national history and identity.

One way to appreciate the undervalued writings of Garro is to compare her work and ideas with those of her more recognized former husband. In the following chapters I place these two great writers in conversation with each other and thus introduce to a wider audience the role of Elena Garro in formulating oppositional narratives of Mexican national history. This dialogical approach reflects ideas articulated by Santiago Castro-Gómez in an essay on "Traditional vs. Critical Cultural Theory." Traditional theories of culture posit "man" as a creator of cultural values, evidenced in customs, language, and modes of thinking (Castro-Gómez, 143). Critical Cultural Theory, as Castro-Gomez calls the opposing view, emphasizes the sociopolitical (conflictive) aspect of culture. In other words, culture is viewed as the battleground where the control of meaning is decided (Castro-Gómez, 147). Notice the vocabulary used by Castro-Gómez: culture as the battleground, the contestatory space, where the cultural memory is formulated, where the struggles for meanings and ideologies take place. Based on this perspective, what makes us select only Paz's reading as the most authoritative viewpoint on La Malinche, on the Mexican Revolution, on the Spanish Civil War and its participants, or on gender relations in general? As a response to this question, this book examines how both Paz and Garro have contributed different perspectives regarding major sociopolitical constructs involved in formulating the cultural memory of the Mexican people.

Memories can be both private and public; that is, memories can belong to an individual but also reflect group history. Cultural memory "is shaped by, and thus conveys or represents, its group history and identity" (Hirsch and Smith, 2), so the agents of cultural transmission—whether people or texts—influence the shape of the future memories of a people. The shaping and reshaping of a collective cultural memory is a process informed by many sources: politicians, academics, historians, journalists, and artists, among others. Canonical intellectuals of twentieth-century Mexico, including Octavio Paz, have been accepted as mediators of the memory of future generations. Today critics recognize that the gender, age, and class (among other characteristics) of a witness or agent of transmission affect the agent's "reading" of events that form cultural memory. Therefore the formation of cultural memories, like the literary canon, is a construct influenced by subjective factors and by the temporal environment. The representation of gender in cultural memory presents a particular problem because past narratives were mostly constructed and transmitted by men. In response to that shortcoming, a focus of feminist literary critics has been to "redefine culture from the perspective of women through the retrieval and inclusion of women's work, stories, and artifacts" (Hirsch and Smith, 3). Many critics of Mexican culture would agree with Margo Glantz that in Mexico women had been excluded from the cultural scene until well into the twentieth century (Glantz, *Sor Juana*, 122); along similar lines I would argue that Garro's voice has been marginalized in comparison to her husband's because of both her gender and the inherent contestatory nature of her ideas.

Although "gender" and "memory" are contested concepts, my study provides concrete examples of how two intellectuals of different genders approach the important issues of the past: national identity, gender, ethnicity, and affairs of state. If culture is a representational environment in which certain ideologies are legitimized, what better way to explore the representation of different ideologies than through a study of the way different wars in a country's history are represented by its key writers? Although many critics have studied the works of Garro and Paz individually, few have compared their perspectives with regard to their focus on a theme that they both experienced personally: war. Rarely do we have a published record produced by two members of the intellectual elite who experienced the same conflicts and impact of a war scene. In the following chapters I analyze their representations of power relations, suffering, violence, and the dynamics of social upheaval concomitant with warfare. In placing these two talented writers in conversation with each other, I hope to introduce to a wider audience the role of Elena Garro in formulating oppositional narratives of Mexican national history.

While I discuss many themes and refer to a broad range of Hispanic writers within the context of Latin American literary history, I have chosen to frame each chapter using the motif of the different wars that affected the lives of Garro and Paz personally and professionally. I chose the theme of war because, as John Limon wrote, "the history of literature began with war and has never foresworn it" (3). Limon begins his story of war-literature with the idea that writing and war have a "perdurable affinity" and that war is "the most vivid of historical markers" (4). Nevertheless, the topic is generally considered a "man's" theme. As Donna Pankhurst comments in "The 'Sex War' and Other Wars: Towards a Feminist Approach to Peace Building," "the roles of women in war and other types of violent conflict remained almost invisible throughout the world. Accounts of war, through news reporting, government propaganda, novels, cinema, etc., tended to cast men as the 'doers' and women as the passive, innocent victims" (13). In general, and certainly in Mexico, women have always borne the major responsibility of transmitting cultural values, including war stories, to the next generation, even though they were rarely responsible for formulating these values and accounts.[11]

In the case of war stories, women are most frequently treated as objects and are seldom the writers of those narratives. In Mexico, as in most countries of Latin America, the many wars and battles that mark its history have been captured in narratives and poems that provide the cultural memory transmitted to generations. In terms of the Mexican Revolution, the first civil war of the twentieth century, the list of writers whose narratives deal with the topic is sizable. Any popular inventory includes figures such as Mariano Azuela (*Los de abajo* [translated as *The Underdogs*]), Rafael Muñoz (*¡Vámonos con Pancho Villa!* [Let's Go with Pancho Villa!]), and Martín Luis Guzmán (*El águila y la serpiente* [The Eagle and the Serpent]) of the early period, and the list continues with more recent names: Carlos Fuentes (*La muerte de Artemio Cruz*, 1962 [translated as *The Death of Artemio Cruz*, 1964]), Jorge Ibargüengoitia (*Los relámpagos de agosto* [The Lightning of August], 1965), Fernando del Paso (*José Trigo*, 1966), and Ignacio Solares (*Columbus*, 1996).[12]

Even when women did write about wars, critical literary reviews often neglected their narratives. In studies of Mexican history and literature, for example, the women who participated in the Mexican Revolution, as well as those who wrote about it, were long ignored. Historians acknowledge now that women participated in the Revolution in many ways (Sarah Buck, Jane Jaquette, Mary Kay Vaughan); the Revolution is the founding myth of the Mexican political state (Knight, "Myth of the Mexican Revolution," 223), so it is important that the cultural memory reflect the real contributions of women both as warriors and as writers.

One of the rediscovered texts is the novel *Cartucho* (Cartridge, 1931) by one of the pioneering female Mexican writers of the early twentieth century, Nellie Campobello, which narrates the battles of the Revolution from the unusual perspective of a young girl.[13] Although *Cartucho* first met with critical success, it later disappeared from cultural memory. To ignore women writers not only preserves the myth that "war is men's business" but also maintains a false picture of national history. By choosing the theme of war, I not only propose to question the mythology of war's gender but also hope to show that Elena Garro was very much involved in exploring and questioning the cultural construction of the myths that form the foundation of Mexican national identity.

Chapter 2, "All in the Family: Paz and Garro Rewrite Mexico's Cultural Memory," deals with the way Mexicans narrate the clash between the Amerindian peoples and the Spanish conquistadors under Hernán Cortés, who arrived in 1519. The Mexicans are unique among Latin Americans because they frame the bloody wars of conquest using the biblical myth of Adam and Eve as their foundational story. Cortés is cast in the role of Adam, and the indigenous woman called La Malinche, who was his guide and translator, is the Mexican Eve.[14] In this chapter I explore in greater depth the differences in the perspectives of Garro and Paz on the foundational couple and their role in the cultural memory of Mexico regarding national identity as well as gender and ethnic issues. I have included a review of the perspective of Paz's grandfather, Don Ireneo Paz, who had presented a nineteenth-century version of La Malinche characterized by a decidedly romanticized view of the "first couple." Octavio Paz reproduced aspects of this earlier construct, especially its view of gender relations, in his essay "The Sons of Malinche," from *The Labyrinth of Solitude*. In contrast, Garro presents in *Los recuerdos del porvenir* and "La culpa es de los tlaxcaltecas" her acknowledgment of the burden of the Malinche paradigm, but the women she depicts rebel against the cultural stereotypes associated with La Malinche. Moreover, for Garro, *mestizaje* (the mixture of Indian and Spanish blood or cultural elements) and indigenist issues were of crucial importance to Mexican national identity. Anne Doremus has maintained that Paz, like his mentor Samuel Ramos, did not look upon *mestizaje* as "a significant factor in the development of the national character. In their view, indigenous culture made little impact on the Mexican psyche" (384). Garro, on the contrary, shows how important indigenous issues are to Mexico.

Two civil wars affected the lives of the Paz and Garro families, the first of which was the Mexican Revolution of 1910–1917. In Chapter 3, "War at Home: Betrayals of/in the Mexican Revolution," I explore how the two writers deal with the Mexican Revolution, a civil war that split the country into many factions that still manifest themselves in Mexico today. The theme of the Mexican Revolution is explored by the two writers in dissimilar ways; their viewpoints are influenced by gender differences and the divergent ideologies of their backgrounds. As documented in the essays of Paz and in Garro's more varied compositions (her essays in *Revolucionarios mexicanos*, the novel *Los recuerdos del porvenir*, short stories from *La semana de colores*, and the full-length play *Felipe Ángeles*), their understanding of the successes and failures of the Mexican Revolution continues to influence narratives of cultural memory.

Chapter 4, "Love and War Don't Mix: Garro and Paz in the Spanish Civil War," deals with the multifaceted topic of a civil war that both Paz and Garro experienced in the battle zone itself: the Spanish Civil War. It was a time of great ferment and attracted participants from across the globe. Latin American intellectuals were not on the sidelines but were actually instrumental in defining the conflict, fighting with both pen and sword. Mexico as a country played a key role in supporting the Republicans and then in accepting the many Spanish émigrés who sought asylum; these refugees would later exert a strong influence on Mexican cultural history. Both Paz and Garro were part of this intellectual milieu, but they had markedly different experiences during their time in Spain, with personal and professional repercussions that shaped their subsequent work and personal relationship. I use Garro's autobiographical *Memorias de España 1937* and her novel *La casa junto al río* (The House by the River, 1983) and poems as well as essays by Paz (including his autobiographical *Itinerario*) to explore the impact of the Spanish Civil War on the developing psyches of these two creative writers.

Chapter 5, "Tlatelolco: The Undeclared War," focuses on a watershed experience for Mexico and for each writer individually. The cataclysmic events that took place on the Plaza de Tlatelolco in 1968, referred to as the Tlatelolco Massacre, have been recognized by most historians, social scientists, and literary historians as marking a decisive transformation in Mexican culture and politics. The lives of both Paz and Garro were dramatically changed by this tragic incident. I explore the impact of this national conflict on their writing and on their personal and public personas. Garro reproduced the traumas of her political and personal involvements in the events of that time by means of the novel *Y Matarazo no llamó* (And Matarazo Did Not Call, 1991) and the play *Sócrates y los gatos* (Socrates and the Cats, 2003). Paz documented his point of view in the poem "México: Olimpiada de 1968" (Mexico: Olympics of 1968, first published in *La Cultura en México* on October 30, 1968) as well as in *Posdata* (translated as *The Other Mexico: Critique of the Pyramid*, 1970) and later essays.

In the first five chapters I concentrate on the literary expressions of Paz and Garro representing their responses to major national and international conflicts that traumatized large groups of people politically, economically, and culturally. In the final chapter, "From Civil War to Gender War: The Battle of the Sexes," I explore the texts that are labeled romans à clef—Garro's novels in which she thinly disguises her own experiences and her turbulent relationship with Paz. While the conflicts that marked their personal relationship seem to have found expression in her writings, Paz appears to have disregarded his relationship with Garro in his writings. In order to learn more about his attitudes toward women, I analyze Paz's works that focus on female figures in Mexican culture.

People who know the details of Garro's biography note that Garro unquestionably reproduced aspects of their personal life in romans à clef, particularly the novels *Testimonios sobre Mariana* (Testimonies about Mariana, 1981) and *Mi hermanita Magdalena* (My Little Sister Magdalena, 1998). I propose, however, that these novels are more than autobiographical documents. They represent a biting critique of the patriarchy and women's role in twentieth-century society.

Whereas Garro plays with her public's curiosity about her exposé of "life with Paz," he, in contrast, is more reserved in his representation of personal data, including the turbulent years with his first wife and daughter. While his poetry looks at women primarily as objects, his most open analysis of male-female relations appears in *The Labyrinth of Solitude*, in which he concludes that women are the "mysterious other" and male-female relations are destined to repeat the Malinche paradigm.[15] I carefully examine the nature of his most consistent interaction with a female figure, found in his major study *Sor Juana Inés de la Cruz o las trampas de la fe* (1982; translated as *Sor Juana or the Traps of Faith*, 1988).[16]

This book introduces the reader to two of the most original, provocative, and critical literary figures of twentieth-century Mexico. In presenting the multifaceted creative worlds of Garro and Paz, and their relationship to each other, I offer a comparison of the ideologies of the two writers and how they influenced cultural memory with regard to gender, ethnicity, politics, and the arts. Their uncivil conflict marking the clash between the dominant tradition transmitted by Paz versus the previously marginalized perspective of Garro serves as a reflection of the battle for cultural memory in Mexico.

"I believe the imagination is a force in
order to arrive at the truth."
ELENA GARRO
in Rosas Lopátegui and Toruño

ALL IN THE FAMILY
PAZ AND GARRO REWRITE MEXICO'S CULTURAL MEMORY

WHAT COULD THE ILLUSTRIOUS, internationally known Nobel Prize laureate Octavio Paz (1914–1998) have in common with a modish Mexican Laura? I am referring to Laura Esquivel (b. 1950), the writer of popular fiction, one of whose novels, *Como agua para chocolate* (1989; translated as *Like Water for Chocolate*, 1992), sold more than four and a half million copies around the world and remained on the *New York Times* bestseller list for more than a year. In 2006 Esquivel published a novel that focused on La Malinche, a historical figure from the Conquest period whose continued presence in Mexican cultural memory is closely associated with the work of Octavio Paz. Similar to other Hispanic and Latino writers, from the sixteenth-century chronicler Bernal Díaz del Castillo to Carlos Fuentes, Rosario Castellanos, and Elena Garro in the twentieth century, Esquivel showed her fascination for the archetypal figure in Mexican culture whom Paz had attempted to redefine in his landmark essay "Los hijos de la Malinche" (The Sons of Malinche, 1950). As Maarten van Delden and Yvon Grenier note, Paz is considered "instrumental in shifting the focus from La Malinche as a historical figure to La Malinche as a cultural symbol" (61). In this chapter I explore how Paz and Garro characterize La Malinche and her role in the Conquest as ways to represent the national identity of Mexico.

La Malinche, an indigenous woman known by many names (including Malintzin and Doña Marina), was a slave living among one of the indigenous groups when Cortés, the leader of the Spanish conquistadors, arrived in her village in 1519. La Malinche came into importance only when Cortés discovered that she could speak both Maya and Nahuatl and that she was also intelligent and "fair" to look upon. He made use of her many talents from 1519 to 1524, especially her abilities as translator and cultural intermediary as he dealt with the many indigenous groups he encountered during his battles to gain control of Mexico. How the story of the Conquest is told and the representations of La Malinche and her role in the Conquest have much to do with the formation/contestation of cultural memory in Mexico that relates to both ethnicity and gender. Contemporary interrelationships of men and women as well as the power relations between Europeans and Amerindians can be traced back to this originary relation between Cortés and La Malinche. These stories of conquest and control center on La Malinche, so it is not surprising that she is portrayed in the writings of Paz and Garro and that they have different perspectives on the traditional cultural memory related to her.

Since 1950 Octavio Paz has been considered the major spokesman for the contemporary popular perspective on La Malinche. He first wrote about her in his seminal essay "Los hijos de la Malinche" (The Sons of Malinche), a chapter in *El laberinto de la soledad* (translated as *The Labyrinth of Solitude*). Unlike Laura Esquivel's obvious appropriation of La Malinche's story in her eponymous novel, Elena Garro's connection to La Malinche was not overt and came about more on the basis of critical readings of the subtexts of her 1963 novel *Los recuerdos del porvenir* (translated as *Recollections of Things to Come*) and the short story "La culpa es de los tlaxcaltecas" (It's the Fault of the Tlaxcaltecas). During their lifetimes, Garro was rarely cited for her revisionist (and visionary) perspective on La Malinche, while Octavio Paz has always been mentioned, referenced, and respected; it is his version that has become canonical. Indeed, it is difficult to find an article that does not refer to Paz and "Los hijos de la Malinche." Interestingly, his grandfather, Ireneo Paz (1836–1924), also contributed two novels to the Malinche paradigm that has developed since the early post-Conquest chronicles of the Spanish conquistadores: *Amor y suplicio* (Love and Torment, 1873) and *Doña Marina* (1883). I reconsider Don Ireneo's portrayal of Doña Marina as well as Octavio Paz's conception of the "Mexican Eve," another of her designations, and then compare their representations with Garro's ideas on the role of this mythic figure in the collective memory of Mexico. Generational and gender issues clearly affect these representations.

La Malinche's role in the formation of national identity is considered vital for all three, and yet the Paz men present her in sexual terms, reinforcing Mexican cultural memory, while Garro attempts to offer a more nuanced view that subverts patriarchal and Eurocentric ideology.

For the past 500 years, after the onset of European expansion into the Americas in the fifteenth and sixteenth centuries, historians, novelists, poets, and artists from all perspectives have tried to explain, interpret, blame, or vindicate La Malinche as part of the notion of what it means to be "Mexican." Cortés and his 600 Spanish soldiers had arrived on the shores of the Yucatán Peninsula in February 1519. In one of his early encounters with the various indigenous peoples, twenty young women, including the indigenous slave woman baptized "Marina," were given as a "gift" of tribute to placate the invaders. This subjection of women, either as a tool of conciliation or as part of the booty of war, has not changed throughout centuries. Although women in war are very often abused as sex objects and/or domestic servants, La Malinche is depicted as being present at all the important events during the years of the Mexican conquest (1519–1521) by the sixteenth-century indigenous painters (especially as seen in the *Lienzo de Tlaxcala*).[1] Cortés wrote very little about her in his own *Letters* to the king of Spain. But one of his soldiers, Bernal Díaz del Castillo, gave her ample recognition for her role in their endeavors as translator and negotiator between Cortés and the indigenous leaders. Thus La Malinche served both as a sexual object—bearing Cortés a son—and as a facilitator during the events of the Conquest. Little historical documentation of the full trajectory of her life exists, yet La Malinche's significance continues to permeate cultural history, from the chronicles of Cortés and Díaz del Castillo in the sixteenth century to contemporary Mexican and Chicana/o Studies.

Of all the states invaded and populated by Europeans during the Conquest period, only Mexico has devised a particular family saga to explain what happened during the initial contact period and the subsequent formation of the new mestizo society. The Mexican nationalist (and basically Eurocentric) explanation is derived from the biblical paradigm of Adam and Eve. Cortés, the leader of the Spanish conquistadors, is equated with Father Adam, while the Mexican Eve and mother of the mestizo nation is identified with the indigenous woman who served in diverse capacities and was variously known as La Malinche, Doña Marina, or Malintzin, depending on the ideology of the narrator.[2] This family-based story has a concrete expression: Cortés and La Malinche did produce a son, who is often (and erroneously) considered to be the "first mestizo," the first child of the "hybrid" community that is the contemporary Mexican nation.[3] Tragically, the children who are the product of wartime subjugations are stigmatized and abandoned, yet in this case their child has been elevated metaphorically as the origin of the mestizo peoples. In addition, the relationship between the Mexican Adam and Eve metaphorizes the political, military, economic, and cultural struggles of the colonizing enterprise. Most often, relationships within this ethnically mixed family have been interpreted to underpin the controlling myth of imperialism: that the European male is superior in all ways and facets (militarily, economically, physically, culturally) to his counterpart in the conquered lands and that the female, taken from the indigenous population, is meant to be controlled and impregnated by the European consort.

The collective discourse based on this narrative has produced the "cultural memory" of the Mexican people. As Jan Assmann suggests, cultural memory is a "collective concept for all knowledge that directs behavior and experience in the interactive framework of a society and one that obtains through generations in repeated societal practice and initiation" (126). Furthermore, as Richard Miller notes in an interview, "people with a shared history and cultural identification create ways of perceiving themselves. People have a cultural memory insofar as they see themselves as part of a collective story. Cultural memory gathers narratives, values, martyrs, leaders and heroes into an account that helps us understand ourselves" (quoted in Williams). Moreover, as Miller reminds us, cultural memory also looks forward, as it shapes "the civic character of future generations in order to continue a common story." The writers from the past have contributed to the development of what is the cultural memory of Mexico today—and today's writers are helping to formulate what that cultural memory will be in the future. In the creation and selection of these memories writers are influenced by their gender, class, ethnicity, and historical moment: all characteristics that make them think a certain way.

A select number of key writers in each generation seem to stand above the rest in shaping their generation's attitudes and perceptions, and surely Octavio Paz is always included on that short list of influential writers. As the British translator Amanda Hopkinson notes in her review of Esquivel's *Malinche*, while the novel "cannot be regarded as having anything seriously to do with its subject," the best thing about the book for her is that it might send readers to Octavio Paz: "then it may even come to serve some literary purpose after all" (no pagination). Hopkinson, director of the British Centre for Literary Translation at the University of East Anglia, refers to the "unsuperseded *Labyrinth of Solitude*." Harold Bloom offers further enlightenment: "The myth of

La Malinche or the *Chingada*, unforgettably expounded by Paz, is alien to the United States, yet it is the center of *The Labyrinth of Solitude*" (5). Although women such as Pocahontas and Sacajawea have served as bridge figures in the United States between the conquering white men and the indigenous worlds, neither one has served as the American Eve or generated a negative body of literature about her sexual exploits. Neither one has been demonized in the way La Malinche has, as being a traitor to her people.

Paz's name and his essay are cited in almost every reference to La Malinche—from reviews in newspapers (such as the Hopkinson piece on Esquivel) to critical essays and scholarly books; a reader can consult such varied texts as Rolando Romero and Amanda Nolacea Harris's *Feminism, Nation and Myth: La Malinche*, which deals with the figure of La Malinche from a Chicana/o perspective; or Benigno Trigo's *Remembering Maternal Bodies: Melancholy in Latina and Latin American Women's Writing*, which offers a counter-reading to patriarchal narratives; or Harold Bloom's *Octavio Paz*. Constant reference to Paz's work is understandable: his reputation, in terms of name recognition and also as an acknowledged Mexican intellectual, has led one scholar to suggest that "all thought on *lo mexicano* in the twentieth century passes through Paz" (Johnson, 50). After reviewing all the references to Paz in which scholars discuss the Malinche paradigm, it might appear that "Paz reflects at great length on La Malinche's role in the formation of the Mexican consciousness" (Fitts, 11). In actuality, Paz is more like Cortés than Díaz del Castillo when it comes to the quantification of his work on La Malinche: he dedicates a mere two pages of *The Labyrinth* to any details about her life and meaning, yet he has become the seminal "unsuperseded" writer on this crucial topic.

Despite Paz's chapter title, I question whether it is appropriate to say that La Malinche is at the center of his work—and I most assuredly also question the way he represents her. I ask why he has become the spokesperson for the meaning of La Malinche, especially when he repeats a compilation of the negative aspects of her persona, which has had detrimental effects on the views of many Mexicans on gender and ethnicity as part of their national identity. I suggest that Garro also appears to question the way in which Paz summarizes the meaning of La Malinche—both as a passive sexual figure and as a *malinchista* who rejects the native to favor the foreign and therefore betrays her *patria* (homeland). While these are the attributes that Paz presents in his brief account, Garro's novel and short story (*Los recuerdos del porvenir* and "La culpa es de los tlaxcaltecas") methodically deconstruct those characteristics and offer alternative behavior patterns. Although subsequent writers—especially women writers like Rosario Castellanos and Sabina Berman and Chicanas like Cherríe Moraga and Norma Alarcón—have challenged the paradigm offered by Paz, Garro was one of the earlier writers to take on this issue.

The Cortés-Malinche paradigm has been considered a root paradigm in Mexican culture and continues to generate historical, psychological, anthropological, and literary studies to this day.[4] Within Paz's own family, his grandfather, Ireneo Paz, also a writer and journalist, was a prominent liberal intellectual and a political activist as well as a model for his grandson.[5] Of the many novels written by Don Ireneo, two were historical novels about the Conquest period that also contribute to the formation of the Malinche paradigm, but in ways that differ considerably from the portrait offered by his illustrious grandson. Always calling her by her Spanish given name, Doña Marina, Don Ireneo more closely follows the positive portrait first offered by Bernal Díaz del Castillo, the Spanish chronicler and friend of the historical Malinche, in *La historia verdadera de la conquista de la Nueva España*, first written in 1568 and translated as *The Conquest of New Spain*. Ironically, it is Elena Garro, at a time when she was still married to Octavio Paz, whose work echoes certain constructive aspects of Don Ireneo's imaginative picture of this key character in the Mexican pantheon of mythic figures.

Not too long before Garro's own death (in 1998, the same year as Paz) she regained some of her lost recognition as a capital figure in Mexican culture, for reasons too complicated to reiterate at this juncture.[6] A review of Don Ireneo's portrayal of Doña Marina and a comparison of Garro's ideas on the role of the Mexican Eve with those of Octavio Paz reveal that this literary Mexican family may share a preoccupation with their memorable mother but that each member projects a different face for her. While their respective contributions may be considered to be "all in the family," nevertheless their different historical moments and gender differences lead to distinct perspectives on the nature of sexuality, subordination (or marginalization), and cultural identity. One way to follow social and cultural concepts is through a study of literary discourse, by tracking the differences in how they represent the Malinche-Cortés paradigm. We can analyze not only their personal feeling about the issue but also how literary texts interact with beliefs, opinions, and behavior. Moreover, by comparing Garro's re-vision of the Malinche-Cortés paradigm with that of Paz, I am also trying to reclaim "buried" or marginalized truths by and about women. This is a fundamental concern for feminists and for those exploring/examining the development in the twenty-first century of Mexican cultural identity.

If Octavio Paz has surfaced as the outspoken theorist regarding La Malinche's role in the formation of Mexican national identity, this is in part the result of his international recognition as a "capital figure" in Mexican culture. Even critics of Paz such as Jorge Aguilar Mora (see *La divina pareja*) and the Chicana Adelaida Del Castillo acknowledge his work in defining areas for interpreting and understanding Mexican culture. It is not surprising that Octavio Paz's essay is always included in any discussion of La Malinche. As Aguilar Mora allows, whatever its shortcomings, *The Labyrinth* "has become an irrefutable manual" (*La divina pareja*, 26).[7] It has become a true "master text," with almost immeasurable impact, and thus deserves careful analysis. *The Labyrinth* is one of the most quoted books by Paz, used in classrooms across the United States, found on the reading lists of specialists and amateurs, and referred to as a manual for knowing the nature of the Mexicans.

The Paz essay entitled "Los hijos de la Malinche" (fourth in *El laberinto*) is translated by Lysander Kemp as "The Sons of La Malinche," even though *los hijos* could just as easily be translated more inclusively as "The Children of La Malinche." That may have been the original referent in the mind of Paz (or maybe not!).[8] Of course, the word "children" often does seem to point to male children in Mexico, in disregard of the female.[9] These sons of Malinche, as opposed to her daughters, include generations of Mexican males who are in control of Mexican discourse and wield power in the country and in cultural pursuits. While all Mexican men do not exercise political, economic, or social power, more often than not they are in control of their families and especially their women. In Paz's view, all Mexican males repeat the paradigm that he proposes in his essay: "It is impossible not to notice the resemblance between the figure of the macho and that of the Spanish conquistador. This is the model—more mythical than real—that determines the images the Mexican people form of men in power. . . . They are all machos, *chingones*" (82). The men represent the conquistadors, Cortés and his brothers, vis-à-vis the Indian women that they encountered and dominated; the present-day *chingón* (the conquistador's avatar) controls the *chingada* (La Malinche, prototype of all Mexican women).[10]

Basically, this is part of what Paz describes in his essay, not so much as a prescriptive order but as a description of patterns of culture that he has found in his own investigations and inquiry into the Mexican psyche: "The strange permanence of Cortés and La Malinche in the Mexican's imagination and sensibilities reveals that they are something more than historical figures: they are symbols of a secret conflict that we have still not resolved" (87). Paz alludes to a description of the relationship between men and women in Mexico that is nothing more than what happened in this first conflict—a battle of the sexes that is an ongoing war repeating the Conquest's roles for males and females. The subjugation of women in modern Mexican culture continues a paradigm whose roots lie in the war of the Conquest.[11]

While most English speakers and Europeans (or perhaps I should say non-Mexicans) have heard of Octavio Paz, not many know about his family. Paz acknowledged the great influence of his paternal grandfather on his formation, especially the books in his grandfather's library; we might assume that he also read narratives written by the elder Paz, including such revealing novels as the historical *Amor y suplicio*, a best seller in its time (Santí, "Octavio Paz," 54), and *Doña Marina* (1883). Although Don Ireneo is not well known among critics and readers today,[12] it is nevertheless informative to review his portrayal of Malinche and compare it not only to the portrayals by his grandson and by Garro but to ideas of the sociohistoric period in which he wrote.

Díaz del Castillo's *La historia verdadera de la conquista de la Nueva España* serves as one of the major subtexts for Don Ireneo's portrait of the woman he calls "Doña Marina." Don Ireneo's approach continues the Romantic ideology and rhetoric of an earlier period, but he reflects his unique historical moment in his treatment of Spain and its relationship to Mexico.

During the first nationalist period immediately after the War of Independence (1810–1821), writers dealing with the Conquest and historical themes regarded Spain as the enemy, as we clearly see in novels such as *Jicoténcal* (1826).[13] In this text, Doña Marina is the malevolent Eve who allows the serpent from Spain to destroy Edenic America. Her actions are seen through the prism of anti-Spanish sentiment, so that whatever she did is reinterpreted in negative ways. The writers of newly independent Mexico generally attempted to destroy the reputation of this Indian woman; because of nationalist anti-Spanish fervor, she becomes the sellout (*vendepatrias*), whose support of the Spanish conquistador shows her rejection of native culture in favor of Spanish ways. While these writers may grant her the status of Mexican Eve, as the mother of the "first mestizo," they most often prefer to associate her with the negative aspects of the Christian view of the biblical Eve. She is represented as the corrupter, a sexually tainted figure responsible for the downfall of a glorious indigenous kingdom (however idealized and fictional that portrait may be). Her conflicted status as the "raped one" (La Chingada), the first *malinchista*, which Octavio Paz later concretized in his 1950 essay, has its most ardent proponents in this early nationalist period.

In contrast, late nineteenth-century Mexican intellectuals, especially during the period called the Porfiriato, from 1876 to 1910, regarded Europeans favorably and included Spain in their good graces.[14] With the support of Juan Prim (1814–1870), the general who was the guiding light behind the Republican revolution of 1868, Spain was attempting to bring about reconciliation with its former colony. In his novels, Don Ireneo encouraged reassessment not only of Mexico's stormy past with Spain but also of its policy toward a newly republicanized Spain, whose nonmonarchical government he clearly favored. His narrator appeals to Mexican readers to erase their negative attitude toward the former "conquerors":

> And if we have a word of pardon and disregard for the Spaniards of three centuries ago who came to torment our grandfathers, how can we not express a feeling of fraternity for the [Spanish] Republicans of today who are instructing us with their deeds, who electrify us with their words, and who place themselves at the head of European civilization? (*Amor y suplicio*, 157)[15]

In both novels Don Ireneo elevates the Spanish contributions to Mexican culture and tempers the cruelty and atrocities of the Conquest. While the young Octavio might have been an avid reader of his grandfather's work and of all the tomes in his library, Don Ireneo's novels have yet to become popular reading, although they do appear in the catalog of the library of Porfirio Díaz himself.[16] Their florid style and old-fashioned treatment of female characters in particular would not make them best sellers today, perhaps, but they do have their attractions for those interested in the figure of La Malinche and Mexican culture in general. It is intriguing to analyze the late nineteenth-century perceptions and compare them with the attitudes more prevalent in the 1950s and 1960s, when Octavio Paz and Elena Garro were writing about similar topics.

Don Ireneo's version of the Conquest narrative reflects his Romantic interest in ontology and addresses his contemporaries regarding their continued concern about the nature of Mexican *mestizaje*. As Aníbal González reminds us, the Romantic and post-Romantic Latin American writers showed a propensity "to seek out ontology through literature, through writing: to demand of writing the answer to the ontological question, 'who am I?'" (53). The ontological search for self-identity was merely a synecdoche for larger questions, such as "What is the nation?" and "What is the national project?" In the political debates and fiction produced during the struggles for independence from the Spanish Empire and in the period of nation-state building in the late nineteenth century, the sexual couplings of prototypical men and women were not only love matches but also symbolic relationships that reenacted the foundation of the nation-state (Sommer). In the first decades of the twentieth century immigration, industrialization, democratization, and urbanization brought about changes that challenged these previous ideals of national identity.

For Ireneo Paz, for example, the interactions of Marina and Cortés were not only an expression of their personal love, of which he had no doubt. They also embodied the behavior of the people and gender that they represented. The male was the strong European intruder who selected, tamed, and impregnated the compliant indigenous female. This love, inevitably, also had to produce the birth of a child that would represent the union of their best traits and would be, as the first mestizo, the forebear of the modern Mexican nation. The parents of mestizo Mexico therefore had to be shown as worthy progenitors, as noble, valiant, and virtuous. This was the task that Ireneo Paz apparently set for himself, as I first demonstrated in *La Malinche in Mexican Literature*, a comprehensive analysis of texts that represent the Malinche paradigm. In *Foundational Fictions: The National Romances of Latin America,* Doris Sommer also shows convincingly that other Latin American novels written after independence "are all love stories" (30) and connect (in one way or another) the nation and the women they portray. The female physical body is linked with the nation, and heterosexual romances serve as the synecdoche for the foundation of the nation.

Reflecting this paradigm, Don Ireneo maps out the political, economic, and military interactions through the use of love stories, in which an Indian woman's choice of a mate indicates the historical fate of the various nation-states involved in the Conquest. Moreover, he repeats this pattern not only for the historical figures but for the characters he has created, who are the main focus of the first novel, *Amor y suplicio.* This narrative does not begin with the arrival of the Spaniards but first relates the historical conflicts among the various indigenous groups. The focus here is on the daughter of the Tlaxcalan leader Maxixcatzin, whom Don Ireneo christens the princess Otila. Historical records show that the Tlaxcalan leader did have a daughter, whose name in Spanish has been given in other documents as Elvira. The point here is that Don Ireneo utilizes an indigenous name for the father but chooses a Spanish name for the daughter, suggesting that she will also become a *malinchista*—one who rejects the Indian and favors the Spanish, as Paz defines it in "The Sons of Malinche" (86).

Indeed, the series of love triangles presented in *Amor y suplicio* follows the trajectory of power relations of the various nations before and during the

Conquest period. In choosing lovers for Otila, Don Ireneo recalls the historical record that places the Tlaxcalans in opposition to the Aztecs; just as the two men are from warring nations, they similarly are in conflict over the hand of Otila. Otila soon rejects even the powerful Guatimozin (historically referred to as Cuauhtémoc), once she has caught sight of a European conquistador. The first time Otila sees Don Juan de Velázquez de León, she compares him to a god (*Amor y suplicio*, 171). Although Otila knows that the Spaniard is no deity,[17] she readily accepts his religious beliefs, language, and culture; his white skin becomes in her eyes a sign of his superiority. While Don Ireneo's narrator does not openly profess the prevailing nineteenth-century racist views of Count de Gobineau,[18] the Spaniards are represented as the essential progenitors of the mestizo because their white skin and European culture make them superior. This is an idea that would also be taken up by José Vasconcelos (1882–1959) and many other members of the Criollo intellectual elite in the postrevolutionary period.

Using the love relations of individuals to parallel the military and social events of nations is not a new literary motif, and it has been studied by scholars in a variety of disciplines.[19] Don Ireneo gives his version a particularly Porfirian and nineteenth-century Romantic ideological cast: the Indian women always choose the European lover over the Indian male and generally show respect for and submission to the male figure.

Don Ireneo's laudatory comments about the Spanish and his presentation of Indian women who prefer only Spanish men do not correspond with the typical views of his Liberal compatriots—intellectuals like Eligio Ancona, for example.[20] For Ancona, a writer of historical novels such as *Los mártires del Anáhuac* (The Martyrs of Anahuac, 1870), Cortés is the greatest enemy of the Mexican people, and Doña Marina has sold out her brothers when she falls in love with the Spaniard and sides with him in the Conquest. Ancona continues the nationalist mindset of the early days of the Mexican nation, while Ireneo Paz's novels show that he is more forgiving of the Spanish role and acknowledges the Spanish contribution to the Mexican mestizo nation. For Don Ireneo, in contrast to the nationalists, Doña Marina is an admirable indigenous consort whose noble lineage and demeanor make her worthy as a mate for a civilized (and civilizing) Spanish forebear. More in keeping with his position as a Mexican intellectual, however, Don Ireneo judges Cortés to be the unacceptable partner for this worthy Marina. Instead, he finds another Spaniard who has more noble characteristics befitting the companion of the mother of the first mestizo—for him, Marina's child.

Ireneo Paz puts into the mouth of Juan Jaramillo, the historical conquistador who officially was married to Doña Marina, the judgment that he would prefer to popularize: "I bring to my side an honest woman who has sinned only because of fate. . . . And I offer to respect her and love her for all the days that remain for me to live" (455–456).[21] Imagine the joy that these sentiments evoke in the heart of this Doña Marina; her past as a slave forms part of the historical record or at least is well known to Mexicans who are familiar with the chronicle of Bernal Díaz del Castillo, whose portrayal of Doña Marina seems to have inspired Don Ireneo. In his version, Doña Marina, pregnant with the child of Cortés, no longer wants him as her husband and the paternal figure for her child. Thus, in an original and amazing turnabout from the treatment in other texts, Don Ireneo's Jaramillo turns out to be the model Spanish gentleman, whose attitude toward Marina is an exemplar of Christian charity.

Jaramillo's willingness to accept Doña Marina, despite her professed love for Cortés and despite carrying his child, has always been a puzzle for most readers and writers of this aspect of the Malinche legend. Cortés's secretary, Francisco López de Gómara, declares that Jaramillo was drunk and was forced to marry her because of Cortés's need to get rid of this no longer useful woman (López de Gómara and Simpson, 346). In Marisol Martín del Campo's *Amor y conquista* (Love and Conquest, 1999), Jaramillo is depicted as a loathsome creature, opportunistic and uncivil, more in keeping with the insinuations of López de Gómara. Ireneo Paz, however, needs to find an appropriate Spanish mate for Marina, given that he cannot easily whitewash Cortés, whose reputation even among Hispanophiles is not untainted. Don Ireneo not only imagines the tender dialogue quoted above to substantiate the true love between Jaramillo and Marina but also allows his Marina to confront Cortés and confess to him that she has chosen another man for her husband! The scene is pure Romantic melodrama and quite unrealistic in its portrayal of sexual relations during the Conquest period. Nevertheless, the ideology of Don Ireneo is quite evident; he has to explain how "his" virtuous Marina could transfer her affections from one man to another and still justify her position as the venerable and worthy mother of mestizo Mexico. Don Ireneo does not appear to want to contradict Bernal Díaz del Castillo, the source for his portrayal of Marina; in a famous citation, Díaz de Castillo relates that he was a witness to Marina's reencounter with the mother who had sold her into slavery and tells his readers that Marina exclaimed to her own mother that

God had been very gracious to her in freeing her from the worship of idols and making her a Christian, and allowing her to bear a son to her lord and master Cortés, and in marrying her to a gentleman, such as Juan Jaramillo, who was now her husband; that she would rather serve her husband and Cortés than anyone else in the world. (86)

Bernal Díaz gives his assurance that these were the true words of Doña Marina, who sounds like a proper and grateful colonial, the same portrait reproduced by Don Ireneo.

In *La Malinche in Mexican Literature*, I comment that in this speech Díaz del Castillo stressed all the aspects of Marina that made her an archetype for indigenous assimilation to Spanish culture (31).[22] Don Ireneo includes each of these characteristics in his portrayal of Marina, so that she appears to be a virtuous Christian lady, more faithful to Christian ideals than Cortés is. Don Ireneo makes every effort to encode the positive virtues associated with the Virgin Mary within his portrayal of Marina, showing her good heart, compassion, and beauty and at one point calling her a goddess (I:25). She exhibits modesty and sexual restraint, completely contradicting the "lascivious Malinche as whore" pattern that became part of the popular legend in the Nationalist period.[23]

Don Ireneo wants his readers to know that Marina did love Cortés, yet she is a praiseworthy mother and puts the well-being of her baby above her own feelings. Cortés and the reader realize that Marina's love for this child—the fruit of their love relationship—motivates her to find a worthy husband for the family she has founded. Don Ireneo follows the historical records by having Marina and Jaramillo accompany Cortés on the trip to Honduras (a historical event which took place in 1524), during which the chronicles document their marriage. But he adds quite clearly that it is Marina who directs Cortés to give her to Jaramillo in marriage. This is not a portrait of a submissive woman but of one with a plan and a mission. His portrayal of such a compelling and moral woman is far more in keeping with his personal agenda regarding Mexican ethnic identity politics than it is with any sense of the realities of the historical characters. Would Marina the slave really have been able to make a deal with the conquistador? Would a woman of her status be able to tell Cortés she was no longer "his"?

Not satisfied with merely stressing Marina's morality, the narrator also prepares the reader to react in a specific way to Cortés's acceptance of Marina's demands: "The two former lovers could not have concluded their meeting in a more heroic manner" (374).[24] Marina and Cortés act courageously, as true heroes, because they sacrifice their own personal desires for the greater good—the protection of the mestizo, the future Mexican population. Thus "[Ireneo] Paz seems to be describing what he considers to be the attributes of the mother of the Mexican people—the dedicated, unselfish love, the intelligence and fortitude, the bravery and beauty—all in one almost perfect female" (Cypess, *La Malinche*, 78).

How divergent is Don Ireneo's portrait from the early Nationalist writers and from that of his grandson! Whereas Don Ireneo reflected the pro-Spanish ideology of the historical moment in which he wrote, Paz was influenced by the pessimistic existentialism that prevailed in post–World War II intellectual circles.[25] Octavio Paz preserves the emphasis on Malinche's great love for Cortés, but he divests her of any agency except giving herself to the conqueror: "It is true that she gave herself voluntarily to the conquistador" (*The Labyrinth of Solitude*, 86). With this comment Paz ignores the reality of the slave class and the realities of any conquered people, especially women who have been subjected to rape and violence in all past and current wars. He assumes that a female slave would have had a choice in how her master would treat her. Is it accurate to state that she gave herself voluntarily? Could the historical Malinche/Marina have rejected the sexual demands of her master?

It is also worth questioning whether we should say that the two were "lovers," as Ireneo Paz glowingly describes them and as the Mexican historians of the early twentieth century also insist.[26] Calling them lovers seems to suggest that there might have been a sense of freely shared love on both sides, ignoring that one was a slave, the other a dominant male partner who was known to have had many other female sex partners and sired other children during their professed love relationship.[27] In this proposed Eden, Adam and Eve were not alone.[28] Yet many of the biographical narratives published in Mexico contemporaneously with Octavio Paz's essay continue the Romantic version of the "affair." Whether they call her "una india ejemplar" (an exemplary Indian) as Jesús Figueroa Torres does in his *Doña Marina* (1957) or "la dama de la conquista" (the lady of the Conquest) as Federico Gómez de Orozco prefers, they reject the negative portrayal of the woman that labels her a *vendepatrias* (traitor). They prefer to see her as the beautiful, virtuous, and loving lady, ever faithful to the brave Spaniard, both of whom must fatalistically come together to bring into being the new "fruit" (using their organic metaphor)—the mestizo.

Octavio Paz shows the conflictive and anguished underside of this material that is part of his country's mythic life and historical remembrances. Paz not only repudiates the Romantic view of Marina as the faithful lover but also "metaphorizes women in general," as David Johnson asserts, "and effectively converts her into a Hegelian object, an object particularly useful to a masculinist historiography endeavoring to make woman culpable for the Mexican condition" ("Woman, Translation, Nationalism," 105). Paz argues that woman is "the Enigma" to man but also the symbol of fecundity and death (60). The supreme symbol of fecundity and death in Mexican culture is La Chingada, which becomes another name for La Malinche in Paz's essay:

> If the *Chingada* is a representation of the violated Mother, it is appropriate to associate her with the Conquest, which was also a violation, not only in the historical sense but also in the very flesh of Indian women. The symbol of this violation is Doña Malinche, the mistress of Cortés. (86)

Paz thus sees as inevitable the association of "woman" as somehow always the Other, the Violated One, with the particular indigenous woman who is labeled the mother of the Mexican people. All women are *chingadas* for Paz because of their innate feminine vulnerability, and La Malinche is another representative of the "cruel incarnation of the feminine condition" (86).

Paz writes from an obviously male perspective when he considers women to be always "open" to violation and capitulation because the male penetrates them in the sexual act.[29] Paz reads this physical act as a symbol of the natural state for the female—acceptance of the superior male, submission, and abuse are her lot. Paz declares that the Chingada is La Malinche and that she is the Mexican Eve, mother to each Mexican. All Mexican women are her daughters—*chingadas* all. And Mexican men are either *chingones* (those who humiliate, castigate, and offend others) or "hijos de la chingada" (dishonored sons of a violation over which they had no control; *The Labyrinth of Solitude*, 75). No wonder "they"—these Mexicans projected by Paz—are lost in the labyrinth: it is a situation of shame and degradation.

"¡Hijos de la chingada!"—the *grito* (cry) of national identity shouted aloud on the night of September 15—becomes for Paz the point of departure for his entire elaboration of the relationship between the Chingada and Marina-Malinche. In one segment (86), Paz implies that to be an "hijo de la chingada" is to be the fruit of a violation and that the first violation, which engendered the first of these "children of the *chingada*," was the rape of La Malinche by Cortés. In his discussion, Paz first seems to qualify who belongs to this sad category of sons (68); but the thrust of the chapter and the reactions of his readers indicate that the prevalent reading for Paz's explication of the phrase "los hijos de la chingada" is that all Mexican men suffer from this sorry state. "To the Mexican there are only two possibilities in life: either he inflicts the actions implied by *chingar* on others or else he suffers them himself at the hands of others" (78).

If we examine these various statements closely we note the lack of consistency in Paz's approach not only to these "hijos" but also to La Malinche, Doña Marina, and La Chingada. On the one hand, he states with great conviction: "It is true that she gave herself voluntarily to the conquistador" (86); yet he also declares that she was violated. After all, in Paz's view, the first of these "hijos de la chingada" was brought forth after the rape of La Malinche by Cortés. Paz also adds that "Doña Marina becomes a figure representing the Indian women who were fascinated, violated or seduced by the Spaniards" (86).

What does Paz want us to believe—was she violated, as a slave might be, or was she so in love with Cortés that she gave herself voluntarily? My questions are not idle remarks; they bring into focus the main negative argument against this woman: that she submitted to the foreigner and rejected the native, starting with the "gift" of her sexual favors. She betrayed the "Indian" first and foremost in the sexual sphere. She is a *malinchista*—open to the stranger and, by extension, to the outside. According to Paz, "the Mexican people have not forgiven La Malinche for her betrayal" (86). He ignores that as a slave Malinche did not have control of her body. While she in all likelihood had few options as a slave, she did become involved in major events. The massacre in Cholula, for example, has been interpreted as if Malinche protected the Spaniards at the expense of the Cholulan warriors, who were ambushed and killed in their own plaza.[30]

Whether or not Paz personally believed in La Malinche's betrayal, the comments in his essay have provoked a negative reaction, if not anger, among many Mexican readers.[31] In exploring the sexual dimension of La Malinche's image as a traitor, Paz did not continue the Romantic reveries of his grandfather and the early twentieth-century biographers of Doña Marina; rather, he reverted to the early nineteenth-century versions in which she is portrayed as the whorish Mexican Eve in whose body betrayal is a natural core. As an intellectual he could have attempted to provide a balanced view of this figure, including both derogatory and positive aspects. Unfortunately, very little in the essay relates to any positive aspect of this woman. It certainly has led to a concretization of her negative status and made even more popular the definition of xenophilia as a particularly Mexican characteristic, also known as *malinchismo*.[32]

Although Paz frames this issue as a national problem regarding the power relationship between men and women, he also seems to have tried to enact this power relationship of male dominance and female submission in the way he attempted to dominate "Helena" Garro, as she was known then. His letters to the young Garro, archived in the Princeton Library, suggest that he wanted to control his future wife's social activities and professional expression.[33] After reading Paz's "anthropological" discussion about the warlike condition of male-female relations in Mexico, it is ironic to learn that on a personal level the war between Paz and Garro was manifested at all levels of their relationship from its onset (for further discussion, see Chapter 6).

Furthermore, if we examine the structure of the essay, we note that the chapter in *The Labyrinth* does not really focus on the historical woman called La Malinche or on specific aspects of the little we know about her life. Concrete references to La Malinche, after the title of the chapter, do not appear until almost the last pages. On pages 77–78 of the 1959 edition (in which the chapter "Los hijos de la Malinche" covers pages 59–80),[34] Paz links La Chingada to La Malinche, after having spent most of the almost twenty preceding pages elaborating on the verb *chingar* and all its forms, meanings, and usages in Latin American culture. Only after clearly establishing how negative it is to be "La Chingada" does he affirm that the first Chingada was La Malinche.

In the brevity of his spatial attention to La Malinche, Paz follows the pattern set not by his grandfather but by Cortés, who referred to that "Indian woman" only twice in the five volumes of his *Letters from Mexico*. Cortés's terseness, however, meant that without other texts La Malinche would have been forgotten. With Paz's text, and the great impact of his interpretation, La Malinche has not been forgotten, just maligned. Ironically, although his commentary consists of only two brief pages, Paz's work has been so influential that it has become *the* hegemonic text to which all subsequent texts must refer. That essay, along with his work in general, has become part of a cultural institution that has been very hard to critique, especially since 1968, in the period after the events known as the Tlatelolco Massacre.[35]

Although Paz's essay continues to be cited almost as an originary text, a growing number of writers and critics mention it only to refute its arguments in their attempt to revise the image of La Malinche as the Chingada or the Mexican Eve. Before briefly commenting on the range of critics who have expressed concerns about Paz's perspective, I should also include a reference to one of the writers whose work appears to support Paz's view of La Malinche as the woman in love and at the same time violated and dominated. Although

Carlos Fuentes (1928) is now generally considered to belong to the group associated with the journal *Nexos* (in opposition to Paz's group in *Vuelta*), *La muerte de Artemio Cruz* (1962; translated as *The Death of Artemio Cruz*, 1964) may be read as offering Fuentes's own riff on Paz's exploration of the importance of the concept *chingar* as well as his ambivalence toward the sexual interactions between La Malinche and Cortés.[36] In this popular novel, Fuentes also combines female sexuality and national politics. Artemio Cruz's marriage to Catalina, for example, is a calculated economic negotiation between men, based not on love but on money and power. It brings to mind the machinations of Pedro Páramo to marry and own the lands of Dolores Preciado in Juan Rulfo's eponymous novel. Offering women and slaves as a commodity or gift as part of political, economic, or military negotiations has been a common practice in many societies. La Malinche herself was exchanged from one group of males to another as part of a military accord.[37]

The relationship portrayed in the Fuentes novel that echoes Paz's representation of the Malinche-Cortés union involves the passionate and patriotic encounter between Cruz, the young revolutionary officer, and Regina, the beautiful *soldadera* (a female soldier of the Revolution or, more informally, a camp follower who cooked, nursed, and provided sexual and emotional comfort). Their coupling is meant to generate the new nation that would arise after a war—not the Conquest but the civil war: the Mexican Revolution. As Artemio chooses to remember it, his idyllic affair was based on love and free will, parallel to Paz's reading of La Malinche giving herself voluntarily to Cortés. Ultimately, however, the reader learns that the encounter was actually a violent rape: Cruz is the ultimate *chingón*, and Regina is La Malinche as Chingada. Postrevolutionary Mexico, Fuentes seems to argue, continues to rely upon a union between men and women that follows Paz's reference to the root paradigm of Malinche and Cortés rather than the glorified romance of Don Ireneo's narratives.

Fuentes was openly intrigued by the Conquest period, as is evident in other works, including his play *Todos los gatos son pardos* ([In the Night] All Cats Are Gray, 1970) and the novel *El naranjo* (The Orange Tree, 1993). Try as he might to appear nationalist and even feminist, Fuentes's works, as Minni Sawhney suggests (172), can be characterized more often as hegemonic texts with an androcentric perspective.[38]

In contrast, Chicana writers have been the most vociferous in their criticism of Paz's version of La Malinche and Mexican national identity. They openly deal with Paz and confront the masculinist perspective of his ideology.

Chicanas who have published their critiques of Paz's negative portrayal of La Malinche include the writers and cultural historians Adelaida del Castillo, Cordelia Candelaria, Cherríe Moraga, and Norma Alarcón.

Adelaida Del Castillo (in 1974), for example, undertakes to rescue women in general and La Malinche in particular from the negative descriptions. She enthusiastically accepts Marina (as she calls her) as "primordial to any conceptualization of '*mexicanidad*' based on '*el mestizaje*' that she initiates . . . any denigrations made against her indirectly defame the character of the mexicana/chicana/female. If there is shame for her, there is shame for us; we suffer the effects of these implications" (141). Del Castillo personalizes her critique of Paz, because she identifies herself with Marina in a positive fashion. She also goes beyond the purely sexual role for Marina and for women. She focuses instead on the religious motivations for Marina's behavior. Paz does not bring these up, although they are certainly important for Don Ireneo, who never misses an opportunity to portray Doña Marina as a devout and practicing Catholic.

For Paz, however, Malinche's religious or political activity is not as important as her sexual role. Anna Lanyon, an Australian writer who has written her own version of the Malinche story with great sensitivity and insight, reminds us of that important nuance of Paz's presentation:

> Malinche, Paz said, had become the symbol, the very embodiment of that violation [of the Conquest]. She had consorted with Cortés and borne a child to him, the first *mestizo*. She had brought forth a new race of sons, but in doing so she had offended their sense of honour. This, Paz believed, was the essence of Malinche's reputation as a traitor. He made no pretence about political treachery. He seemed to sense that this was always an invalid accusation. Malinche was a traitor to her sons because they saw in her the shame of a violated woman. (200–201)

It is an ongoing irony of war that women who are raped are blamed for their own violation and loss of honor. Paz reminds us that in Mexico women still carry this unjust onus. How ironic, too, that some writers continue to repeat the view that La Malinche/Marina is the initiator of *el mestizaje*. Historical documents and common sense would lead us to reject the notion that no mestizo, child of the two peoples, was born until the birth of Martín Cortés, son of Malintzin and Cortés, in 1522. Martín may be the first whose life is documented, as Don Luis Leal suggests,[39] but he could not have been the first mestizo born on Mexican soil. Mestizos were probably born nine months after the first Spaniard arrived. Moreover, we do know of the documented case of the shipwrecked Gonzalo Guerrero, who mentions the children he sired with his unnamed indigenous wife. We should ask, then, is Martín Cortés considered the first mestizo because of his upper-class status, his Catholic religion, his mother's status as a purported princess, and his father's importance as conquistador? As Don Ireneo has tried to suggest in his narratives, being the mother of the first mestizo would be an unquestionably positive role.

In Paz's presentation the designation of Martín as the "first mestizo" is no longer simply the sign of La Malinche's positive role as mother of the mestizo nation, as Don Ireneo would have it, but is the proof of her violation and status as the first Chingada. He has cast her in the mold of the patriarchal, colonized woman that Bernal Díaz del Castillo first suggested, but without the context of admiration and respect. This reading of La Malinche follows the stereotype of the representation of the patriarchal woman—an inferior being who is in the thrall of the superior male. Jason Wilson states that mostly non-Mexican readers see Paz as an iconoclast in regard to "conventional, societal values and morality" (66). But I would suggest that in regard to gender relations Paz maintains a traditional perspective both in his personal life and in his professional writings.[40]

We discern in his position with regard to ethnicity and gender that Paz holds the view of a superior European male who acknowledges the submissive and dependent state of the ethnic female. "She" is the one to be disadvantaged and stripped of any cultural content; "she" certainly has no expression of political agency. Such a critique of his gendered use of La Malinche conforms to Paz's general philosophy, as noted by Jorge Aguilar Mora (*La divina pareja*, 42) and William Katra (8), reflecting the ideology of a middle-class establishment writer who does not ground his observations in a social or geographical context. For non-Mexicans Paz's discussions of the "macho" and La Malinche have been particularly influential but also detrimental. I draw this conclusion from Paz's discussion of his concept of machismo in "The Sons of La Malinche." Not unexpectedly, the idea of the macho Mexican male is inextricably linked with the history of La Malinche. For Paz, Mexican historical patterns explain the development of machismo. The behavior pattern associated with the macho has its roots in the Conquest and is derived from the sexual behavior of the Spaniards vis-à-vis their dominance of Indian women, beginning with Cortés's exploitation of La Malinche. Most readers would deduce from Paz's argument that the macho and La Malinche are related, that being a Mexican male means treating the female as a figure to be dominated and controlled.

Finally, it is also important to remember the great irony of Paz's scrutiny of La Malinche as La Chingada, the open one, the *malinchista*. "She embodies the open, the *chingado* . . . to our closed, stoic, impassive Indians. Cuauhtémoc and Doña Marina are thus two antagonistic and complementary figures" (86). If Cuauhtémoc represents the one who is closed to alien influences and La Malinche is the one who embraces the foreign, then Paz could well have said, with a Flaubertian flourish, that "La Malinche, c'est moi." Moreover, it is noteworthy that Paz uses this term to refer to the relationship between himself and Sor Juana (*Sor Juana or the Traps of Faith*, 526–527; see Chapter 6). Many readers would agree with Luis Leal that Paz is a "universal man of letters" ("Octavio Paz and the Chicano," 115). Paz has always been associated with outside influences. Alejandro Sela Obarrio suggests even more bluntly his relationship with Malinche in his focused study "La Malinche y Octavio Paz," saying that in his life and artistic work Paz "is seen as extremely 'affected by foreign influences'" (124).[41]

An assessment of Paz's career and worldview, including his choice of a second spouse, makes public that he is more akin to a Malinche than to a Cuauhtémoc. As Paz suggests, for him La Malinche represents openness, interest in the foreign, while Cuauhtémoc is the symbol for "closedness" to interventions or to foreign influences. Let us consider, then, that at crucial times in his career Paz did not react with "closedness" but left his country. He was an ambassador who represented Mexico, yes, but he traveled widely and lived many years outside his country. At one point, he was considered "Mexico's most widely traveled poet" (Chiles, 57). He was very influenced by movements originating beyond Mexico's borders, including surrealism, Indian culture and philosophy, and others.[42] He even compiled his investigations on India's history, religions, philosophy, and Sanskrit erotic poetry, among other topics, in *Vislumbres de la India* (1995), translated as *In Light of India* by Eliot Weinberger in 1997. He would have reacted negatively to being labeled a *malinchista* rather than a "global citizen"; but at the same time, his perspective on La Malinche and her so-called "choices" led him to equate her with the same phenomenon in a negative way.

In contrast to Octavio Paz, both Don Ireneo and Elena Garro empower their Malinche to choose the partner she prefers, changing her from a submissive, violated woman to a figure of resolve and power. Her sexuality is not represented in terms of violence or lasciviousness but is expressed independently of Cortés. While Ireneo Paz's Marina chooses the Spaniard, Elena Garro's Malinche reverts to her indigenous lover. The difference in the selection of the spouse is significant. Garro's rejection of the paradigms offered by Don Ireneo and Octavio Paz is a major change that refutes not only Don Ireneo's continuation of the Díaz del Castillo paradigm but also the stereotype of the violated woman put forth by Paz.

In her texts written while she was still married to Paz, Elena Garro does not openly confront the patriarchal views of her then husband, but she does present a veiled review of some of his premises that ends up questioning (in *Los recuerdos del porvenir*, 1963) and finally subverting (in "La culpa es de los tlaxcaltecas," 1964) the basic approach put forth by Octavio Paz. As a reader of Mexican culture, I find in Garro's novel and short story an apparent rewriting of Paz's essay on La Malinche and a subversion of the key ideas: that La Malinche was so in love with Cortés that she "gave herself voluntarily," in Paz's famous phrase, and that she betrayed her "people" for him. Garro's Malinche figures exhibit some similarities with the tradition; but key differences from the archetypal figure enshrined in cultural memory demonstrate the degree of Garro's independence from male control and power, as represented by both Octavio Paz and Don Ireneo. In her own way, Garro is rejecting a patriarchal, Eurocentrist cultural memory and attempting to redirect her country's attitudes toward women and the indigenous peoples.

Garro's novel *Los recuerdos del porvenir* received the Villaurrutia Prize in 1963 and is still her most celebrated text. In 1966 Octavio Paz commented: "[I]t is a work of extraordinary truth, one of the most perfect creations of contemporary Spanish American literature" ("Novela y provincia," 143–144).[43] The positive evaluation appears sincere and has been validated by both a receptive readership and positive critical affirmation. On one level, the novel can be categorized as a historical work whose context is the Cristero Rebellion,[44] but it also re-creates mythic patterns that permeate Mexican culture, as I first noted in my earlier study of the Malinche paradigm (*La Malinche*). My essay "The Figure of La Malinche in the Texts of Elena Garro" was the first to show explicitly that Garro's novel moved beyond the Cristero uprising to incorporate the Malinche subtext.

The novel is difficult to summarize. It works on many levels, and its structure, narrative discourse, and use of time do not reflect the practices of the typical historical novel of its time. Its surface story takes place during the 1920s in the small town of Ixtepec, in Garro's home state of Puebla, and portrays the impact of the Mexican government's attempt to uphold the anticlerical laws of the 1917 Constitution. A military cacique, Francisco Rosas, is sent to govern the town. He arrives with his army and a coterie of women, among whom is his beautiful mistress Julia. The townspeople resent these outsiders, just as they refuse to obey the laws against the church. Narrated by the town of Ixtepec itself, part 1 of the novel focuses on the townspeople's reactions to Rosas and Julia, while part 2 describes more fully the town's attempts to help the priest, Father Beltrán, and Roque, the sexton, to escape Ixtepec and join the Cristeros fighting in the area. Critics have generally focused on the complexities of the unusual narrator, the roles of Isabel Moncada and Julia Andrade, and the themes of memory and patriarchy.

If Ireneo and Octavio Paz both dealt with the "strange permanence" (Paz, *The Labyrinth of Solitude*, 87) of La Malinche in Mexican culture on an overt level, Garro's texts illustrate that it is a major subtext influencing male-female relationships. She does not refer directly to La Malinche in this novel or in the short story "La culpa es de los tlaxcaltecas," but the motifs, patterns of behavior, and themes clearly lead the attentive reader to what I have called the Malinche-Cortés paradigm. Garro reacts to the androcentric perspective of La Malinche by first creating a patriarchal context for her characters then subverting this authoritarian world. For example, Conchita in *Recollections of Things to Come* offers her memory of this misogyny in a meaningful internal monologue:

> She remembered her father and her grandfather speaking about how unbearable women were because they talked so much . . . her grandfather and her father went on talking for endless hours about the inferiority of women. (169)

In this short, ironic observation by Conchita, we learn that generation after generation of Mexican men, from grandfather to son to grandson, have held the view that women are inferior and talk too much. Never mind that the grandfather and Conchita's father are the ones who speak "endlessly" while she, the female child, is speechless, or that the men's actions are in direct contrast to what they say.[45] This misogyny provides the cultural context for the attitude toward La Malinche, who not only "talked too much"—she was a translator and spoke when no one else did—but was also a woman, a member of that inferior "tribe" against whom men must always be on guard. "Clearly the most devastating aspect of the treatment of women has to do with the repetitive and continual nature of the stereotyped portrayal . . . they are seen to forever repeat the same story—that of La Malinche" (Cypess, *La Malinche*, 120).

In her depiction of androcentric society, "the future was the repetition of the past" (*Recollections*, 58). Although the military battles of Conquest were over, Garro shows that the patterns of behavior documented in that conflict have persisted, especially when it comes to male-female relations. The same kinds of gender and ethnic relations that erupted in the Conquest also marked the period of the continuation of the Mexican Revolution known as the Cristero Rebellion (1926–1929). Garro adds a point that is not found openly in Paz's text, however: the repetition will occur, she suggests, until a new sociocultural pattern develops that eliminates such harmful relations and thus prevents their reoccurrence or, perhaps, their regularity and acceptance. In actuality, Paz's comments in *The Labyrinth* are descriptive but have been taken to be proscriptive; Garro is arguing for change and suggesting ways to transform the paradigm in favor of more equitable power relations.

Paz finds that women are to blame for the Mexican condition of inferiority or at least for a feeling of being betrayed by their progenitors, Adam/Cortés and Eve/Malinche; Garro, in contrast, shows that women have always been treated with discrimination. In the narrative world of the novel, Martín Moncada, patriarch of one of the households in the town of Ixtepec, looks at his wife in a Paz-like manner: "as a strange and delightful being who shared her life with him but jealously guarded a secret that could not be revealed" (*Recollections*, 26). A more strident antifeminism comes from the mouth of the figure who represents Cortés, the *chingón*, in Paz's categorization of behavior. Gen. Francisco Rosas is an outsider to Ixtepec, a conquistador who takes over the town and rules it despotically. For him, "all women are whores" (*Recollections*, 241), echoing Paz's report that for Mexicans all women are *chingadas*. Rosas treats women as if they were all Malinches, to be subdued and raped according to his will. Rosas's characterization follows closely the portrait of the *chingón* as it is presented in *The Labyrinth of Solitude*. As the novel ends, the narrator even has Rosas thinking as a Paz Mexican, that he was "condemned to walk alone, forsaken by fortune" (*Recollections*, 282). Garro, in opposition to Paz, gives voice in *Recollections* to the reactions of the women, creating a dialogue that was not present in *The Labyrinth of Solitude*. The representation of women in her novel is complex, including women who repeat the Paz paradigm of submissiveness but also women who rebel against the stereotype, even in a warlike context.

Garro introduces a secondary woman character who represents a clear description of the sad lot of Mexican women. Sitting silently at meetings when the men are allowed to speak at will, Conchita in her feminine stillness represents the opposite of the active, dynamic, and openly, fluent/talkative Malinche. Yet in her silence she is perceptive and ready to be rebellious. Her comments express the notable difference between the androcentric world and her own sad destiny: "what happiness it is to be a man and be able to say what one thinks, she said with melancholy" (*Recollections*, 22). Unlike La Malinche, also known as "Cortés's *lengua* [tongue]," Conchita never took part in the conversations but sat quietly, witnessing. She seems to be Paz's passive woman (85), yet the reader knows that beneath her submissive surface she entertains rebellious thoughts and perceptive views about women's role.

While Conchita's powerlessness to speak contrasts with La Malinche's use of voice, the actions of both Julia Andrade and Isabel Moncada (the main women characters of the novel) parallel the legendary sexual behavior attributed to La Malinche. As carefully shown in my previous essays, Julia and Isabel are both portrayed within the Malinche paradigm (Cypess, "The Figure of La Malinche" and *La Malinche*). We know very little about the early life of Julia before she arrives in town as the mistress of Rosas and even less once she disappears from historical documentation. In that regard, she resembles the original La Malinche: no definitive documentation tells us when or how she died.[46] Rosas and his entourage are living in the Hotel Jardín (Garden Hotel)—an ironic allusion to the Edenic Mexico of the past, which legend says was violated by the conquistadors. Julia, like La Malinche, is the conquistador's woman and is blamed for everything bad that happens in town; but it seems absurd to the reader that the townspeople should blame Julia for their misfortunes.

For much of the story Julia is very much La Chingada, the woman forced into submission, passive, who offers no resistance to violence, to paraphrase Paz. Does the presence of Julia prove, then, the eternal presence of a Malinche who suffers guilt by association with the conquistador? Is she one of the long line of *vendidas* who prove again that Malinche is the "Mexican woman," in Paz's terms?[47] Although Julia is called "the messenger of misfortune," Garro re-creates aspects of the negative pattern only to prove its inaccuracy for contemporary women.

The "new" woman that Julia represents soon asserts herself when she takes advantage of the opportunity to escape from the Hotel Jardín, her anti-Eden, and abandon Rosas. Whereas Cortés discarded La Malinche when she was no longer useful to him, Julia escapes before Rosas has the chance to betray her. Another stranger arrives in town: Felipe Hurtado, who is the opposite of Rosas. He comes to rescue Julia rather than subjugate her. We learn that Julia did not willingly give herself to Rosas, because she welcomes the escape provided by Hurtado. Unlike La Malinche, who was given to another man when Cortés no longer needed her services, Julia *chooses* to leave with a man of her own preference. Clearly, Garro is subverting the role of women proposed by Paz's essay.

As if in retribution for the offensive treatment suffered by La Malinche at the hands of the *chingón*/conquistador, Garro presents scenes in which General Rosas is pining for Julia. His behavior directly contrasts with the comportment of the men in La Malinche's life, from his open expression of his love for her to his drunken behavior, which brings to mind the Jaramillo episode in the Malinche legend. According to some stories, and as cited by Cortés secretary, López de Gómera, Jaramillo was reputed to have been drunk when he married La Malinche after she had already given birth to Cortés's child, as if he could not go through with the ceremony in a sober state. Rosas, on the contrary, drinks himself silly because Julia appears indifferent to his love. As the bartender discloses to the amazed townspeople, "The more he loves her, the more she distances herself from him. Nothing pleases her: neither jewels nor delicacies" (*Recollections*, 91). When Rosas confesses to Julia "I live just for you," she answers, "I know" (*Recollections*, 92), a strange dialogue indeed, with the macho acting humbly, admitting his own weakness to the woman. Yet more often than not she is his captive, physically imprisoned in the lost paradise that Ixtepec/Mexico has become.

Unlike the original Malinche, for whom the second husband was no different ethnically or militarily from Cortés, this avatar is rescued by a marginal figure coming from the outside: Felipe Hurtado, who has not been contaminated by the negative environment of Ixtepec (Anderson, "El ahogado," 103). Julia and Felipe successfully escape the wrath of General Rosas because of the force of their own love relationship. Somehow, before Rosas can seek vengeance on Hurtado and kill him, chronological time literally and magically stands still in Ixtepec: in the frozen darkness, Felipe escapes with Julia. The description of the scene of their hurried departure focuses on the magical qualities of that moment when time did not progress, when the inevitable routine of the everyday suddenly was arrested. Garro seems to be telling us that under certain circumstances the past does not have to predict the future, that destiny is not preordained. Just as the historical Malinche faded into a void, so do Julia and Felipe; but the new Malinche purposefully brings about her own erasure from history in order to live with the man she loves.

Although Paz alleged that La Malinche freely chose Cortés as her partner, belying any relation to her historical status, it is more rational to consider that the historical Malinche, as a slave, had little choice in the selection of her male partners. Garro's Julia comes closer to behaving as we might have hoped for the real Malinche—escaping from history because she has found a reciprocal love relationship. In one sense, Garro might be regarded as restating Don Ireneo's portrayal of Doña Marina and Juan Jaramillo, who also find love and reject the "gran chingón." From a feminist perspective, however, it is true that Julia still is tied to a man in order to escape the "circular hell" (*Recollections*, 255).

In *Recollections*, Garro develops another Malinche avatar in the rendering of Isabel Moncada, whose final trajectory differs from that of Julia but more closely resembles that suffered by the historical woman La Malinche as she has been portrayed in legends and popular culture. Isabel is an unlikely Malinche at first glance: she is the daughter of one of the bourgeois families in Ixtepec, neither a slave nor an outcast like the prostitute Julia. Isabel, like Conchita, is clearly aware of the marked differences between the genders that their culture enforces:

> Isabel disliked having differences made between her and her brothers. The idea that a woman's only future was matrimony she found humiliating. For them to speak of marriage as a solution made her feel like a commodity that had to be sold at any price. (*Recollections*, 17)

Isabel views her own position in twentieth-century Mexico as no better than a "commodity," reminding readers that La Malinche was indeed treated as an article of trade with commercial value, to be bartered, sold, or given away to strangers. Within her culture, she did not have the right to determine her own future, and the textual references to Isabel also indicate that as a woman her behavior was almost "predetermined." For no logical or experiential reasons, Isabel suffers from a sense of guilt and is labeled a traitor: "before him [her father], Isabel lowered her eyes, feeling guilty" (*Recollections*, 156). Long before Rosas enters the town, Nicolás, her brother, calls her a "traitor" (27). His attitude toward his sister seems to prove that for certain cultural patterns "one generation follows another, and each repeats the acts of the one before it" (*Recollections*, 243). This inevitability, which Paz would consider a predetermination of behavior, or what modern theorists would call essentialist cultural identity (as Diane Fuss and Judith Butler critique it), would account for the permanence of the Malinche-Cortés paradigm that affects male-female relations in Mexico. In *Los recuerdos* and also in "La culpa es de los tlaxcaltecas" (as demonstrated below), Garro offers a nuanced response to such proposals of predetermination.

Given that the re-creation of the Malinche paradigm in aspects of both Julia Andrade and Isabel Moncada's behavior shows the impact of cultural memory, we might infer that Garro supports the Paz idea of the repetition of the past in the present and future. After all, the very title of the novel suggests that rather than the future being predicated on past memories, the future is no different from the past: *Los recuerdos del porvenir* (Recollections of Things to Come). Nevertheless, Garro seems to be teasing the reader with this procedure of recalling the characteristics that cultural memory attributes to the Malinche paradigm, only to subvert it. Robert Anderson provides a hint of what is taking place when he notes that the novel juxtaposes two ways of behaving in the face of oppression and fear. Anderson observes that Felipe Hurtado and Julia Andrade are successful in escaping because they embrace "illusion, free will and reciprocal love." Isabel and General Rosas, however, both suffer a loss of illusion, love, and free will, a "tragic petrification, opacity, and inertia" causing their downfall (Anderson, *"La señora en su balcón y Los recuerdos del porvenir,"* 134).[48]

Julia, in contrast with Isabel, was able to shake off the stereotype of the Malinche paradigm because she found a reciprocal love in the person of Felipe Hurtado. They were able to escape the strictures of both chronological time and historical reality, proving that the Malinche-Cortés paradigm can be eluded when there is equality between the partners. In contrast, the Isabel-Rosas relationship is a disquieting variant on the popular version of the Malinche legend. Isabel appears to throw away all traditional bourgeois strictures when she pursues Rosas. Garro teases her reader by first fashioning an Isabel with characteristics that replicate the Malinche paradigm. When Isabel learns that Julia has disappeared, Isabel feels a strong desire to run to Rosas: "If she could have done so, she would have rushed to Francisco Rosas' side" (*Recollections*, 156). She distances herself from her family, as La Malinche was supposed to have done, in order to be with this stranger. She also becomes a prisoner of Rosas, however, confined to the Garden Hotel, a postlapsarian garden of Eden and place of sin and betrayal. Her brothers, Nicolás and Juan, did not want to be separated from her; but they are destined to die in the course of the battle of the Cristeros and to blame Isabel because of her betrayal: her selection of General Rosas as her man.

Nevertheless, while Isabel "performs" aspects of the Malinche paradigm, in the end Garro implies that the behavior of Mexican women need not conform to the parameters constructed from past experiences. Although all the indicators may be there—the presence of a Cortés-like conquistador, the awareness of the betrayal motif, forbidden sexual relations—Garro suggests that women can break away from the inevitability of the Malinche pattern. While Julia escapes with the help of a man (a sign of the reality of Mexican women's lives in the twentieth century), Isabel, in another scene of magical realism, appears to have turned into stone: "In her rush to find her lover, Isabel Moncada got lost. After looking for her for a long time, Gregoria found her lying far down the hill, transformed into a stone" (*Recollections*, 287).

This conclusion to the trajectory of Isabel's path has been read in many different ways.[49] It is her maid, Gregoria, who suggests that Isabel has turned to stone. She is not a reliable narrator, as Amy Kaminsky reminds us ("Residual Authority," 104). On the one hand, the report that Isabel has been transformed into stone implies that she is being punished for not conforming to traditional female behavior in her relationship with Rosas (Gregoria's attitude serves as a repository of tradition). On the other hand, becoming a monument offers many other interpretations, as Amalia Gladhart summarizes in her essay "Present Absence: Memory and Narrative in *Los recuerdos del porvenir*." As Gladhart explains, "In the evacuated form of Isabel Moncada, we see a monument that attempts to narrate a national myth, but that is unable to do so. She becomes a kind of cenotaph or empty tomb, a marker for one buried elsewhere . . . she stands as a memorial to official violence" (96). I would add that Isabel as stone stands as a memorial to the violence done to women in the name of La Malinche by official history. Like La Malinche in the eyes of the Mexican nation, she was punished for her choice of a mate and all that implied in terms of culture, religion, and class. But Garro still shows this woman as a questioning, reactive being, who struggles against the hegemonic views of her society. That performance is not an easy one; nor does it necessarily lead to success.

Garro stresses even more forcefully the important difference between her Malinche figures and the Malinche of cultural memory in her short story "La culpa es de los tlaxcaltecas," through the way in which the woman character chooses her mate.[50] Again, in this text no individuals bear names from the Conquest period, but it soon becomes evident to the alert reader that this story of love and betrayal repeats events dictated by a cultural memory of the Malinche-Cortés root paradigm. The story can be read as an allegory of conflict and resolution in which the choice of mate implies different attitudes about national identity and the intersection of ethnicity and gender.

Laura as the Malinche avatar, her present husband (Pablo), and her first husband (an unnamed Indian from the Conquest period) appear to play out the traditional roles referred to by both Don Ireneo and Paz, only to enact new patterns of behavior at the end. Instead of contrasting the actions of two women who wrestle in opposing ways with the Malinche paradigm, as in *Recollections*, here one woman's different actions in regard to her spouses are examined in two distinct periods, which happen to coexist. Laura exists first as a woman of the twentieth century but declares that she is confronted with "la otra niña que fui" (that other girl that I was, 11) because of an encounter with her "other husband," an Indian from the Conquest period. While many critics have analyzed the magical realism elements of this story,[51] I would like to focus on the ways in which Garro offers a direct challenge to the archetypes presented by Don Ireneo and Paz. Garro's provocative character Laura rejects Pablo and his hegemonic, androcentric ideology in favor of returning to her first love, the indigenous male, and to a Mexico that is faithful to the indigenous past (Cypess, *La Malinche*, 166).

In this story, unlike the texts of the male writers, Laura has a female confidante, the kitchen maid Nacha. It is also significant that the story has another female character: Margarita, who is Laura's mother-in-law. Her role, in contrast to that of Nacha, is to represent the patriarchal female; she acts according to the cultural script for females, being frightened of the unknown, ready to placate her son, and reliant on the male perspective, for example. Nacha, most likely ethnically indigenous or mestiza and therefore linked more closely to the indigenous world of the Conquest than Margarita or Pablo, whose ethnicity is Creole or white, serves for Laura as both sounding board and validator. For the reader, Nacha also authenticates what takes place in the story, an important function in the world of magical realism.

Reminiscent of Don Ireneo's Malinche figures, Laura tries to explain to Nacha why she would have married a man such as Pablo.[52] This discussion of mates echoes the scenes in Don Ireneo's novels in which the indigenous women look at their indigenous companions and see them as inferior to the Spanish conquistadors, whom they then accept as their husbands. In contrast, Laura, in her own words, confesses that she fell in love with Pablo, the white man, only because he reminded her of the Indian man she had first known (compare this outlook to the opposite one expressed by Don Ireneo's Otila in *Amor y suplicio*). After marrying him, Laura soon realized that he was not like the other man, but someone strange and unappealing. It is instructive to examine the exact text of Laura's complaints:

> [I]t seemed he would change into the other man whom he looked like. But it wasn't true. Immediately he became absurd, without memory, and he merely repeated the gestures of all the men of Mexico City. . . . How many times does he start arguments in the movies and in restaurants? . . . On the other hand, my cousin husband never, but never, becomes angry with his woman. (11)[53]

The character traits that Laura attributes to Pablo—his jealous rages, his absurd behavior, his physical abuse—lead the reader to judge him to be a stereotypical "macho" in the style that Paz depicts in "Los hijos de la Malinche" (as shown in Chapter 4, that is how he himself treated his young fiancée and wife). Clearly, as Laura describes him, Pablo behaves like a jealous male who is always afraid that he is being betrayed. For Laura, this pattern of behavior marks the "men of Mexico City." For them, all women are Malinche figures according to the stereotype—women who are untrustworthy, sexually promiscuous, and requiring domination.

Almost all explorations of the Malinche-Cortés relationship assume a story much as Paz describes it: the young woman falls in love with the Spanish conquistador and ignores her family, her *patria*, and her blood ties, in order to follow him and do as he commands. For both of the Paz men, Malinche's choices, motivated by "love," serve as an allegorical expression of the military, social, and political conditions that inform national identity. Her gesture is read as a synecdoche for the actions of the indigenous peoples vis-à-vis the Europeans: the female is in the thrall of the male, and the Amerindian is dominated by the European. Until the twentieth century, very few Mexicans would have questioned this pattern or suggested possible changes; even among the Indigenists, who supported Amerindian culture, women were still considered inferior.[54]

As a response to this cultural memory that Paz suggests will always be part of Mexico's future, Garro offers a different and surprising conclusion. In this story, Laura undertakes a number of voyages—through time and space—that also impact the cultural and social trajectories of modern Mexico. We cannot really say that Laura goes back and forth in time, because the two temporal zones appear to exist on the same plane; but her movements are from the center (Mexico City) to the periphery, back to the city, and then finally to another place, where she is united with her indigenous husband and all he represents. I have explored these moves in another context,[55] but now I would like to review what Garro's reconfiguration of the Malinche figure entails. Instead of reacting within a traditional paradigm, Laura rejects the patriarchal behavior of Pablo, much as the Marina of Don Ireneo's novel is repulsed by the immoral Cortés. But the new twist is that—rather than turning her attention to another "man of Mexico City," to another conquistador—this new Malinche chooses the indigenous man. This revolutionary choice is fraught with meanings that reflect the difference between the Pazian—traditional male—attitude toward ethnicity and gender and Garro's more progressive perspective.

While Paz's essay attempts to convince us that the past predicts the future and that the cultural performance of La Malinche and Cortés must perforce continue through eternity, Garro's stories offer us a different conclusion to a long-term cultural memory, as indicated by Laura's specific actions. One in particular holds great significance because it involves one of the few concrete references to Mexican historical documents. In her heightened state—called craziness by her mother-in-law, depression by the doctor—Laura insists on reading "la Historia de Bernal Díaz del Castillo," as the text is called in the story ("La culpa es de los tlaxcaltecas," 28). Can it be that Laura's reading of Díaz del Castillo, whose representation of Doña Marina served as a subtext for Don Ireneo, is a subtle reminder of Don Ireneo's positive representation of the indigenous woman? Reference to Díaz del Castillo, as the text that feeds the positive view of Marina for Mexican cultural memory, can certainly be a sign of Garro's rejection of the negative view of La Malinche that Paz includes in his essay. In addition, it suggests that Laura may be rereading the canonical texts as a way to recall the original behavior of the archetypal woman whose actions she is being compelled to imitate by the force of cultural memory. At the same time, the reference to Díaz del Castillo stimulates the reader to re-member the past as recorded in his text but then to reread the actions of Laura that discard the earlier version as inadequate.

Don Ireneo, following Díaz del Castillo's account of Doña Marina, repre-sents the Eurocentric version of how the good indigenous people were sup-posed to behave—accepting the European cultural "gifts" as they were brought to the Americas. Díaz del Castillo acknowledges some of the splendors of Mex-ica culture, including the marketplaces and the canals. Along with most of the chroniclers, however, he celebrates European cultural traits and largely dismisses the importance of non-European cultural legacies with regard to constructions of national identity. His Marina is happy to accept a Spanish consort and the elevated status accorded to her in Don Ireneo's version. Paz also believes in the greater attractiveness of the Spanish male. Garro stands alone in reconfiguring the trajectory for her Malinche—she chooses the in-digenous male over the Spanish male. Laura had been performing as a white woman married to a member of the Spanish elite living in the center of cul-tural life. In an unexpected move, however, she rejects that life in order to resume a more authentic existence with her first husband. "But the journey from the margins to the center of power is part of the reason La Malinche was labeled a traitor, and for Laura, too, her journey from the periphery to the center marked one kind of betrayal—that of the original Malinche in terms of cultural memory—her disdain of the indigenous population in favor of the Spanish peoples. But Laura, unlike la Malinche, has a second opportunity to review the trajectory of her actions, both geographically and emotionally" (Cypess, "The Cultural Memory of Malinche," 154). Supported by the subaltern Nacha, she leaves the house of the patriarch, the center, and disappears with the Indian, her first husband. Laura takes advantage of an option that La Malinche did not have—to exercise her own agency by leaving her patriarchal home and reuniting with the Indian husband.

Garro also deals with the character trait that is an essential part of the Malinche paradigm—her supposed betrayal of her "people" as the key act of the Conquest period. Laura confesses to Nacha: "I am like them, a traitor." Nacha responds, "I am also treacherous," which places them both on an equal plane.[56] But is it because of their gender that they are traitors or because of their ethnicity? Garro explores the idea of betrayal beginning with the story's title, "La culpa es de los tlaxcaltecas" (It's the Fault of the Tlaxcaltecas), and proves that infidelity can be viewed on many levels. Collective memory usually directs us to think first of women as traitors. Garro's story begins with that assumption only to subvert the idea.

Laura and Nacha call themselves "traitors," but other characters turn out to act that way, while Laura and Nacha are exonerated. For example, Josefa, one of the maids, acts disloyally to her mistress in order to curry favor with the master of the house, the dominant figure. Nacha and Laura, in contrast, join together as confidantes against all the others and play out new courses of conduct that belie cultural memory. In their relationship to each other, Laura and Nacha do not act disloyally or mistreat each other. Nacha attempts to attend to her mistress's needs as best she can, trying to intuit what to give her or what to say, and Laura feels an intimacy with Nacha that is not evident in any of her other relationships in the Aldama household. When Laura disappears at the conclusion, after having reunited with her indigenous husband, Nacha also leaves the Aldama house in a poignant display of solidarity. Because "betrayal" is often viewed as a female to male action, Laura and Nacha's solidarity is generally overlooked by critics.

Garro promotes an even more subversive position in regard to betrayal when it comes to the female-male relationships. Is Laura acting like a "typical female" and betraying her husband Pablo by accepting her first husband's invitation to return with him? Our answer should be tempered by considering that Pablo is false-hearted in his behavior toward his wife—physically harming her, refusing to understand her confused state, and interpreting her actions within a patriarchal paradigm. Laura rightly ends this abusive relationship in order to return to her roots by going off with the indigenous man of the story, whom she had abandoned earlier for the white man.

These women represented by Garro were first formed in the Malinche paradigm set into place by a Mexican nationalist and patriarchal system depicted by Don Ireneo and Paz. The women show signs of being passive and subordinate to the male authority figures, the *chingones* who force them to act as *chingadas*. It is a tribute to Garro's genius that she responds as she does to the Paz thesis. She does not deny the "strange permanence of Cortés and La Malinche in the Mexican's imagination and sensibilities." But, if they are "symbols of a secret conflict" (*The Labyrinth of Solitude*, 87), Garro attempts to explore the nature of that conflict and the ways to resolve it more fully, from a feminist perspective. As we have seen from the comments of Isabel and Conchita in *Recollections* and the harsh treatment of Julia by Rosas, Garro appears to blame patriarchal society for the oppression of women and for the bad reputation of La Malinche.

One reason why writers like Paz emphasize the strange permanence of the Malinche-Cortés paradigm has to do with the belief that in Mexico "there is no single time; all of our times are alive, all of our pasts are present" (Fuentes, quoted by Wucker). Garro's texts may also seem to be supporting this belief in cyclical time, or in the concurrent nature of all times in Mexico, which would mean that the present is predicted by the past and that the future will be the same as the past and the present. Although this belief is suggested by the title *Recollections of Things to Come*, the different endings for Julia and for Isabel prove that change can occur and that the past need not foretell the future. And Laura's experiences certainly propose a revolutionary turn. As the narrative suggests, she lived first as an Amerindian woman of the Conquest period married to an indigenous man and later as the wife of a twentieth-century male of the Mexican upper class. Against the teachings of her national culture, Laura chooses to return to the indigenous male and his way of life. On the one hand, it might appear superficially that this is an indication of the circularity of life; but on the other hand, considering that Laura experiences life with the upper class and decides to reject that path, her decision is not a repetition of the past. On the contrary, through Laura's actions Garro proposes a rejection of Mexican (sexual and ethnic) history as it was depicted by both Don Ireneo and Octavio Paz.

Don Ireneo Paz implicitly accepts and supports Europhilia and patriarchy in his treatment of gender and ethnic relations, and Paz broadens these concepts in "The Sons of Malinche." While most critics focus on his description of the transgressions of La Malinche—her betrayal and sinful sexuality—Paz also describes the behavior of the Mexican male, the *chingón*, in essentialist terms. His essay reveals how Mexican notions of gender and masculinity have developed and persisted from the Conquest period. The inferiority of the Amerindian as a valid spouse—whether male or female—is a powerful notion imbedded deep in Mexican cultural memory, from the time of what psychologists might want to call the "primal scene" of the Mexican mestizo nation: the coupling of La Malinche and Cortés. Literary texts no less than sociological and psychological studies attest to the power of that cultural memory, whereby the woman, whatever her ethnicity, is considered inferior, especially in the hierarchical relationship of a Mexican marriage (Collier with Quaratiello, 220).[57] Moreover, within the context of a Europhilic patriarchy, Amerindian and mestizo males are denied patriarchal status. They are "effeminized" as a way to justify their subjugation (Adorno, 232).[58] Rather than being treated as privileged males, being Indian categorizes them as feminized and therefore weak, vulnerable, submissive to the "real" male—the conquistador.

Garro's reconfiguration of the Malinche paradigm seems to reflect what contemporary theory tells us about the notion of a "national imaginary"—the idea that the characteristics of a cultural community are created in the performance of actions rather than being a reflection of essential "national attributes." Despite their differing evaluations of the meaning of La Malinche (a *chingada* according Octavio Paz or a tropicalized version of a Spanish *doña* according to Don Ireneo), both men seem to understand gender, ethnicity, and national history as an essentialized "given" with regard to their conception of cultural identity.[59]

In contrast, Garro, in exploring different choices for her female characters and positing questions about the "givens" of Mexican identity, rejects the notion of an essential identity that cannot be changed. The Malinche paradigm may be imposed upon the men and women, but not because it is part of an essential nature. Rather, the pattern is a culturally determined "fictive entity" based on a cultural script that we can learn and unlearn. In regard to the cultural script, for too long the accepted Mexican perspective concerning the Conquest has been to consider it a "necessary war"—a conflict that brought death and destruction to the indigenous peoples but was indispensable in bringing about the positive advancements to American civilization that the Spanish/European contributions signified. Any possible positive attributes of the indigenous peoples were overlooked, while Spanish/European civilization was considered superior in all spheres—religious, economic, political, military, and artistic. In this reading, La Malinche's role was to facilitate the Spanish success; certainly, Don Ireneo and Octavio Paz see her in terms of support of the Hispanic tradition, while Garro, in contrast, subverts this perspective.

Garro's readers are encouraged to reevaluate what had been handed down as inevitable: "the strange permanence of Cortés and La Malinche in the Mexican's imagination and sensibilities" (Paz, *The Labyrinth of Solitude*, 78). The ultimate lesson for the Malinches of Mexico is that choice is part of the agenda for women and that they have an opportunity through their actions—and not because of a predetermined script—to plot their future.

"To love is to fight."
OCTAVIO PAZ
"Piedra de sol" (Sunstone)

WAR AT HOME

BETRAYALS OF/IN THE MEXICAN REVOLUTION

WHILE READING ABOUT THE INTERNECINE WARFARE and treachery that marked the Conquest period, we cannot help but note that the same factionalism, violence, and betrayals also took place during the years after Mexican independence from Spain (1821) and certainly form part of the history of the Mexican Revolution, the next great war that both Garro and Paz incorporated into their texts. The chaotic nineteenth century, however, was not a fertile theme for them, despite being marked by the War of Independence (1810–1821); the declaration of a Mexican Empire by Agustín de Iturbide (1822–1823); the Mexican-American War (1846–1848); the War of Reform (La Guerra de Reforma, a civil war fought from December 1857 to January 1861); a foreign invasion (known as the War of the French Intervention, 1862–1867), in which the French installed as emperor the Hapsburg Archduke Maximilian and his wife, Carlota; and finally the dictatorship of Porfirio Díaz, which began in 1876.[1]

The Porfiriato, as it is called, brought over thirty years of peace to Mexico, but at a profound cost to the 95 percent of the population not favored by Díaz's policies. The creation of a new class of capitalists and an elite group of intellectuals, the "científicos" (scientists), provided a veneer of intellectual progress as well as foreign satisfaction with Díaz's favoritism in regard to financial deals. But by the turn of the century Mexicans of all classes began to express their dissatisfaction with the authoritarianism and oligarchic tendencies as well as the corruption of the Díaz regime (see Knight, *The Mexican Revolution*). The era of Porfirian Mexico, notwithstanding its patina of progress, depended upon the Machiavellian skills of the dictator to suppress dissension and to outmaneuver opponents; but by 1910 the eighty-year-old Díaz was no longer infallible. He misjudged the depth of dissatisfaction among the elites as well as the growing resentment among the workers, peasants, anticlericals, and democrats. Despite Díaz's elaborate and carefully orchestrated celebration of Mexico's 1810 War of Independence from Spain, by the end of 1910 his enemies were prepared for the battles that would ensue in order to bring down his government. The official history and concomitant myths of the civil war known as the Mexican Revolution were about to be born. Its many critics and victims would include members of the Paz and Garro families, while the two writers themselves would also contribute to the construction of the national myth of "La Revolución."

The first of the great social upheavals of the twentieth century, the Mexican Revolution was one of the bloodiest conflicts in the history of North America, with an estimated 500,000 to more than 1 million lives lost (McCaa). Its successes and failures as well as its chronology are still being discussed in the sociopolitical and literary arenas. It set the stage for modern Mexican history, and contemporary Mexico cannot be understood without reference to the Revolution. The cast of characters involved is practically innumerable, the bibliography of historical writing, film, art, literature, and music is vast, and the numbers of writers who have attempted to express their ideas are legion and among the most renowned in Mexican letters. The lives of both Octavio Paz and Elena Garro were directly affected by the Mexican Revolution. Paz's grandfather, Ireneo Paz, who had fought as a soldier in the War of the French Intervention (1862–1867), was a journalist as well as a novelist during Porfirian times and then supported Francisco I. Madero (1873–1913), a member of the elite landowning class who opposed the reelection of Díaz in 1910.[2] Paz's father, Octavio Paz Solórzano, sided with Emiliano Zapata and, as a lawyer, contributed to the area of agrarian reform. On Garro's mother's side, her uncles were all revolutionaries with Francisco "Pancho" Villa, while another of Garro's uncles, Benito Navarro, fought alongside Gen. Felipe Ángeles, who later would figure as the hero in one of Garro's plays. Thus both writers not only were affected personally by the actual war but also dealt with the theme in a number of their texts, especially Paz's *The Labyrinth of Solitude* and Garro's novel *Recollections of Things to Come* and the play *Felipe Ángeles* (see the discussion below).

In order to understand more fully the context in which Paz and Garro were educated, readers may consult the myriad historical texts dedicated to the conflict, the outbreak of the revolutionary movement, the war itself, the institutional changes imposed by the victors, and the legacy of the Revolution. While there are many opinions about the character and conditions of the Mexican Revolution, it certainly engendered a rich tradition of artistic treasures. Key names in Mexican history, art, literature, film, and song have entered into a universal knowledge base, including iconic representations of the generic Mexican *soldado* and his *soldadera*, with their wide sombreros, bullets strung across their breast, and guns blazing.[3] Beyond all the stereotypes, scholars, aficionados, and revolutionary buffs have an enormous lode of studies, documents, and material cultural artifacts in the cultural arena to ponder.

The figures that are of most importance politically and militarily and often appear as characters in the many literary works about the Revolution include Porfirio Díaz (1830–1915), Francisco I. Madero (1873–1913), Pancho Villa (1878–1923), Emiliano Zapata (1879–1919), Venustiano Carranza (1859–1920), Victoriano Huerta (1850–1916), and Álvaro Obregón (1880–1928). Thus, unlike Cortés, La Malinche, and other figures of past centuries, men like Madero, Obregón, Villa, and especially Zapata have survived in Mexican cultural memory with varying degrees of esteem.[4] José Emilio Pacheco is quoted as saying, "In Mexico, Pancho Villa lost the war, but he won all the literary battles"—a comment that acknowledges the many literary texts that include Villa as a character (quoted in Taibo, 850). Zapata in particular is the figure who has most successfully remained a *positive* folk hero, becoming the inspiration for the popular insurrection that began in Chiapas on January 1, 1994, by the Ejército Zapatista de Liberación Nacional (EZLN: Zapatista Army of National Liberation). The rebels consider themselves to be the intellectual heirs of Zapata and his dedication to land redistribution.[5]

In the field of literary studies, "the literature of the Revolution" marked significant changes in the nature of the Mexican narrative in terms of both content and theme and style. Every student of Latin American Studies has read at least one novel of the Mexican Revolution by eyewitness figures such as Mariano Azuela (*Los de abajo* [translated as *The Underdogs*]), Francisco L. Urquizo (*Tropa vieja* [Old Troop], 1943), Martín Luis Guzmán (*El águila y la serpiente* [The Eagle and the Serpent], 1928; *La sombra del caudillo* [The Shadow of the Tyrant], 1929; *Memorias de Pancho Villa* [Memoirs of Pancho Villa], 1940), Rafael Muñoz (¡*Vámonos con Pancho Villa!* [Let's Go with Pancho Villa!], 1931), and Nellie Campobello (*Cartucho* [Cartridge], 1931; *Las manos de mamá*

[My Mother's Hands], 1938), one of the few women in an almost exclusively male cohort.[6] Subsequent writers also used the Revolution as a theme or as background, mostly to explore its failures, as in the later works of renowned writers Juan Rulfo (*Pedro Páramo*, 1955), Carlos Fuentes (*La muerte de Artemio Cruz*, 1962 [translated as *The Death of Artemio Cruz*, 1964]), and Elena Poniatowska (*¡Hasta no verte, Jesús mío!* [Here's to You, Jesus!], 1969).

The Mexican Revolution touched the lives of Paz and Garro personally in various ways; in their writings, they also represent its impact through different literary expressions. Although Paz is known as the consummate poet, we see the early development of his ideas about the Revolution primarily in the essay. A key number of Garro's fictional pieces—novel, short story, and drama—as well as a collection of essays incorporate her thoughts about the significance of the Mexican Revolution for herself and her country.

While Paz was born in 1914, during the war years, Garro's date of birth has been a source of debate. According to her own words in some interviews, she was born in December 1920; but her birth certificate says December 1916.[7] Although she may not have witnessed the actual battles, she certainly heard stories directly from the protagonists of the war itself, as did the young Octavio Paz.

The Revolution had a direct and irrevocable impact on the life of Paz and his family and changed their path, largely because of their personal connections with Emiliano Zapata. Paz's father, Octavio Paz Solórzano, was intimately associated with Zapata and his struggle for agrarian reform. The northern heroes Felipe Ángeles and Francisco "Pancho" Villa were the figures of admiration for the Garros (see the discussion below), while Madero and Zapata were esteemed in the Paz home. As already noted, both Paz's grandfather and father were affiliated with these major figures in the conflict against Porfirio Díaz. Francisco Madero, who had been the first to call for free elections that led to the overthrow of Díaz, was supported by Don Ireneo (in spite of his long history of association with Porfirio Díaz). Octavio Paz Solórzano, trained as a lawyer, supported Emiliano Zapata and worked for agrarian reform.

As Enrique Krauze recounts, Paz's father was very different from his grandfather, the wise and powerful patriarch. His father was "the macho, the caudillo, the terrifying man, the 'hell-of-a-guy,' the man who left his wife and children under the spell of the Revolution" ("Octavio Paz," 232). According to Krauze, "In 1914, the year his only son was born, Octavio Paz Solórzano joined the peasant army of Emiliano Zapata. He would rise to be Zapata's personal emissary in the United States" (232). Paz also paints a dramatic picture of the wrenching moments in his life related to the Revolution:

I was only a few months old when the ups and downs of the Revolution forced us to leave Mexico City; my father took up with Zapata's movement in the south while my mother took refuge, with me, in Mixcoac, in the old house of my paternal grandfather, Ireneo Paz, patriarch of the family. When I was a child, many old Zapatista leaders would come to visit us, as well as many campesinos, whom my father, as a lawyer, would defend in their lawsuits and petitions for land. He participated in the activities of the Revolutionary Convention. Later he became the representative for Zapata and the Revolution of the South in the United States. My mother and I joined him in Los Angeles. We stayed there almost two years.[8]

The infant Octavio and his mother, Josefina Lozano, moved from Mexico City proper to stay with his paternal grandfather in the then sleepy suburb of Mixcoac, because his father had left the family to join the army of Zapata. This led to an important stage in the development of the young Octavio: he came under the direct influence of Don Ireneo, a noted journalist and writer with an extensive library. When young Octavio and his mother joined his father in Los Angeles, it turned out to be a traumatic time for the young boy, according to his recollections in a number of personal interviews. He incorporated these memories in his *Itinerario* (1993; translated as *Itinerary*, 1999). After their return to Mexico, they once again lived in Mixcoac.

When Octavio was in the United States, he was treated as a foreigner; ironically, when he returned to Mexico he was again a foreigner, but this time in his own country. These experiences were crucial in the development of his ideas about the importance of the critical perspective. He developed these ideas along with his exploration of the nature and development of Mexican and Mexican American identities in his most quoted and contentious book, *El laberinto de la soledad,* first published in 1950 and revised in subsequent editions. While the ideas in the essays have received criticism from the onset, Paz himself offered his own reevaluation of his controversial ideas, notably in *Posdata* (1970), translated as *The Other Mexico: Critique of the Pyramid* (1972). For example, in the "Note" published as the introduction to *The Other Mexico,* Paz attempts to elucidate: "Perhaps it would be worth the trouble to explain (once again) that *The Labyrinth of Solitude* was an exercise of the critical imagination: a vision and, simultaneously, a revision—something very different from an essay on Mexican-ness or a search for our supposed being. The Mexican is not an essence but a history" (*Labyrinth,* 215). Despite this caveat, Paz's essay has been read as a primer on Mexican-ness and criticized for its shortcomings and its essentialisms.

Playing with subtleties of language involving "rebellion," "revolution," and "revolt," Paz has had a great deal to say about the differences among them in relation to the Mexican Revolution and the Russian Revolution (see *The Labyrinth*, 339). Interestingly, the tradition in Mexican historiography had been to call the 1810 war that brought independence from Spain the "War of Independence," which can be compared with the "American Revolution" that was fought against England. As noted by the well-known Mexican historian Enrique Florescano, "the idea of revolution as an accelerating process of history and a renewing agent for society" was taken from nineteenth-century liberals, "who in turn had received it from the French revolution, the great movement that favored violent disruption over slow evolutionary processes" (310). Florescano reminds us that "revolution" had a pejorative meaning before 1910; "it evoked political chaos, unbridled action by the masses, the limitless ambition of leaders, and the assumption of power through violent means" (310). Florescano credits Guillermo Palacios as the first Mexican historian in the twentieth century to scrutinize the meanings of the word "revolution" in the way Madero used it: for him it had a political connotation. According to Florescano, before Paz wrote about the term it meant a "profound social shake-up, a wave capable of knocking down the strongest parapets" (314). It acquired the meaning of a "sort of hurricane that seemed to have been born from the foundations of history" (314).[9]

While Paz delved into the implications of these words in *Alternating Current*, *Conjunctions and Disjunctions*, and *The Other Mexico*, in his interview with Claude Fell he presents a succinct and clear discussion of his conception:

> Revolutions, daughters of linear and progressive time concept, mean the violent and definite change of one system by another. Revolutions are the consequence of development, as Marx and Engels never tired of saying. Rebellions are acts of marginal groups and individuals: the rebel does not want to change order, as does the revolutionary, but would dethrone the tyrant. Revolts are the daughters of cyclic time: they are popular uprisings against a reputedly unfair system and they aim at restoring original time, the inaugural moment of the pact among equals. (*Labyrinth*, 339–340)

Paz concludes that the first upheaval during the years 1910–1929 was a "bourgeois and middle class revolution to modernize the country" but that there was also a revolt of the Mexican peasants in the South, led by Emiliano Zapata, who was defeated and assassinated in 1919 (340).

Given the centrality of the Mexican Revolution within the history of twentieth-century Mexico and the centrality of Paz "as one of the most influential cultural figures in Mexico in the second half of the twentieth century" (Kuhnheim, 201), readers would expect to consult Paz for an understanding of the Mexican Revolution. Indeed, as in the case of his impact on our perspective of the figure of La Malinche, countless essays on the Mexican Revolution and Mexican culture of the twentieth century, written in many countries, pay homage to Paz by including a reference to his work. Paz is selected as *the* spokesman for the Mexican people, even into the twenty-first century.[10] Many in the younger generation of Mexican intellectuals resent this reliance on Paz, especially because his ideas have been codified and taken by others outside of Mexico to be the essential idea of what Mexicans are. In awarding him the Nobel Prize in 1990, the Swedish Academy called *The Labyrinth of Solitude* "an exploration of Mexican identity that has become a standard text in courses on Mexican history and political science since its publication in 1950" (quoted in Leal, "Octavio Paz," 314).

As supporters of Paz insist, however, he did not intend for his essay to become a mythologized text but for it to be a "work in progress" that showed his thinking at a certain point in time.[11] Nonetheless, it has become more than an essay on national identity and holds a privileged place as a best seller, with more than 1 million copies in print in Spanish alone, as Enrico Mario Santí notes, as the "centerpiece of his lifelong reflection on Mexico" ("Ten Keys," 18). Although Anthony Stanton reminds us that Paz engaged in a "series of changing personal reinterpretations . . . throughout his life of his best known text" ("Models of Discourse," 210), most readers are familiar with Paz's ideas as they appear in the 1959 second edition, which was used for the 1961 English translation by Lysander Kemp.[12] Chapter 6 of the second edition includes his thoughts on the Mexican Revolution in the section "From Independence to Revolution." Chapter 7, on the Mexican intelligentsia, also continues his critique of the results of the Revolution; in practical terms, Paz was often critical of the postrevolutionary problems of Mexico and the role of the Partido Revolucionario Institucionalizado (PRI: Institutional Revolutionary Party), the political party that developed after the military phase terminated, for which he worked in various capacities.

The Uruguayan writer Hiber Conteris has written one of the most detailed essays about Paz and his critique of the Mexican Revolution. He argues that Paz analyzed institutions, forms of organization and government, political structures, and social composition along with its impact on economic development in contemporary Mexico (146). Conteris says that Paz developed his political reflections based on concrete points and then offered generalizations. For Yvon Grenier, who has also studied aspects of the essays in depth, Paz did not offer explicit political commentary, because he opposed political dogma (Grenier, "Octavio Paz and the Changing Role of Intellectuals," 133).

Grenier would agree that "Paz does not fit into categories of right or left, but as a political thinker, combines European intellectual traditions not often popular in Mexico" (Kuhnheim, 202). In *La divina pareja* (The Divine Pair, 1978), the Mexican writer and critic Jorge Aguilar Mora suggested a possible reason why Paz did not write any detailed elaboration of the history of the Mexican Revolution: Paz had a characteristic tendency to juxtapose "history" versus "myth" and to prefer myth, thereby ignoring real social problems. The Brazilian critic Bella Josef appears to agree with Aguilar Mora, commenting that Paz's interpretation of the Mexican Revolution is "miticopoética" (mythopoetic, 50). This concept stresses Paz's preference to "metaphorize," in Aguilar Mora's words, what takes place rather than engage with historical reality (see Stabb, 52–53). Aguilar Mora is critical of Paz's detachment from real events, although he does admit that the essay itself "has a certain complexity" (*Divina pareja*, 26). Of course, Paz did perform a grand political gesture in 1968, when he dramatically and sincerely renounced his ambassadorship to India as a result of the Mexican government's involvement in the massacre of students at Tlatelolco.[13] This was both a personal and public act (discussed in Chapter 5). Without a doubt, Paz has inspired criticism and controversy as well as adulation.

Paz's view of history as he expressed it in *Labyrinth* shows the influence of Sigmund Freud and Claude Lévi-Strauss as well as the Mexican historians Samuel Ramos and Leopoldo Zea. "Paz's task in historical analysis becomes one of revealing the latent meaning of history in the manner a psychoanalyst would analyze a dream for its latent content" (Espinosa, "Ideology in the Works of Octavio Paz," 81). Fernando Espinosa appears to be in agreement with Aguilar Mora's assessment, suggesting that what Paz does is "attempt to transcend historical reality by reducing it to a fabric of interwoven archetypes" (81). While his tendency to mythologize is present, I would suggest that Paz often launches his analyses of Mexican issues with a personal association, as seen clearly in the chapter "From Independence to Revolution." Paz privileges "Zapatismo," calling Zapata "one of our legendary heroes" (142). This was unusual in the 1950s, as the French critic Claude Fell notes in his 1975 interview with Paz originally titled "Vuelta a *El laberinto de la soledad*" (Return to the *Labyrinth of Solitude*).[14] Paz explains in his discussion with Fell that his father was a personal friend and supporter of Zapata and thus his perspective stems from personal circumstances. In his discussion of Zapatismo with Fell, as a "return to origins" (*Labyrinth*, 338), Paz leaves the specificities that he was able to call up in *Labyrinth* (144) to revert to the mythic. Perhaps it is useful to compare the two approaches, for in one he seems to be the Paz of Hiber Conteris and in the other the detached writer that Aguilar Mora criticized.

> The idea that the official propaganda has given of Zapatismo is quite false and conventional. As I tried to explain in *The Labyrinth of Solitude*, what distinguished Zapatism from the other factions was its attempt to return to the origins. There is, in all revolutions, this impulse to return to a past that is confused with society's origins. . . . The first demand of the Zapatists was *return* of the land; the second, a subsidiary demand, was for *distribution. Return*: back to the origin. (*Labyrinth*, 338–339)[15]

In *The Labyrinth* Paz is more specific about what the actual program of this great hero was. He offers this analysis:

> Zapata's traditionalism reveals that he had a profound awareness of our history. He was isolated both racially and regionally from the journalists and theorists of the epoch, and this isolation gave him the strength and insight to grasp the simple truth. And the truth of the Revolution was actually very simple: it was the freeing of Mexican reality from the constricting schemes of liberalism and the abuses of the conservatives and neoconservatives.
>
> The Zapatista movement was a return to our most ancient and permanent tradition. It was a profound denial of the work of the Reform, in that it was a return to the very world from which the liberals had wanted to cut themselves loose. The Revolution became an attempt to integrate our present and our past, or—as Leopoldo Zea put it—to "assimilate our history," to change it into a living thing: a past made present. This effort at integration, this return to sources, contrasts with the attitude of the intellectuals of the time, who not only failed to understand the meaning of the revolutionary movement but even went on playing with ideas that had no function whatsoever except as masks. (*Labyrinth*, 144)

In these comments Paz quotes Mexican scholars, addresses specifics of Mexican history, and shows his keen awareness of the impact of the nineteenth-century Liberals and the Reform movement on the agenda of the revolutionary players. Paz was also privileging Zapata at a time when supposedly most Mexicans thought of him as a "bandit from the south" (Quiroga, 83).[16] In discussing these same issues with Fell in 1975, Paz refers to the mythic dimensions rather than Mexican specificities. When he wrote his original discussion of Zapata, he was a young intellectual living outside of Mexico and trying to understand the players of the Mexican Revolution as a major cataclysm. By the time he spoke with Fell, Paz had become canonized, especially in foreign circles, as the spokesman for Mexican intellectuals, as much for his enormous outpouring of poetry as for his political positions. He had consolidated his credentials as a "rebel spirit" (Perales, 63) by resigning his ambassadorial post in 1968 as a result of the Tlatelolco Massacre, by lecturing as the Charles Eliot Norton Professor at Harvard University, and by founding *Plural* (in 1971), a literary review in which he and his followers were able to explore their political, esthetic, and social ideas.

In his conversation with Fell, Paz maintains the basic points that he had expressed in 1959; he criticizes the Mexican intelligentsia of that time as having been unable to formulate a "coherent system" (*Labyrinth*, 145). For that reason he states that the Mexican Revolution, unlike the Russian Revolution, did not have an ideological base. He calls the people the only source of revolutionary health and blames the Carrancistas, the triumphant faction, for "thwarting the spontaneous desires of the people" by resorting to Caesarism or a personality cult. He believes that this still rules Mexican political life, despite the law forbidding reelections. Paz acknowledges the brutality and crudeness of the revolutionary leaders and their incoherent agenda; yet despite these flaws, for Paz the Mexican Revolution was an important event precisely because it enabled the Mexican (and he uses the singular form of the noun) "to reconcile himself with his history and his origins" (147). For Paz, the Revolution proves all the ideas that he previously had expressed in the preceding chapters of *The Labyrinth* in relation to Mexican identity: the solitude of the Mexican, his behavior during fiestas, his attraction to death. And if the "Mexican" treats his woman as Cortés did La Malinche, as the conquistadors behaved toward the indigenous women, then the Mexican idea of love is also expressed in the Revolution as a rape. Paz expresses these immoderate ideas in poetic language, calling the revolution

> the brutal, resplendent face of death and fiestas, of gossip and gunfire, of celebration and love (which is rape and pistol shots). The Revolution has hardly any ideas. It is an explosion of reality: a return and a communion, an upsetting

of old institutions, a releasing of many ferocious, tender and noble feelings that had been hidden by our fear of being. (*Labyrinth*, 148–149)

The key points of previous chapters of *The Labyrinth*—"Mexican Masks," "The Day of the Dead," "The Sons of La Malinche," "The Conquest and Colonialism," and "The Present Day"—are succinctly recapitulated in these phrases, so that the centrality of the Revolution for contemporary Mexico is substantiated. I find it significant that Paz does pay attention to problems of ethnicity and class in his assessment but is never concerned with gender issues. As stated in "The Sons of La Malinche," for Paz, the icons of femininity in Mexico are both passive figures: the Virgin of Guadalupe and La Chingada. Women are passive in his depiction of the Mexican universe; in the following observation, as in so many of his comments, women are not a concern in national life:

> In one sense, then, the Revolution has created the nation; in another sense, of equal importance, it has extended nationality to races and classes which neither colonialism nor the nineteenth century was able to incorporate into our national life. But despite its extraordinary fecundity, it was incapable of creating a vital order that would be at once a world view and the basis of a really just and free society. (*Labyrinth*, 175)

In those few words, Paz does describe the significant contributions of the Revolution for modern Mexico—and its role in incorporating more ethnic Mexicans (mostly indigenous peoples) and lower classes as well into the definition of "national identity." He does not consider the role of women in the Revolution or in the nation. As Stanton suggests, he "tends to sacrifice detail to the great design . . . particularly in the analysis of Paz's treatment of the Revolution" ("Models of Discourse," 228); in his cosmovision, women are not agents of change, as noted in his perspective on La Malinche in Chapter 1. For some critics, Paz's description of the Revolution's deeper meaning is that "Mexico needs a paternalistic political structure because the masses—Villistas and Zapatistas—are immature (their aspirations are 'confused' and 'stammering')" (Parra, 35). Nevertheless, Paz acknowledges that the "accomplishments" of the Revolution, such as they were, still did not create a "just and free society," especially with the endurance of the PRI as the only political party during the twentieth century.

As Stanton reminds us, Paz's interpretation of the Mexican Revolution can be read as "idealized and utopian," a "mythic and poetic view that idealizes one specific faction of the complex and contradictory movement: that of *za-patismo*" ("Models of Discourse," 230). Thus, rather than being a historian of the Revolution, and beyond his recognition of the importance of Emiliano Zapata's agenda, Paz later became known as a critic of the Partido Revolucionario Institucionalizado, the political party that was so ironically named—both revolutionary and institutionalized. Despite his ongoing criticisms, Paz worked for the government in various official capacities from 1944 until 1968, the infamous time of the Tlatelolco Massacre (see Chapter 5). By the end of his life, he was sometimes seen as an ally of the PRI, if only because he often critiqued the Left's "excessive devotion to ideology" (Van Delden and Grenier, 104).

Although Paz did not write expansively about the Mexican Revolution as such, his observations are always quoted; as incisive as they could be politically, the comments were also culturally significant and remain relevant to this day. At midpoint in the chapter he describes what he observes for his mid-century generation—the influence of the actual participants of the bloody events:

> Only recently has it been possible to see that such opposite figures as Emiliano Zapata and Venustiano Carranza, Luis Cabrera and José Vasconcelos, Francisco Villa and Álvaro Obregón, Franciso I. Madero and Lázaro Cárdenas, Felipe Ángeles and Antonio Díaz Soto y Gama are all part of a single process. . . . the brutality and uncouthness of many of the revolutionary leaders has [*sic*] not prevented them from becoming popular myths. Villa still gallops through the north, in songs and ballads; Zapata dies at every popular fair; Madero appears on the balconies, waving the flag; Carranza and Obregón still travel back and forth across the country in those trains of the revolutionary period . . . (*Labyrinth*, 147–148)

These observations regarding the vitality and longevity of the figures of the Mexican Revolution, which Paz offered at a midpoint in the twentieth century, still hold true today, especially for the populists Villa and Zapata.[17] As noted, the popular insurrection that began in Chiapas on January 1, 1994, is being waged by a group called the Ejército Zapatista de Liberación Nacional, in recognition of the role that Zapata played in fighting for "Land and Liberty."

As Paz ends his chapter on the Mexican Revolution from a more philosophical perspective, he concludes with a grand observation:

> By means of the Revolution the Mexican people found itself, located itself in its own past and substance. Hence the Revolution's fertility, compared with

our nineteenth-century movements. Its cultural and artistic fertility resulted from the profound manner in which its heroes, bandits and myths stamped themselves forever on the sensibility and imagination of every Mexican. (*Labyrinth*, 148)

Paz had a way of synthesizing complexities and formulating ideas that makes him eminently quotable. In current studies of the Mexican Revolution or any aspect of Mexican life, whether by historians or literary scholars, Paz's general ideas about the government and about revolution in general are quoted and considered important springboards toward an understanding of Mexican thought. He strives for objective lucidity, we might say, the opposite of what we find in Garro's texts. Her works are often characterized by excesses of emotion, angst and despair, with only an occasional laugh possible, often brought about by a specific cutting remark.

Whereas Paz was utopian and idealist, Garro's many texts that involve the figures and myths of the Mexican Revolution certainly show her readers its traumatic and terrifying aspects. Paz may have been able to declare, in an oxymoronic poetic riff, that the Revolution was a fiesta and "an explosion of joy and hopelessness, a shout of orphanhood and jubilation, of suicide and life" (*Labyrinth*, 148). But Garro's many texts tell more about the explosions of hopelessness, orphanhood, and suicide. She exhibits an artistic productiveness with regard to this central event in Mexican history. Encompassing the essay, novel, short story, and drama, her trajectory begins with its origins followed by representations of the subsequent stages that inform the social, political, and cultural upheavals as well as the emotional and personal repercussions of the Revolution. Moreover, she adds to the early contributions of Nellie Campobello by also informing us about the diverse roles of women during the time of the Revolution, incorporating their stories as an integral part of the whole. Readers of Azuela's *Los de abajo* or Guzmán's *El águila y la serpiente* or Rafael Muñoz's *¡Vámonos con Pancho Villa!* do not see well-rounded women characters. With Garro's texts we can tell that Mexican women did indeed take part in the Revolution as more than the stereotypical *soldadera* Adelita or the mother figure waiting at home.

Garro also shares with Campobello an interest in daring figures of the Revolution. Whereas Campobello was loyal to Villa and wrote about him in *Apuntes sobre la vida militar de Francisco Villa* (Notes on the Military Life of Francisco Villa, 1940), Garro's nonfiction attention to the rebel fighters of the Mexican Revolution can be found in a series of reports that she produced between

February and May 1968 for the weekly journal *¿Por Qué?*, founded and directed by Mario Menéndez Rodríguez (Zama, 8). Patricia Zama found these biographical essays, published as "Los caudillos" (The Chiefs/Bosses), which later became the book *Revolucionarios mexicanos* (Revolutionary Mexicans, 1997). Interestingly, these sketches were written and published early in 1968, the momentous year of student rebellion throughout the world, most notably in the United States, France, Czechoslovakia, and Mexico. Garro would play a role in the events. As described in Chapter 5 (on the Tlatelolco Massacre), her life would change irrevocably, bringing with it difficulties for her career as a writer and intellectual in Mexico. It is one of the notable ironies of history that Garro was describing the great heroes of the Mexican Revolution and their failures to change the sociopolitical climate during the very year when the students and the intellectuals of Mexico were calling for a real revolution in the way society was constituted in Mexico. They hoped to bring about an end to the sham that the PRI ruling party put forth, extolling the successes of the Revolution and the freedom and well-being that Mexicans supposedly enjoyed.

While the PRI tried to boast about the successes of Mexico in that critical year of 1968, most Mexicans were unhappy with their government's excess spending in face of the poverty of so many citizens. As explained in greater detail in Chapter 5, in his written response to the events of 1968 (*Posdata*) Paz attributed the turmoil that led to the massacre at Tlatelolco to the unfulfilled promises of the Mexican Revolution. Because the Revolution had not solved the country's problems, the ruthless encounter at the Plaza of Three Cultures was an inevitable outcome. Interestingly, Garro's *Revolucionarios mexicanos* also describes the reasons for Mexico's endemic problems of political violence and corruption; but it was written before the violent clash at the Plaza de Tlatelolco, so she focuses on the major figures involved in the historical process of the Revolution and how their tragic fate set the tone of corruption and venality of the ruling party. Writing within the "great men creating history" paradigm accepted at the time, Garro dealt with men because there were no women in the official historical record. Moreover, at that time the figures she selected were more tarnished than the shining folk heroes they would later become.[18]

Garro's *Revolucionarios mexicanos* encompasses five chapters; two concentrate on particular figures who initiated the recall of dictator Porfirio Díaz: Ricardo Flores Magón and Francisco I. Madero. She then describes the provisional presidency of Francisco León de la Barra, who served from May 25 to November 6, 1911; and the government of Madero ("El itinerario de De la

Barra y el gobierno de Francisco I. Madero"). She follows with the "Decena Trágica" (Ten Tragic Days, February 9–17) which culminated in the imprisonment and assassination of Madero and his vice president Pino Suárez, resulting in the ascent of Victoriano Huerta as president. Her final section, "¿Cuál fue el castigo de los asesinos del Presidente Madero?" (What Was the Punishment for the Assassins of President Madero?), is a challenge for her Mexican readers; she poses a moral issue concerning the crimes related to the death of Madero that have never been resolved. In this chapter Garro addresses one of the fundamental issues that cultural historians have called a Mexican sociopolitical phenomenon and one that Paz himself also discussed in reference to the Tlatelolco Massacre. The contemporary leaders of Mexico, like Aztec caciques, are guilty of reprehensible violence and the deaths of innocents, acting above the law (Lomnitz, 128).[19] Garro continues this representation of corrupt revolutionary leaders when these repugnant characteristics are attributed to the enemies of Felipe Ángeles in her play.

As Garro writes each of the five sections, she includes ample historical data and references to documents to substantiate her narrative, but she clearly has an ideological objective. Considering that she had written about one of the forgotten heroes, Felipe Ángeles, in 1954,[20] she might well have been gathering information all those years in order to be able to write with such detail about the various well-known and not a few nefarious figures that she highlights.

While Paz mentions the name of Flores Magón only briefly in *Labyrinth* and does not pay attention to Madero,[21] Garro offers a nuanced portrait of both men. She calls Flores Magón, the man who was an early anarchist in Mexico and a founding member of the Liberal Party from 1892 to 1900, "the first great Mexican socialist, martyr to the worker's cause" (*Revolucionarios mexicanos*, 45).[22] As editor of opposition newspapers, he was soon forced to flee Mexico by the Díaz government because of his revolutionary anarchist ideas. Once in the United States he was harassed by U.S. authorities, which led to various arrests and his jail terms; he was moved to the federal prison of Leavenworth, Kansas, where he died in 1922, under unclear circumstances. Garro repeats the version told by his brother Enrique that his body showed signs of being tortured in prison, although the U.S. authorities claimed that he died of a heart attack (*Revolucionarios mexicanos*, 44). Flores Magón is remembered today as a great revolutionary figure, and Garro's portrait of him shows his unwavering allegiance to the cause of the workers in Mexico—and how both the governments of Porfirian Mexico and the United States colluded to persecute him. She also reveals her own steadfast support of workers' rights, which would lead her to clash with typical "macho" political leaders (see Chapter 4).[23] In fact, as Elena Poniatowska recalls, the workers Garro championed often saw her as the female Emiliano Zapata (*Las siete cabritas*, 118). (Considering how often literary critics credit Paz with "reviving" the heroic side of Zapata, I wonder whether this positive comparison of Zapata and Garro might rankle Paz supporters.)

In her series of essays Garro shows the continuous use of political assassinations in Mexico and the elimination of those who hold ideals. In the final chapter ("¿Cuál fue el castigo de los asesinos del Presidente Madero?") she is fearless in facing hard facts. More similar to Don Ireneo Paz's sympathies than to Octavio's, Garro shows herself to be an ardent supporter of Madero: "The legality, the clean fight for ideas, the profound respect for life, the exercise of power in the name of values—all had died with Sr. Madero. Tragically, the country regressed to the position from which President Madero had begun his struggle" (170–171).[24]

The word "tragic" is repeated throughout this chapter, with Garro stressing Madero's humanity and his intent to democratize the country. Garro uses her portrait of Madero as a great statesman to lament the absence of such leaders in her day (174–175). She states clearly that the "ley de fuga" (law of flight), which was first put into practice by Porfirio Diaz (174), was subsequently responsible for killing not only Madero but those perceived as enemies of the government or any caudillo with enough power to put the law of flight into practice. The same law was used to kill Felipe Ángeles, as Garro shows in her play by that name.

The essays in *Revolucionarios mexicanos* give Garro's readers a keen sense of the various betrayals that marked the revolutionary battles and the fate of the men involved in the armed conflicts and political machinations. The play *Felipe Ángeles*, first published in 1979 although it was probably initiated around 1954 (Muncy, "The Author Speaks...," 24), from a chronological perspective continues the account that the essays initiated. Her main character also suffers betrayals from his fellow revolutionaries and finally is condemned to death.

As a child, Garro heard stories at home about Felipe Ángeles (1868–1919), a figure associated with Madero and later with Pancho Villa, the "Centaur of the North," serving as one of his chief military and intellectual advisors.[25] As Toruño details it,

The name of General Felipe Ángeles, says Garro, was familiar to her since her childhood, given that one of her uncles, Benito Navarro, fought under him.

... Elena's uncles on her mother's side were all revolutionaries with Villa. The only one who survived was the one who fought with Ángeles.[26]

Whereas Paz invoked Zapata from his childhood memories, Garro uses this heroic figure from her family's past, whose exploits she felt had not been sufficiently highlighted, as the basis for her first historical drama.[27] The material that Garro includes acknowledges that Ángeles became one of Villa's principal military and intellectual advisors. He participated as chief of artillery in the great military triumphs of 1914: the capture of Torreón, the battles of San Pedro de las Colonias and Paredón, and the capture of Zacatecas in May 1914. Ángeles participated in the October 1914 Convention of Aguascalientes (called to bring an end to hostilities) as Villa's representative. It resulted in a complete break between Villa and Carranza. Ángeles remained with the Villa faction as civil war broke out again in early 1915. In his first independent command, he captured the city of Monterrey in January 1915. Villa's forces were decisively defeated in the spring of 1915 by Carranza's ally Gen. Álvaro Obregón, however, and Ángeles was forced to flee Mexico and remain in Texas. There he attempted to make a living as a dairy farmer. Ángeles returned secretly to Mexico in 1918 and tried once again to work with Villa, but he became disillusioned with Villa and the entire project of the Mexican Revolution. He was betrayed and arrested by the Carranza government and was court-martialed in a show trial in Ciudad Chihuahua. Knowing that Carranza would never pardon him, Ángeles made an impassioned defense in response to his enemies' case for the prosecution. The court-martial condemned him to death, and he was executed on November 26, 1919.

Although Garro says that she chose to write about Ángeles because he had been an overlooked figure in the history books at that time,[28] it is interesting to note that Paz also refers to him, but with scant details, in his chapter on the Revolution (*Labyrinth*, 133). Just as Paz may be important in revitalizing the figure of Emiliano Zapata, Garro rescues Felipe Ángeles. Garro's only historically based play clearly shows her support of the ideals of the Mexican Revolution and her dissatisfaction with those who would betray these principles for political gain.

A careful reading of the play *Felipe Ángeles* indicates that Garro was not only rescuing a general that she considered to be falsely portrayed in authorized documents; in addition, she shows the valuable interventions of women, another group whose role in the Mexican Revolution has been underrepresented in official narratives.[29]

Throughout the play, the underlying idea is that those who wield the power also determine the discourse so that "history" is in effect the invention of the victors. Here is an exchange between two revolutionary generals that clearly shows Garro's distrust of official history:

> Gavira: We won the battle. The defeated ones never are right. History is with us.
> Diegues: History is a bitch, general. We can't trust her. (19)[30]

Diegues's lack of trust in the historical record comes in response to the way the official newspapers have reported the story of Felipe Ángeles and his supposed "betrayal" (11). Of course, the Spanish word *historia* can also mean "story," so Garro plays here with the dual meanings—referring to an event as both/either fiction or actuality. The hero of the drama, Felipe Ángeles, says it poetically: "[P]erhaps we can invent the history that we lack. History, like mathematics, is an act of the imagination" (52).[31] For Garro, *historia* has been invented by the victors; it appears as an act of the imagination. It is interesting to compare this view with Paz's view as expressed in *The Labyrinth*. He seems to be suggesting that it is possible to unravel the "true" meaning of history by taking advantage of psychoanalytical tools (Espinosa, "Ideology," 83). In his autobiographical poem "Nocturne of San Ildefonso," however, Paz writes: "History is error," an idea more akin to Garro's point. Garro strongly supports the idea of the construction of history: the documents which narrate events are produced by humans who are influenced by their ideology. And if there is an invisible history, it is also the product of a culture, of a cultural memory. This idea is further developed in reference to the novel *Recollections of Things to Come* (1963).

Many plays have been written about the Mexican Revolution, as discussed by Marcela Del Río in her detailed study *Perfil del Teatro de la Revolución Mexicana* (Profile of the Theatre of the Mexican Revolution).[32] Just as the majority of novels were written by men and focused on the major male figures, the well-known dramas of the Mexican Revolution—such as Rodolfo Usigli's *El gesticulador* (The Imposter), for example—are based on the exploits of men. While Felipe Ángeles is clearly the hero of her play, Garro nevertheless creates women characters who subvert the traditional depiction of women in the canonical revolutionary narrative. Señora Revilla, for example, in contrast to the typical woman depicted in the traditional literary texts,[33] not only dares to form a committee in support of the innocence of Felipe Ángeles, a brave and unexpected act. She also questions the very goals of the Revolution in speaking to one of the generals who fought in the battles: "The Revolution? Do you call 'Revolution' a clique of ambitious men who are sacrificing anyone who opposes their personal interests?" (115).[34]

Revilla and two other women are part of the committee to free General Ángeles. The committee appears to be motivated by the concerns of the women that justice be done, despite the "clique of ambitious men"; importantly, Garro does not show any men as part of this committee. Moreover, by expressing concern for a nonfamily member, by their interest in politics and the issues of the day, these women subvert the stereotypical portrayal of their gender in the usual texts on the Mexican Revolution. Garro offers a more complex, nonpolar (whore or mother) representation of Mexican women.[35] Furthermore, Garro creates a dramatic image in the play that reveals her attitude about how the Revolution has been portrayed in the canon. The trial of Ángeles takes place in a theater; although this is a historical fact, Garro uses it to explore the concept of the performative nature of the trial and charges against Ángeles. She notes that the government made up a script about Ángeles's treason just to have the excuse to kill him (as so many revolutionaries did). Just as Ángeles says that history is "an act of the imagination," the case against him is also shown to be an invention of his enemies. Garro calls attention to the idea of historical creation and at the same time implies that the "official history" in Mexico is only a creation of the winning side.

Another important theme of the play, which was already present in her essays on revolutionary figures, relates to the corruption and opportunism of many (historical) characters. Moreover, Garro's Ángeles declares that the "generals" like Carranza hoped to achieve absolute power for themselves, contrary to his belief that the Revolution was meant to do away with authoritarianism, which was also one of the goals of Madero: "Ángeles: He [Carranza] thinks that the Revolution is a means to achieve absolute power and I believed that it was a means to eradicate it" (26).[36]

As Julie Winkler notes, "one of the play's messages is that the Revolution destroyed its best and brightest, while allowing the less capable and morally corrupt figures—the Carranzas and the Huertas—to survive and rule instead (and, incidentally, to write the histories that excluded figures like Ángeles)" (*Light into Shadow*, 114).

Although the failures and betrayals of the war years occupy center stage in the play, Garro does include a more hopeful idea. Señora Revilla adds a point that is of great importance to the historical Garro, as we shall see. When General Ángeles expresses to Revilla his need to believe that his death will not have been in vain, she replies with comforting words: "There are many years to come. Many crossroads. Many men yet to be born, and there will be someone who will search for your path and give it new life again in time" (33).[37] Garro implies that although many heroes of the Mexican Revolution were sacrificed or assassinated, they would come to be appreciated someday. Indeed she focuses interest on the martyrdom of General Ángeles so that her character expresses what she as dramatist has accomplished. As we shall see, moreover, Garro had felt in her own life that she had been a victim whose story had to be told—but that is for a later chapter.

Garro's most famous and award-winning novel, *Recollections of Things to Come*, continues the story of the Mexican Revolution in the postconstitutional phase, the period of the Cristero Rebellion (1926–1929).[38] This is the work upon which her early fame rests: the novel was awarded the prestigious Xavier Villaurrutia Prize in 1963. Paz himself called it "one of the most perfect creations of contemporary Hispanic American literature" (Stoll, 11).[39] It is the most scrutinized piece among all her works and has been analyzed from many perspectives in well over a hundred critical pieces.[40] While its historical subtext is readily seen, in one of the early essays on the novel Frank Dauster perceptively notes that *Recollections* is a subversive novel because of the way it critiques Mexican myths, especially the way it destroys the stereotype of the humble, self-sacrificing woman (57). Indeed, the feminist perspective of the novel has generated many studies from the 1980s onward. Its enigmatic nature is addressed by many critics, who discuss on the one hand its reflection of a concrete sociopolitical environment with the concomitant violence and destruction of a devastating war and on the other hand the magical reality of many of its scenes. Such scenes lead some readers to consider *Recollections* to be a precursor of Gabriel García Márquez's *One Hundred Years of Solitude* (1967).[41] I would like to address not only how this complex work contributes to a study of the Mexican Revolution but how it uses that historical event to critique issues of time and subvert the collective memory of the Mexican people with regard to gender issues.

On the anecdotal level, *Recollections of Things to Come* recounts the stories of the townspeople of Ixtepec (the name of a real village in Garro's home state of Puebla), who support the priests and the Catholic agenda and their battle with government forces in the Cristero Rebellion. As in her short stories, Garro shows the human toll of the violence that has marked the lives of Mexicans as a consequence of the Revolution. While *Recollections* has been examined for its insights into the Cristero Rebellion, its most obvious historical referent, it also serves as a key text that makes use of the Malinche-Cortés paradigm as it plays out in Mexican cultural memory (see Chapter 1). Garro includes details that form part of Mexican cultural memory and help her readers to perceive the story of the women protagonists—Julia and Isabel—as references to the Malinche/Cortés paradigm. *Recollections* is a foremost example of a text that relates to a specific moment of historical reality yet at the same time offers a vision of what might be called "invisible history" in Paz's terms.

It is tempting to associate the allusive nature of Garro's texts with the concept proposed by Paz in the final section of *Posdata* about "invisible history." He sees living history as symbolic of a deeper history of Mexico, the "true history." Paz explains his idea with reference to Tlatelolco:

> The double reality of October 2, 1968: it is a historical fact and it is also a symbolic acting-out of what could be called our subterranean or invisible history. . . . All of the histories of all peoples are symbolic. I mean that history and its events and protagonists allude to another, occult history, and are visible manifestations of a hidden reality. (*Labyrinth*, 291)

Garro's novel—at once a detail-filled chronicle of the destructive consequences of the Revolution and a recollection of the key Malinche paradigm emanating from the Conquest period—seems to put Paz's idea into narrative form. The two female protagonists—Julia Andrade and Isabel Moncada—are the kept women of the town's military invader, General Rosas, much as La Malinche was the "mistress" of Cortés, encouraging readers to see the Malinche paradigm as a subtext of the novel.[42] The major difference, and not a minor matter, however, is that Paz considers this "occult history" to be the "true" one, while Garro, more the postmodernist *avant la lettre*, does not assume that there is one true history but that multiple versions of the facts exist. Her characters often discuss different versions of one event, so that readers have to judge for themselves what might have happened and evaluate how events affect people in different ways. Garro also questions memory itself, identifying it with the theme of betrayal that marks so much of Mexican history and her own narratives: "Memory is treacherous and at times inverts the order of events or brings us to a dark inlet where nothing happens" (*Recollections*, 197).

Garro's treatment of time is also nuanced in ways that separate her view from the traditional Paz perspective. For example, Ross Larson has suggested that "time and space are distorted by Garro in order to reveal the continuing presence of Mexico's primitive past" (*Fantasy and Imagination*, 99). Many readers see her treatment of time as similar to what Paz suggests and what Carlos Fuentes seems to have captured so well in stories like "Chac Mool":[43] acknowledgment of the inescapable presence of the pre-Hispanic past that inhabits the present (Larson, *Fantasy and Imagination*, 94).

Garro also seems to imply that the past appears to invade the present, as it does in her short story "La culpa es de los tlaxcaltecas" and in some phrases from *Recollections*. Her evocation of past events in the present and the repetition of the past in the present, however, are not meant to indicate either that the repetition of the past is "unpreventable" or that "the future was the repetition of the past," an often-cited phrase from *Recollections* (58). When reading that comment in Garro's narrative out of context, it would seem that she is supporting a view of time as an endless, repetitive cycle of sameness. But I suggest that Garro in effect is critiquing those who would pledge their allegiance to the cyclical nature of Mexican history. Her work is an attempt to show how dangerous, ill-advised, and much too easy it is to rely on the past as the harbinger of the future. As Robert Anderson comments, "*Recollections* also indicts those who fail to take possession of their days, only to become mere automatons" ("Myth and Archetype," 221).

In his perceptive study of the prophetic nature of Garro's novel, James Mandrell synthesizes what distinguishes Garro's vision from that of Paz or Fuentes: "When time stops recapitulating the past, when Ixtepec ceases to repeat itself, illusion and the future take over. The future is the illusion that will allow the inhabitants of Ixtepec to escape the misery of their existence" (232). Mandrell continues his analysis of her unique presentation by pointing out that for Garro change is possible but requires "imagination and insight beyond most people, who are mired in the violence and ennui of everyday life" (233). One of her most quoted passages includes this dual perspective; read quickly or out of context, part of the comment supports the idea that people seem to repeat the acts of previous generations. Garro adds a twist to this idea, however; if acts are repeated, it is only because people do not realize that they need not repeat them; people need only awaken to the reality that they can change things, can transform their future:

> One generation follows another, and each repeats the acts of the one before it. Only an instant before dying, they discover that it was possible to dream and to create the world their own way, to awaken then and begin a new creation. . . . And other generations come to repeat their same gestures and their same astonishment at the end. (243)

Garro's narratives are not meant to lull the Mexican people into accepting as a given a repetitive cycle of sameness and inevitability but, on the contrary, to serve as a wake-up call—to change their behavior. I would certainly read these several texts by Garro on the Mexican Revolution in that context: as her effort to communicate a need for change after picturing what the past had been like. Garro is looking at ways to "escape from the strictures of time and historical reality," as Mandrell observes; she "explores in narrative terms the possibility and the means of altering the present state of things by exploiting a momentary rupture in the fabric of history" (231).[44] The narrator of *Recollections* suggests that when the Revolution began, "the door of time opened for us" (31). In the anthropological terms of Victor Turner, a liminal moment took place that could have changed the social script, the status quo. Garro's critique of the way things were at the time of the Revolution and through the period of the Cristero Rebellion shows that she does not accept the status quo and the beliefs that maintain the inequalities of class, race, and gender in Mexico. The novel exposes "the existence of economic injustice and strong racial prejudices [which] make the Indian's lives the most degraded in the society" (Mora, "A Thematic Exploration," 92). Those who wield power in Ixtepec are the newly rich mestizos (greedy bourgeois families like that of Rodolfo Goríbar), who kill with impunity any of the Indians who overstep their bounds, especially those who were asking for agrarian reform—a theme close to Garro's heart. Garro shows how unacceptable their treatment of the Indians is when one of them makes the comment: "Poor Indians! Maybe they aren't as bad as we think" (76).

While Paz notably thinks of the circularity of time, current events repeating paradigms established in the past, Garro challenges that concept. Indeed, she is in contestatory dialogue not only with the Paz concept of time but with the established view of the Revolution that Mexicans are fated to repeat its violence and maintain the social inequalities already inherent in the Mexica world. Think of that famous quotation from *Los de abajo* that is used to represent the popular belief of Mexican collective memory regarding the inability to change Mexican sociopolitical structure:

> Villa? ... Obregón? ... Carranza? ... X ... Y ... Z ... ! What's it to me? ... I love the Revolution like I love an erupting volcano! The volcano because it's a volcano, and the Revolution because it's the Revolution! ... But what do I care what stones wind up on top or on the bottom after the cataclysm? ... (80)

Azuela's crazy poet Valderrama suggests that there are no differences among the various leaders, a subversive idea to their followers, of course. But the point (for Azuela) is that the Revolution brought/brings no change, that the Mexican people engage in violent and cataclysmic events—the Conquest, the war against Spain, the Mexican Revolution—only to remain as before. Azuela's other poet-spokesman, Solís, provides another image for the Revolution that again stresses people's inability to govern their own actions. Solís claims that the Revolution is a hurricane: "and the man who gives himself to her is not a man anymore, he is the miserable dry leaf swept by the wind . . . " (38). With this image of a "dry leaf" the fighter is reduced to someone who does not govern his own actions. "The poetic image nullifies the revolutionary's significance as a historical agent," as Max Parra states in his commentary on this aspect of the novel (33). Garro's narrator, the town of Ixtepec itself, also refers to the image of a leaf at a time of stasis and atemporality: "I really do not know what happened. I was outside of time, suspended in a place without wind without murmurs, without the sound of leaves or sighing" (*Recollections*, 138). At this point in the narrative the town is describing a key moment in which Julia has just escaped with Felipe Hurtado and time literally has stopped. The leaves are still, the wind is quiet, so the town appears to be in a moment of stasis, when the power of the military cannot prevail. The people who are cowed by the generals are like the lifeless leaves depicted by Azuela, while the people who are willing to act, to follow through on their desire for love and freedom, do escape the stasis, the eternal present of inaction. Felipe Hurtado and Julia have dared to defy General Rosas, thereby escaping from cyclical time.

While Garro's approach to temporal issues has elicited many studies, her treatment of gender and race in particular is significant and distinguishes her work from that of Paz and from that of most of the (male) writers of that generation. As Jean Franco reminds us, Garro's work "challenges the state's appropriation of meaning by evoking more ancient loyalties—to family, religion, and 'imagined' communities which do not coincide with the nation" (*Plotting Women*, 134). In *Recollections* the conflict between official history and collective memory, between social expectations and personal desires, is represented most clearly in the presentation of its women characters. As Winkler notes, "Women comprise the first and most obvious of the marginalized groups in *Los recuerdos del porvenir*" ("Insiders, Outsiders," 178). All the female characters, whether members of the bourgeoisie and "good mothers and daughters" or social outcasts (the prostitutes and the kept women of the invading soldiers), appear to have little autonomy as typical women in a patriarchal society. Whereas the canonical novels of the Mexican Revolution all but exclude women or use their bodies as representations, Garro includes commentary about the victimization of women. Moreover, she also shows them attempting to change their fates as victims, however unsuccessful some may be. Rarely in the novel of the Mexican Revolution is there a figure like Julia, who manages to escape oppression, or an Elvira Montúfar, who expresses the liberation brought by widowhood (23).

Compare the women we meet in *The Death of Artemio Cruz* by Carlos Fuentes. He presents his readers with Regina as the beloved of Artemio Cruz, but we soon learn that he raped her and forced her to follow him, as Julia follows Captain Rosas. Regina is killed and remains only as a memory for Artemio. Artemio's own wife, Catalina, might well feel the liberation of the widow Elvira Montúfar, but that part of her story is not included in Fuentes's novel. Most closely resembling Montúfar is the heroine of another novel by a woman, Ángeles Mastretta, whose *Arráncame la vida* (1985), translated as *Tear This Heart Out* (1997), follows the pattern of showing a woman liberated after the death (or possible murder) of her husband. One other striking contrast in comparing Garro's *Recollections* with other novels of the Mexican Revolution is that reading her novel enables us to see relationships among mothers and daughters, brothers and sisters, as well as all the scenes of brutality and victimization associated with war.

While scenes of violence pervade *Recollections*, one of Garro's short stories from her first collection, *La semana de colores* (The Week of Colors, 1964), synthesizes the cruelty and carnage of the Mexican Revolution as it affects two young girls. "Nuestras vidas son los ríos" (Our Lives Are the Rivers) is one of two stories added to the second edition of *La semana de colores* (1987); the other, "Era Mercurio" (It Was Mercurio), is also a political story that refers to a friend of Garro's, the PRI politician Carlos A. Madrazo (1915–1969) and his battle against corruption in Mexico prior to the student uprisings in 1968 (for the import of that story and its connection between Garro and Madrazo and their involvement in the convoluted events of 1968, see Chapter 5). While "Era Mercurio" includes historical figures and realistic references, no dates or realistic motifs are mentioned in "Nuestras vidas son los ríos," for the name of the young general who is shot by the firing squad is not part of the historical record.

Although the main point of the story, as Winkler suggests ("Elena Garro," 35), centers on the education of two young sisters regarding the reality of death, the Revolution is important in the story in revealing Garro's perspective on the war and its participants.

Garro always professed admiration for the brave men who fought for their ideals in the Revolution, and in this beautifully written short story she pays homage to that type of person in the character of Gen. Rueda Quijano, a man twenty-six years of age who goes to his death with a detachment that belies the finality of his fate. For the young girls, Leli and Eva, who read about the scene of his demise and see his photograph, his physical beauty seems incongruous with his violent and premature death.

Although the general is somehow rescued from oblivion because his photo and the story of his death become part of the reality of these young girls, the lesson they learn is not just about the decisiveness of death. They have already discovered the sadness and certainty of death in their own home and among the members of their family; their aunt died young and their uncle Boni at thirty-one is contemplating suicide. He reads to Leli from the great Spanish poet Jorge Manrique lines whose metaphysical elegy gives the story its title: "Nuestras vidas son los ríos." The elegy is celebrated in the Hispanic world for the way it synthesizes an eternal theme: the inevitability of death for human beings and how this common fate brings equality to all—rich or poor, woman or man, and in Mexico, campesino or landowner, Indian or white.

In her further use of canonical Hispanic subtexts, such as the reference to the Golden Age Spanish dramatist Pedro Calderón de la Barca's *La vida es sueño* (Life Is a Dream), Garro creates a story on the theme of death that is at once Mexican and universal. The reference to the Mexican Revolution, however, and its quick dispatch of so many young Mexican nationals grounds the story in a political reality despite its rich poetic imagery. Death may be a "blue sea bathed in yellow suns" (173–174) that all people will finally reach,[45] but how we get there is brought up as an issue not to be ignored. When the girls ponder details of the general's death, Eva assures her sister that the government killed him:

"Have you seen the Government?"

"Yes . . . I saw it once . . . Rutilo told me: the nasty government is a big killer . . . "

"He killed General Rueda Quijano."

"He killed him for good"—Eva said these words with a solemn voice. (166)[46]

The reaction to this allocation of guilt is revealing. Garro's young girls personify the government in much the same way the eminent Mexican writer

Juan Rulfo does in his short story "Luvina," found in his collection *El llano en llamas* (1953; translated as *The Burning Plain*, 1967). Compare their evocation of the government as a real person who is evil with the same attitude found in this conversation in "Luvina," a short story that shares the same depressing, deadly environment as Rulfo's masterpiece *Pedro Páramo* (1955):

> "You say the government will help us, teacher? Do you know the Government?"
> "I told them I did."
> "We know it too. It just happens. But we don't know anything about the Government's mother." (119)[47]

In both "Nuestras vidas son los ríos" and "Luvina" the speakers reveal a prevalent attitude regarding the government as an indifferent father figure that cares little for its citizens and brings harm to them. Garro shares this viewpoint with Rulfo and with most of the writers and intellectuals of Mexico. The personification of the government as a male figure fits the rhetoric that was established during the Porfiriato; as Juan Bruce Novoa reminds us, Don Porfirio spoke of the "pueblo" (people) as his children and became, in effect, the "great father" of the nation (39), replacing Cortés, and with no reference to a mother figure in that age of patriarchy.[48]

While Garro treats the themes of death and political responsibility in ways that recall the great Mexican master Rulfo, her use of young girl narrators also compares with the perspective of another (woman) writer who dealt more directly with scenes of the Mexican Revolution. Nellie Campobello's *Cartucho* (1931) recounts the adventures of a young girl growing up amidst the battles and fiery figures of the Revolution in the North—Villa territory. Whereas Rulfo was immediately accepted as a major figure, Garro more gradually became integrated into the canon. Campobello had been ignored as a writer for a number of decades but has been rediscovered; her innovative perspective on the Revolution has been studied in a number of monographs.[49] Like Garro, she offers us the reactions of children who are faced with the senselessness and violence of war. Most war fiction—from the *Iliad* to Ernest Hemingway's *For Whom the Bell Tolls* (1940), for example—deals with men in battle and the repercussions of their experiences. Perhaps the best way to expose the horrors of war is to see its effect on the most innocent members of a society—its children. Campobello was one of the first writers in Mexico to show the effects of war on children by her use of a child narrator who recounts anecdotes of the war zone around her. Her stories also show many women protagonists—not as the perpetrators of such violence (although women did fight as *soldaderas* in the Mexican Revolution) but more often as the helpmates, as the ones who help to ease the wounded or bury the dead.[50] As Mary Louise Pratt reminds us, Campobello's contribution lies not only in filling her pages with women—which she did—but also in using women and children as "testigos privilegiados" (privileged witnesses) to the horrific events that affected them despite their inability to change the course of war (260).

For both Paz and Garro, their major prose pieces clearly relate to the Mexican Revolution. While Paz is most often quoted, mainly because of his long-standing canonical position, it is Garro who presents to the reader the lives of those marginalized figures who have been neglected in the history books—not only the women but even the generals who were on the "wrong" side of the campaigns. Her characters are diverse and more reflective of the complexities of the struggle and show the numerous capabilities of women in particular. Moreover, while most readers and critics turn their attention to the novel as the genre that treats this sweeping historical theme, Garro was imaginative in her use of the material and created not only a novel but also a play, short stories, and a series of essays that highlight her perspective on the importance and impact of the Mexican Revolution.

The Revolution was supposed to have brought closure to a period of dictatorship and discrimination, yet we can see that Paz and Garro as well as many other writers and intellectuals continued to question whether it really did contribute benefits to Mexican society.[51] As Patrick Dove reminds us, Paz suggests that by means of the Revolution the Mexican nation went through a "catastrophic transition from oligarchy to bourgeois democracy, [similar to] an adolescent facing a rite of passage into adulthood: 'This time of transition and radical uncertainty is both a philosophical and an ethical moment, and it presents the nascent nation with a two-fold question: "What are we, and how can we fulfill our obligations to ourselves as we are?"'" (92). For Dove, Paz's twofold question presupposes the idea of modernity as an absolutely new beginning. But Paz also indicates that the Revolution has in many ways failed to live up to this promise of a total renewal and a second origin and that modern Mexico remains caught within a contradiction: "We have an exuberant modernism with a deficient modernization" (Paz quoted in Dove, 92). Whereas Paz brings to our attention the contradictory nature of Mexican modernity, he still believes in the redemptive or corrective potential of art and the possibilities of future wholeness (Dove, 96).

In summary, Paz wanted to believe that "[t]he Mexican Revolution was an explosive and authentic revelation of our real nature" (*Labyrinth*, 135). Despite repeating this phrase in different ways in the chapter, Paz also discredits all the revolutionary leaders as being bereft of ideas, "with no ideology except that of a hunger for land" (Quiroga, 82). But for Garro, in contrast, revolutionary leaders such as Madero and Felipe Ángeles did have important ideas that were distorted and marginalized by greedy, authoritarian, power-hungry generals. Moreover, as a woman in a patriarchal society who tried to speak for the marginalized figures of her country—the indigenous peoples, the workers, the landless—Garro realizes the limitations of political structures. Her message rests on the need to encourage *all* Mexicans to challenge the belief in a circular, repetitive course of history. While Paz certainly helped Mexicans to appreciate the importance of Emiliano Zapata and to reconsider the concept of revolution, Garro's vision has much to tell us about the real interactions of women, Indians, and workers in relation to the Mexican Revolution and the more self-seeking actions of the revolutionary generals. Her message still resonates today.

"Politics is a great enemy of love."
PAZ
The Double Flame

LOVE AND WAR DON'T MIX

GARRO AND PAZ IN THE SPANISH CIVIL WAR

ELECTION RESULTS LEADING TO ARMED fighting and the dissolution of law and order, conflicts over the ownership and use of land, bloody warfare, hunger in the streets, and international crises marked the period of the Mexican Revolution but also characterized the years of the Spanish Civil War. Comparisons between the two have proven fruitful for a number of reasons. Although each was brought about by different historical, social, and cultural circumstances, the Mexican Revolution (circa 1910–1920) and the Spanish Civil War (1936–1939) are both considered major upheavals in the twentieth century. According to Octavio Paz, the Mexican Revolution was not associated with a specific ideology (Fell, 339). In contrast, the opponents in the Spanish Civil War were more clearly divided between the Nationalists or Falangists (fascists of Spain) and the Republicans, mostly socialists and Communists.[1]

Throughout Europe and the Americas, the war in Spain was viewed as the battle between the forces of democracy and fascism, or communism versus fascism. Frankly, this would not seem the venue to choose as the place to bring your new bride, except for an aspiring young poet driven by the romance of mingling with the members of the intellectual leadership in the arts and perhaps naïve about the risks. Despite having lived through the traumas of the Mexican Revolution, Paz and Garro, who married in May 1937, immediately set off to a Spain beset by a civil war whose outcome was far from certain. In this chapter I review the international, national, and personal contexts of this momentous war and how Paz and Garro assimilated their wartime experiences not only into their written work but also into their future political and esthetic perspectives. Being in Spain was liberating for Paz and led to progressively more important career choices, while Garro's encounters with the major international literary icons provided disconcerting evidence of the subordinate status of women. Her personal experiences would later be expressed in narrative, where she challenged patriarchal principles and women's inferior status. She elected to subvert the established cultural memory of the war and its participants by writing about her own observations on major political events and individuals that affected her personal and artistic life.

The Spanish Civil War has been called "the last romantic war of contemporary history" (Camino, 92). Paz and Garro were among the many young people who hastened to Spain to support the Republican cause in any way possible. They arrived during one of the bloodiest and most harrowing years of the Civil War. The year 1937 marked the terror bombing of Guernica on April 27 by the German Condor Legion as well as two major intense battles in the immediate area around Madrid: at Jarama (January to February) and Brunete (July, preceding the arrival of the young couple). They joined other intellectuals and writers who had also been invited to attend the Segundo Congreso Internacional de Escritores Antifascistas para la Defensa de la Cultura (Second International Congress of Antifascist Writers for the Defense of Culture) and were eager to join like-minded thinkers. As incongruous as the idea of holding a conference in defense of culture during a war may sound, the meeting did take place and influenced the lives of Paz and Garro personally and professionally.

Paz established lifelong friendships and developed his enduring attitude about Communist injustices, while Garro's struggles with patriarchal gender relations during her Spanish journey became one of the several themes that pervade her work. The theme of war often exaggerates the differences between the genders, as Sandra Gilbert and Susan Gubar remind us: "not only did the apocalyptic events of this war [World War I] have very different meanings for men and women, such events were in fact different for men and women" (*No Man's Land*, 262). The experiences of Garro and Paz in the Spanish Civil War bear this out.

Paz considered the Mexican Revolution (which the two young people had already experienced) to be the first major civil war of the twentieth century

(*Labyrinth*, 175).[2] The Spanish Civil War is usually viewed as the opening chapter of World War II, because it involved the first major military contest between leftist forces and fascists. The repressive Díaz government in Mexico had been condemned by more liberal, leftist factions; in Spain, in contrast, a series of right-wing insurrections within the military attacked the democratic government of the Second Spanish Republic, elected to power in 1931. Fighting began on July 17, 1936, and for three grim, bloody years the battles raged in all parts of Spain. Yet the war involved many more participants than just the native Spanish people. The defenders of the democratically elected Republic, called the Loyalists, were mostly from Spain's working class and peasantry but also included socialists, trade unionists, Stalinists, Trotskyites, and anarchists, joined by many Spanish writers and intellectuals who felt ideologically attuned to the Loyalists. In addition, scores of writers and idealists from Europe and the Americas, sympathetic to the Republican ideology, rushed to Spain to back the cause. Unfortunately, in the official political realm, the democracies of Europe abandoned the legitimate government of Spain, supposedly fearful of its links to communism (Lambie, "Vallejo," 131). Only two countries, the Soviet Union and Mexico, supported the Loyalists for specific reasons, as noted below.

The rebels in this war, the anti-Republican forces known as the Nationalists, were composed mostly of political and social conservatives, including the fascist Falangist Party, the Catholic Church, the upper ranks of the military, and some who hoped to restore the Spanish monarchy. Their allies were fascist Italy and Nazi Germany, who supplied them with troops, tanks, and planes. Germany field-tested some of its most important artillery in Spain, as the Soviets did on behalf of the Republicans. Gen. Francisco Franco (1892–1975), leader of the Nationalist coalition, was seen as advancing the cause of fascism in Europe.

Because of this internationalized context as the contest between fascism and "socialism" or progressive liberalism,[3] Spain (which had been disregarded as a political backwater for so long) suddenly became a site of intense global interest. Unlike the Mexican Revolution, in which the United States was the major foreign power to intervene, mostly based on the fear of Pancho Villa,[4] in Spain volunteers arrived from many countries. Most of them were on the Republican side, although 60,000 Italians, 20,000 Portuguese, and 15,000 Germans plus about 2,000 French monarchists and Irish Catholics were sent by their governments to fight with the Nationalists. The Great Depression and the threat of fascism on one hand and Stalinism on the other were all factors that stimulated a global interest in Spain.[5] According to Hugh Thomas in his masterly study *The Spanish Civil War*, about 32,000 men and women fought in the International Brigades, including the American Abraham Lincoln Battalion and the Canadian Mackenzie-Papineau Battalion, which were organized in conjunction with the Comintern to aid the Spanish Republicans (942). Perhaps another 3,000 fought as members of the anarchist Confederación Nacional del Trabajo (CNT: National Labor Confederation) and the Partido Obrero de Unificación Marxista (POUM: Workers' Party of Marxist Unification). George Orwell is perhaps the most famous name among those fighting with POUM, although, as discussed below, one of Octavio Paz's childhood friends was a member of POUM and became the subject of one of Paz's most famous poems associated with the Spanish Civil War: "Elegía a un compañero muerto en el frente de Aragón" (Elegy to a Companion Dead at the Aragon Front).[6]

Even before writing that poem, however, Paz was one of the first poets to respond to the news of the attack on the Spanish Republic with the publication of "¡No pasarán!" (They Shall Not Pass!) in 1936. The historical context and the esthetic impact of this poem are discussed later in this chapter.[7] The texts I use here to study the impact of the Spanish Civil War are primarily Paz's poems, because his international reputation began with the poems stimulated by the Civil War. I also refer to some of his essays that make reference to the war. Garro's major written response to the war is found in her *Memorias de España 1937*, one of her only outright autobiographical texts.[8] Published in 1992, the eighteen brief chapters of this text chronicle from Garro's perspective the events that occurred in the year they spent in Spain during the Civil War, ending with their return to Mexico. While a number of her post-1968 narratives are set in European sites, *La casa junto al río* (The House Next to the River) specifically takes place in Spain in the post–Civil War period and includes references to the war itself. All her texts, however, show the influence or repercussions of her experiences in Spain. It was the scene of her first interactions with the intellectuals of the day as a married woman and clearly brought out the restricted roles accorded women in patriarchal societies.

Paz and Garro were only two of the many writers whose experiences in Spain are reflected in their texts. The theme of Spanish Civil War is treated by many of the major Latin American writers of that time and brought together diverse writers across the globe who ordinarily might never have interacted personally. As the war raged on, Spain and the Republican struggle became a cause célèbre among the prominent left-leaning intellectuals throughout the Americas and Europe. In addition to Orwell, who wrote "Homage to

Catalonia" as a result of his experiences, the French writer André Malraux volunteered in Spain and organized the Air Force of the International Brigades; his novel *L'Espoir* (Man's Hope, 1937) paints a picture of Republican Spain in combat based on his own experiences. Ernest Hemingway is unmistakably the most famous writer in North American cultural memory associated with the Spanish Civil War. *For Whom the Bell Tolls* (1940) is perhaps the iconic novel of the period.[9] But beyond the easy association with Hemingway and Orwell, the name of the English poet Stephen Spender (1909–1995), who would meet Paz and Garro in Spain, may come to mind, along with the eminent North American writer John Dos Passos (*Adventures of a Young Man*, 1939), who had become interested in Hispanic issues when he first went to Mexico in 1926.[10] Langston Hughes, who also knew Spanish from his several trips to Cuba, served as a newspaper correspondent for the *Baltimore Afro-American* during the Spanish Civil War to cover the African American volunteers in the International Brigades (1937) (see Presley). Although the artistic community was largely leftist, several prominent writers supported Franco, such as Ezra Pound, Roy Campbell, and Lucien Mauvault.

As Luis Mario Schneider explains in his comprehensive book *Segundo congreso internacional de escritores antifascistas* (Second International Congress of Antifascist Writers), the First International Congress in Paris in 1935 had been attended by such prominent writers as Thomas Mann, Heinrich Mann, E. M. Forster, Aldous Huxley, Stephen Spender, Waldo Frank, Virginia Woolf, Boris Pasternak, John Dos Passos, Sinclair Lewis, Selma Lagerlöf, Carl Sandburg, and Ernest Hemingway, as well as Pablo Neruda, José Bergamín, Rafael Alberti, and María Teresa León (Schneider 38). One of the themes that occupied the writers at this conference was the role of the intellectual in a socialist society, but there was also a tacit approval of the Stalinist Soviet ideology (Schneider, 39). They agreed to reconvene in Madrid in 1937, not anticipating that Spain would be suffering the horrors of a civil war by that time. When war broke out, the organizing committee was determined to bring all its members to Spain, no matter what the risks, because it wanted to show unequivocal support for the Republican cause (Schneider, 41). This unique organization was the catalyst for assembling so many writers and intellectuals in a war zone despite the misgivings of the Republican government, which not only had to deal with the challenges of conducting a war but also had to worry about protecting so many noncombatants from countries around the globe.

A partial account of all those who officially attended this Second International Congress highlights that writers and intellectuals from both sides of the

Atlantic attended, bringing Spain and the Americas together as never before. Well-known Spanish figures of the period who attended included Antonio Machado, José Bergamín, Rafael Alberti, Jacinto Benavente, León Felipe, Margarita Nelken, and María Teresa León. Latin American countries were represented by figures who are all recognizable today, such as the already famous Pablo Neruda and Vicente Huidobro (Chile); César Vallejo (Peru); Carlos Pellicer, José Mancisidor, and Octavio Paz (who was then the youngest and least known of the Mexican contingent); and Alejo Carpentier, Nicolás Guillén, and Juan Marinello (Cuba). The French delegation consisted of André Malraux, Julien Benda, Claude Aveline, León Moussinac, André Chamson, and Tristan Tzara; the United Kingdom delegates were W. H. Auden, Stephen Spender, Ralph Bates, Edgell Rickword, and Silvia Townsend Warner; and the Soviet contingent consisted of Ilya Ehrenburg, Mikhail Koltsov, and Aleksei Tolstoy. Also in attendance were Ambroglio Donini (Italy); Louis Fischer, Malcolm Cowley, and Anna Louise Strong (United States); Nordahl Grieg (Norway); Ludwig Renn, Anna Seghers, Egon Erwin Kisch, and Leon Feuchtwanger (Germany); and Denis Marion (Belgium). (For the complete list of delegates, see Schneider, 77–79.)

The Cuban Juan Marinello (1898–1977), who was president of the delegation from Latin America, observed in one of the last speeches at the conference: "If years ago, all roads led to Rome, today, all roads lead to Madrid" (quoted in Schneider, 228). Indeed, the young married couple found themselves in the company of an august group of distinguished writers when they arrived in Europe in 1937 as participants in the Second International Congress. Meeting such illustrious companions would turn out to be quite a momentous time in the life of the young poet. It may seem ironic that the Mexican Paz first became internationally recognized as an up-and-coming poet as a result of his journey to Spain, reversing the path of the conquistadors, who had searched for glory, fame, and fortune by going to the New World. Ignoring all the risks involved, Paz eagerly accepted the opportunity to venture forth in 1937, even into the cauldron of war.

It was also a momentous year for Elena Garro, whose life changed dramatically: after being a choreographer and aspiring artist in her own right, within a secure environment of her close-knit family and circle of friends, she lost her independent identity to become the "wife of." The arrangements for their marriage occurred precipitously in 1937. As soon as Paz returned from the Yucatán in late spring,[11] they immediately went off to Spain and the war. Some might want to read the conjoining of these two events (their marriage and then living in a war zone) as a harbinger of the stormy nature of their relationship during the years of their marriage.[12]

Although Garro had never left home before, going to Spain was a reconnection with her paternal roots: her father, José Antonio Garro Melendreras, had come from the "mother country." Paz had left Mexico and his home in Mixcoac once before, as a boy of six, when his parents took him first to San Antonio and then to Los Angeles because of his father's involvement with the Mexican Revolution and the agrarian program of Emiliano Zapata (see Santí, "Octavio Paz"). That experience had not been pleasant for the young child and had tainted his ideas about what it meant to be a foreigner without mastery of a language. So powerfully negative was that first incursion outside of Mexico that Paz stated in an interview that going to work in the Yucatán in 1937 was the first time he had lived outside of Mexico City (Santí, "Primeras palabras," 7). Contrary to what Paz recalls and professes in his conversation with Santí, he mentions in other essays and his references in *Itinerario* (his intellectual autobiography) that he became politically involved in helping the indigenous population of his own country because of friends who were involved in the cause.

Paz went to Mérida in the Yucatán Peninsula with Octavio Novaro Fiora del Fabro and Ricardo Cortés Tamayo, to help establish schools for the Mayans. After only three months, he received a telegram from Elena, his fiancée at the time, saying that he had been invited to attend the Second International Congress of Writers in July 1937 in Madrid, Valencia, and Barcelona.

It may seem curious that this young man with one published volume of poems would have received such an invitation to attend a prestigious conference with some of the most renowned cultural figures of the time. Although he was only in his twenties, by 1937 Paz had already published *Luna Silvestre* (Wild Moon), a collection of poems; many of them are erotic, in the vein of Pablo Neruda's type of love poetry in their intimist nature. Privileged to have enjoyed the library and the tutelage of his distinguished grandfather (the journalist, novelist, and man of letters Don Ireneo Paz), Paz was even more fortunate as a student in the Escuela Nacional Preparatoria, which boasted some exceptional professors, including the lauded poet José Gorostiza as well as distinguished scholars of the time, like Pedro Argüelles, Alejandro Gómez Arias, Antonio Díaz Soto y Gama, and Samuel Ramos. One of Paz's favorite teachers was Carlos Pellicer, already a published poet, whom Paz would later call Mexico's "first really modern poet" ("La poesía de Carlos Pellicer," 75). Although Paz had begun to study law like his father before him, he soon abandoned that path and expressed the view that he would become a poet. His seriousness about literature was quite evident. As early as 1932 he founded the first of his many literary reviews, *Barandal* (Balustrade), which, according to Guillermo Sheridan, had a Marxist bent ("Octavio Paz in Yucatán"). It is also interesting to note that the journal counted on the collaboration of a diverse group of poets, including some from the circle called the Contemporáneos (which included Salvador Novo, Carlos Pellicer, Xavier Villaurrutia, Jaime Torres Bodet, Gilberto Owen, José Gorostiza, Jorge Cuesta, and Bernardo Ortiz de Montellano) as well as Spaniards like Juan Gil-Albert and Antonio Sánchez Barbudo.[13]

Thus the young Paz worked with the members of the Contemporáneos (Novo, Pellicer), whose esthetic was cosmopolitan and against the "social poetry" that was becoming popular as interest in communism grew in the 1930s. Through his activities in the journal, Paz also became known to a group of Spanish poets. For the young Mexicans of his cohort, the poets of the Spanish Generation of 1927 (Federico García Lorca, Rafael Alberti, José Bergamín, Juan Gil-Albert) were read and appreciated. Paz was selected as a representative from Mexico to the prestigious conference as a result of his collaboration with writers who would make his work known in Spain.

Although Paz and Garro were personal friends of many of the Contemporáneos and Paz would later write about a number of them in positive terms, at that moment in the thirties the poets associated with that vanguardist group represented for Paz the previous generation; he was not so sanguine about their importance and tried to distance himself from them, especially because of his political interest in communism at that time.

For those readers who know Paz as the venerable Nobel laureate whose pronouncements on Mexican culture and esthetics are found everywhere, it may be easy to believe that in the 1930s Paz was as cosmopolitan as Contemporáneos such as Pellicer and Villaurrutia, as one early critic of Mexican writers supposed. Maurice Halperin included Paz in his list of poets whose chief contact with Mexican reality was in "the government offices or polite drawing rooms of Mexico City" ("Social Background," 877). In the case of Paz, interestingly, that evaluation does not jibe with his early activist stage. Paz was writing in a very different style from a Villaurrutia or Novo (see the discussion of his poems of the thirties below). As José Quiroga writes: "Paz rejected the 'pure art' of the Contemporáneos" (3). Because of Paz's noted tendency to revise his work and to control the poems that appear in his collections and anthologies, some of his early poems (the pieces that might be called *comprometidos* in Spanish, meaning politically committed) are *not* the ones he deigned to include in his official oeuvre. For example, the poem that brought him to the attention of the organizers of the Second International Congress ("¡No pasarán!") is not included in his official collections.[14]

By 1937 Paz had revealed on the one hand his desire to put his social concerns into action and on the other his disquiet about writing lyric poetry when he was living in such important revolutionary times. Even if Mexicans were no longer involved in the armed conflicts of the Revolution, they were certainly still living in a momentous and activist age: in the national political arena, under the presidency of Lázaro Cárdenas (1934–1940), and certainly in the esthetic realm and in Paz's chosen genre, poetry.

Mexico under Cárdenas moved to the left politically after having been ruled by a series of conservative presidents. Cárdenas might have been a general and the founder of the Partido de la Revolución Mexicana (PRM: Party of the Mexican Revolution, which later became the PRI), but in action he was a socialist with a progressive program of building roads and schools, organizing the modern secular school system, and promoting land reform and social security for workers. Cárdenas gave firm support to the Zapatista maxim "Tierra y Libertad" (Land and Liberty).[15] The government also expropriated and redistributed millions of acres of hacienda land to peasants. Union workers gained in wages and extended rights. In 1938 Cárdenas nationalized the railways and created Ferrocarriles Nacionales de México (National Railways of Mexico), which was placed under a workers' administration. Significantly, he also nationalized the petroleum industry, creating PEMEX (Petróleos Mexicanos: Mexican Petroleum). Cárdenas is praised for his part in fomenting Mexican economic independence, but he also forged an independent role for Mexico in international affairs.

It was fortuitous indeed for Republican Spain that Cárdenas was president at the time of the Spanish Civil War: he supported the Republican opponents of Franco, supplying them with weapons, food, and oil. Moreover, after the war Cárdenas accepted thousands of Spanish immigrants and refugees, which was as important for Mexican intellectual life as it was for the Spanish émigrés whose lives were saved.[16] Mexico also defended Spanish Republicans at the League of Nations, unlike most of the Western nations, which had declared policies of nonintervention in Spain. As Garro sorrowfully describes the politics in *Memorias*: "It was useless for the French workers to organize demonstrations in order to protest: 'Planes for Spain.' No one paid attention to them. The Committee of Non-Intervention opposed sending arms to the Republicans and Roosevelt was an enemy of Republican Spain" (133).[17] Only Mexico, her country, sent arms and planes.

If Mexican politics was forging an innovative and unexpected path, in the area of esthetics all of Latin America seemed ablaze in the thirties. As the cultural historian Carlos Monsiváis reminds us,

> In the thirties poetry in Spanish experiences a moment of splendor. In that time, in addition to the Mexicans, the Chileans Gabriela Mistral, Pablo Neruda, and Vicente Huidobro, the Peruvian César Vallejo, the Argentines Jorge Luis Borges and Oliverio Girondo, the Cubans Nicolás Guillén, Emilio Ballagas, and José Lezama Lima, the Ecuadorian Jorge Carrera Andrade, the Guatemalan Luis Cardoza y Aragón, the Nicaraguans Salomón de la Selva and José Coronel Urtecho were writing. And in Spain the Generation of 1927 was in force, those whom the Spanish Civil War would break up, but not before a brief stage of intense creation by Federico García Lorca, Rafael Alberti, Vicente Aleixandre, Gerardo Diego, Luis Cernuda, Jorge Guillén, Pedro Salinas, Emilio Prados, Dámaso Alonso, León Felipe. And before them were the writers Antonio Machado and Juan Ramón Jiménez.[18]

It was an exciting time to be writing poetry and to believe that poetry could make a difference in the world. The great Cuban writer and internationalist José Martí (1853–1895) had also shown with his own example that writers could be and should be involved in revolutionary struggles. Martí proclaimed "the brotherhood of oppressed peoples and denounce[d] the social abyss between those who had power and those who were completely lacking it" (quoted in Herlinghaus and Plesch, 139).[19] Martí, the poet-soldier who died fighting for Cuban independence at the end of the nineteenth century, is one example of Latin American writers who believed that poetry was capable of transforming the world and that creating a poem was a revolutionary act. As a revolutionary poet, Martí "was organizing a war, dialoguing with the poor, seeking to destroy an empire, anticipating the imposition of another, and galloping on horseback toward his death in battle" (Fernández Retamar et al., 69). Similarly impassioned about supporting the Republican cause, Paz, like the poets Neruda, Vallejo, Carpentier, and Langston Hughes, emulated the paradigm of Martí.

In Latin America as in Europe, at the time of the Spanish Civil War poetry "was regarded as an important means of mass-communication, reaching a wide audience through the radio and the press as well as readings at the front" (Warner, 119). Poetry was a "privileged instrument" (Salaün, 11). Some estimates suggest that over three thousand poems were motivated by the war, and the various anthologies and critical studies are too numerous to mention, attesting to the stimulating literary zeal of the time. It is interesting, moreover, to note the impressive numbers of noteworthy poems written in the first rush as the war began, in contrast to the genre associated with wartime in Mexico, which was mostly in narrative form. For example, Azuela's *The Underdogs* is considered the representative text for the Mexican Revolution, while the Spanish Civil War poems by Alberti and Lorca in Spain, Neruda's *España en el corazón* (Spain at Heart), and Vallejo's *España, aparta de mí este cáliz* (Spain, Take This Cup from Me) are renowned.[20]

Of the major writers that Paz met in Spain, he mentions that he felt great camaraderie with Arturo Serrano Plaja (*Itinerario*, 58), but it was the (ten years) older Neruda who was initially crucial to Paz for his "career" impact. When Paz recounts the possible reasons for his being selected to attend the conference even though he was not a member of the Liga de Escritores y Artistas Revolucionarios de México (LEAR: League of Revolutionary Writers and Artists), he suggests first that Rafael Alberti and Serrano Plaja had read his poems and knew him; only after what seems a bit of hesitation does Paz also admit the possible influence of Neruda:

> Neruda also knew about me and years later, referring to my presence at the congress, said that he "had discovered me." In a way that was true: at the time I had sent him my first book, which he read and liked, and generously told me so. (*Itinerary*, 47)[21]

Perhaps Paz's reference to Neruda as almost an afterthought has to do with their subsequent falling out (discussed below), but at that time in Paz's life Neruda was a more substantial influence than either Serrano Plaja or Alberti. In 1937 Paz had sent Neruda his *Raíz del hombre* (Roots of Man), and Neruda reacted positively to the work (Stanton, "La poesía de Octavio Paz"). The young poet wrote in a similar vein: just as Neruda had written love poems that were controversial for their eroticism, Paz's poem was openly erotic. A comparison of these two stanzas shows how the young Paz seems to echo the more mature poet.

These are lines from the poem "Raíz del hombre":

Amante, todo calla
bajo la voz ardiente de tu nombre.
(Beloved, all is silent
under your name's scorching voice.) (*Obras completas*, 11)

And this is Neruda's final stanza of Poema 15, "Me gustas cuando calles" (I Like for You to Be Still):

Me gustas cuando callas porque estás como ausente.
Distante y dolorosa como si hubieras muerto. (Neruda, 38)

I like for you to be still: it is as though you were absent,
distant and full of sorrow as though you had died. (Neruda, 39)[22]

It is not only the use of the verb *callar* (to be quiet) that is noteworthy but the play of ironies that marks the poems. For Paz, the beloved's physicality is more powerful than words, yet words can bring the beloved to the lover. For Neruda, too, the words act as a link to join the beloved and the lover, after a lack of words almost implied the absence of the corporal presence of the beloved. Each poetic voice also addresses an inherent ambiguity in the beloved. They share a similar approach to the body and the use of images like stars, blood, and trees. Stanton concludes: "There is no doubt that this 'first book' that Neruda receives is *Raíz del hombre*, the poems of which he would have perceived echoes and resonances of his own poetry" ("Poesía de Octavio Paz." 654).[23] Neruda not only gave Paz encouragement but—especially after the success of Paz's poetic response to the Spanish war: "¡No pasarán!"—supported the initiative to invite him to the Second International Congress. Neruda's support is not inconsequential, because he was an important figure. He had been living in Madrid in 1936 as the consul from Chile and had also participated in the First International Conference, held in 1935 in Paris.

In an essay in *Letras Libres*, the cultural historian and critic Carlos Monsiváis outlines the importance of Paz's meeting with Neruda:

For Paz the meeting with Pablo Neruda in Europe was decisive. Neruda's influence was like an inundation that spreads out and covers miles and miles— waters that are confused, powerful, hypnotic, formless. Paz meets Neruda in Paris and sees him again in Valencia, in the Second International Congress of Antifascist Writers, and then again in Mexico, where he is consul of Chile. But what Neruda brings in regard to his poetic genius and friendly attention, he mitigates with his partisanship and his demand for obedience. Paz fights with him and distances himself from a type of poetry and social commitment. Neruda detests the "purists," cultivators of "art for art's sake." Paz defends the right of free expression. And he disengages himself from an esthetic and an ethic founded in the political utility of poetry, bringing himself closer to the construction (or better said, the perfection) of his original voice. ("Octavio Paz y la izquierda," 31)[24]

Paz's transition from writing in a so-called Neruda fashion—with regard to both erotic poems and political topics—to finding his own voice and becoming friends with many poets and intellectuals resulted in a public dispute with Neruda in 1943. At that time Neruda was leaving Mexico after having served as consul general in Mexico City since 1940 and having had a social relationship with Paz and Garro. Paz wrote a surprising farewell commentary about Neruda in *Letras de México*, considering their earlier friendly relationship. By then Paz had already distanced himself from his earlier, more politicized poetic stance:

> His literature is contaminated by politics, his politics. . . . It is very possible that Señor Neruda will one day succeed in writing a good poem about the war news, but I doubt very much that that poem will influence the war. . . . what separates us from him is not his political convictions but simply his vanity . . . and his salary. (quoted by Poniatowska, *Octavio Paz*, 40)[25]

In contrast with Paz's early admiration for Neruda, Garro was not very approving when she first met the Chilean poet in Spain. We should remember that the days in Spain, despite the ongoing war, were part of their first year of marriage—the honeymoon period. It was difficult enough to be in the middle of a war zone, surrounded by combatants, and have to suffer in sweltering, uncomfortable lodgings. When Garro asked Neruda to change accommodations with them, he refused. Garro comments that though he called her "m'ijita" (literally "my little daughter" but in popular parlance "little one" or even "sweetheart")—a term of endearment (or was it just a putdown?)—he refused to help her. Her response was to write that she "hated him" and that he was a selfish egotist (*Memorias*, 19).

While Garro's concerns about the room may seem petty within the context of a war zone, she does not seem to have misjudged Neruda, as proven by subsequent references to his troublesome behavior in Spain. For example, she tells her readers that he abandoned his Dutch wife and their daughter (29); he also acted badly toward Vicente Huidobro (23) and César Vallejo (83).

It took Paz longer to realize that he and Neruda were not on the same wavelength poetically and personally. Paz had written an extensive positive note in 1938, published in the Marxist Mexican journal *Ruta* (Route), called "Pablo Neruda en el corazón" (Pablo Neruda in Our Heart), a clear reference to Neruda's poem "España en el corazón" (Spain in Our Hearts) that had been published in Chile in 1937. Stanton suggests that his praise of Neruda was also a way for Paz to distance himself from the Contemporáneos ("Octavio Paz y los 'Contemporáneos,'" 1004) and their kind of "pure poetry."

As Stanton reminds us, "The conflict between pure poetry and social poetry marked an entire period in Hispanic letters. When Paz begins to write, at the beginning of the decade of the thirties, the balance already had leaned visibly in favor of those who opposed artistic purity" ("Octavio Paz y los 'Contemporáneos,'" 1004).[26]

One of the poems that Paz wrote while in the Yucatán, "Entre la piedra y la flor" (Between the Stone and the Flower, 1937), shows a social conscience: he recounts the hard life of the henequen workers whose lives he witnessed. Henequen, also known as sisal, was the chief crop of the workers whose lives Paz was attempting to improve by being a teacher. In an interview, Paz comments on what he tried to do with this poem: "I was very much impressed by the misery of the Maya farmers tied to the cultivation of henequen and the vicissitudes of the worldwide sisal trade" ("Excéntrica—Escritor de la Semana: Octavio Paz").[27]

Paz's anticapitalist beliefs during his early youth are reflected especially in the early versions of the poem, conceived in 1936 and published in 1940.[28] The five sections focus on the hard life of the henequen workers (I), their struggle to tame the land (II), the poetic voice's frustration in trying to tell their story (III), the negative influences of a capitalist society that measures things on a money scale (IV), and the poet's desire to do away with such an objectionable society (V). The poetic voice expresses its strong emotions, displeasure, and anger by repeating key phrases in each section. In section IV, for example, the word *dinero* (money) is repeated and defined and finally expressed with metaphors that show its power in human life, as the poet relates money to "magic," "the word," and "blood."

Significantly, the 1976 revision of the poem includes only four sections and contains more memorable lines:

El trabajo hace las cosas:
el dinero chupa la sangre de las cosas.
(Work makes things:
money sucks the blood out of things.)[29]

Paz's laments about the role of money and the free market system make it clear that in this poem he was experimenting with what is called "social poetry" as practiced by Neruda, as compared with the *poesía pura* (pure poetry) associated with the Contemporáneos, the generation before Paz.[30]

The poem that brought Paz to the attention of Neruda and the Committee for the Second International Congress of Antifascist Writers is more in the vein of "social poetry," although, as Stanton suggests, Paz always resisted poetry with a thesis ("La prehistoria estética," 33). Nevertheless, like "Entre la flor y la piedra," Paz's "¡No pasarán!" is an example of "committed poetry," with a social message. Despite its significance in his early career, Paz did not include this poem in his later anthologies; this exclusion perhaps reflected a response to criticism of him by the Contemporáneos. According to Stanton, when the poem first appeared Paz was taken to task by writers in Mexico such as Bernardo Ortiz de Montellano, a member of the Contemporáneos and a firm believer in "pure poetry," and Rubén Salazar Mallén, a not infrequent critic of Paz; both thought the poem was an example of Paz's pandering to social issues in order to get an invitation to the Second Congress ("La poesía de Octavio Paz," 651). Paz himself responded to the charge, no doubt offended by the suggestion that he had been manipulative and insincere. It is true that most of his poetic work until that point had not been political in theme, but he certainly did have a social conscience, as seen from the work he did in the Yucatán.

One of the few defenders of the poem was the leftist writer Efraín Huerta (1914–1982), who worked with Paz on the journal *Taller Poético* (Poetic Workshop) and wrote a brief laudatory note, calling it a "gran poema de Octavio, un poema perfecto" (great poem by Octavio, a perfect poem), noting its social message, and focusing on that aspect. Huerta adds: "[H]e has brought to the people of Mexico and Spain the most effective means of communion and understanding. He has created an authentic poem of limitless perspectives" (quoted by Stanton, "La poesía de Octavio Paz," 652).[31]

At the time Huerta wrote his praise, the supporters of the Republican cause agreed with him: over 3,500 copies of the poem were distributed for propagandistic purposes (Stanton, "La poesía de Octavio Paz," 652).

From its very title, "¡No pasarán!" (They Shall Not Pass, which is also used as a refrain), Paz invokes in his readers the real situation of the Spanish Republicans who were attacked by the Falangist forces. Paz was aware that the phrase "¡No pasarán!" (which had been used in World War I) had become recontextualized during the siege of Madrid in 1936. Dolores Ibárruri Gómez, a Communist political leader, gave a passionate speech to rally the Republican forces and declaimed, "¡No pasarán!" As a result of her zeal she became known as La Pasionaria, and the phrase became associated with the Republican cause. Paz's poem also expresses encouragement and support for the Republicans. It is a cry for solidarity among all the citizens, "camaradas" of all of Spain ("toda España") and all the globe ("De todas las orillas del planeta, / en todos los idiomas de los hombres").

Paz describes how these volunteers from around the world, as well as ordinary Spanish citizens, are gathered together to request that "they" should not pass (another variation of the refrain: "os pide que no pasen"). "They" as the subject of the various forms of the verb "pasar" is not described, but those who are being defended against the attack, who are defending Spain, are identified as "amigos" and "camaradas." Moreover, they are addressed in the second person plural, a verbal form used in Spain but not in Mexico, where Paz was located while writing. This distinction is a challenge to express in English, which no longer has unique forms for formal and informal subjects. In the original, then, the poem reflects the Peninsular Spanish theme in the form of the verbs ("detened," "reconquistad"), the direct objects ("os" is second person plural, familiar), and the particular references to places: the cities of Spain (Badajoz, Irún), and of course the very title and refrain "¡No pasarán!" Also, the choice of the verb "reconquistad" (reconquer) is sure to bring up the concept of the Reconquista (Reconquest) in Spanish cultural memory; this is a reference to the period in which the Spanish forces of the fifteenth century were successful in ousting the Moors from Spanish soil. Paz suggests with this allusion that the Spanish Republicans should oust the usurpers. It is ironic that Paz selects a verb with clear religious allusions—the Reconquest that ended in 1492 was very much a religious war—and uses it against the Falangist forces, which purported to represent the interests of the church in the Civil War.

Offering one of the few critical readings of the poem, Stanton suggests that the poem has some "esthetic defects"—notably its use of binary oppositions and the selection of rather conventional adjectives such as "terrible grito" (terrible cry) and "ternura caliente" (heated tenderness); he nevertheless reminds us that the poem was written with sincere fervor and was meant to be read aloud ("La poesía de Octavio Paz," 652–653). One feature of the poem that will reappear in Paz's work in prose as well as poetry is his specific evocation of the war in the use of realistic motifs (the geographical references and the military vocabulary), combined with a vision of war that is universal and metaphysical.

One of the poems that Paz did later accept as more representative of his work of this period is "Elegía a un joven muerto en Aragón" (Elegy to a Young Man Dead in Aragón; first known as "Elegía a un compañero muerto en el Frente de Aragón" [Elegy to a Companion Dead on the Aragon Front]). First recited to an audience of Spanish Republicans, "Elegia" was inspired by Paz's initial belief that his old friend José Bosch had been killed in battle in Spain.

In the first lines of stanza one, the voice of the poet repeats the idea that the dead man is a young friend of his, someone with whom he sympathized, his comrade, and someone whose life was cut short at a young age. This young comrade and the poet shared a future of hope and possibilities that was shortened by the bullets that the poet imagines.

One point that seems disturbing in the poem relates to the implications of the final line: "Has muerto entre los tuyos, por los tuyos" (You have died among your own, for your own). Suddenly the dead young man is no longer a representative of the same world as that of the poet, although they had been comrades. At one point the poet even corrects himself, emphasizing that they both share the same worldview: "Has muerto cuando apenas / tu mundo, nuestro mundo amanecía" (You have died when scarcely / your world, our world was dawning). "Your world" (the milieu of the young man) is also the poet's—it is "our world" after all. But the young man who had once faced a happy future with his friend is now dead. The final line seems to detach the poet from his friend's sacrifice. Whether this was a conscious or deliberate distancing tactic is not clear from the emotions expressed earlier. Although the poetic voice seems to make use of this tragic moment to express his personal grief—after all, this is not an elegy for an unknown soldier—a full reading of the poem suggests that he distances himself from the friend, his death, and the world in which that event took place.

Written in Spain, "Oda a España" (Ode to Spain) also openly expresses Paz's solidarity with the Spanish Republican cause. It appears to have been written as a direct result of an immediate emotional reaction, but Paz did not consider it worthy enough to be reworked and included in his later anthologies. Throughout his career, he consistently practiced a form of self-editing, as both Santí and Stanton have documented. The one poem that brought him to the attention of the organizers of the Second International Congress and led to his subsequent friendship with important writers—"¡No pasarán!"—is not included in his official collections. In his later years he confesses to Enrico Mario Santí his strong desire to have these pieces expunged from his literary record; he wants his readers to forget his early "outbursts." That is not the word he uses, but his commentary to Santí implies that these poems represent spontaneous work meant for publication in newspapers and journals and not the kind of carefully controlled "literature" with which he wanted his name to be associated.

It is not that Paz's ideas about Spain changed so much through the years, but many critics do see a difference in his political ideology. Santí suggests that Paz felt liberated by leaving behind these early experiences. Perhaps his stormy marriage to Elena Garro that marked that period had something to do with his need to suppress that phase of his life (Santí, "Los pininos"). In a conversation with Santí, who was charged with preparing a volume of his early essays ("Los pininos," 23), Paz proposes that the only reason he wanted to suppress certain texts was not for their political content but because they were not up to his standards (18). Now that those poems are readily accessible in editions by the Fondo de Cultura Económica, readers can assess them independently of Paz's own judgments.

The poems about the Spanish Civil War are concrete demonstrations that the Paz of the thirties believed in poetry as experience, "como algo que tiene que ser vivido" (as something that has to be lived; Müller-Bergh, 119). He later rejected this esthetic, however, just as he rejected the strict Stalinist ideology of those who were writing in the "social realism" style. As early as the forties, Paz seemed to have rejected his pro-Republican poetry. The success of his campaign against his own early political work about Spain is evident. Paz is not usually included among the select company of Latin American writers whose poetry is identified with the Spanish Civil War, including Neruda, Vallejo, Guillén, Carpentier—all major writers who had been in Spain at the same time as Paz.

At this juncture it is important to note that the battle between "poetry" and "politics" is played out in a number of ways not only in Paz's work but for many of the writers of the twenties and thirties. The polemic took on a particular gendered cast in Mexico, interestingly, when some critics promoted the idea that the kind of writing produced in the postrevolutionary period was "antimasculine" or "effeminate," with reference to the cosmopolitan writing of the Contemporáneos, many of whom were known homosexuals. In a 1924 article titled "El afeminamiento en la literatura mexicana" (Effeminacy in Mexican Literature) the writer and politician Julio Jiménez Rueda complained that the intellectual in Mexico had degenerated and there were no longer real men using the pen. Francisco Monterde, another distinguished writer and critic at the time, responded quickly to Jiménez Rueda's complaint about the absence of a "virile literature" by pointing out that Mariano Azuela had written a novel worthy of such a classification—*Los de abajo*, one of the first novels in the category "literature of the Mexican Revolution."[32] Of course, this whole debate to determine whether literature is virile or effeminate has much to do with the social construction of gender identities and *machista* attitudes toward homosexuals in Mexico. Moreover, this attempted marginalization of the Contemporáneos may also have had the purpose of excluding their work from serious critical commentary—and ultimately, participation in the canon—through judgments about who is going to be published and read. The question of canon formation related to the Contemporáneos was presented in a gendered vocabulary; yet, ironically, women writers were not even considered to be part of the discourse. We see this clearly in the career of Nellie Campobello and her marginalization vis-à-vis the narratives of the Mexican Revolution, but Garro herself claimed to have been marginalized because of her "war" with Paz.[33]

Writer and critic Guillermo Sheridan, biographer of Octavio Paz and also a collaborator in Paz's journal *Vuelta*, offers a comment that shows Paz rejecting the political use of antihomosexual posturing: "[I]t is incredible the number of 'writers' who have raised their prestige by denouncing homosexuals as criminals" (Sheridan, *Los Contemporáneos ayer*, 259).[34] In the thirties, however, when the poets of the Contemporáneos represented the previous generation for Paz, he was not so confident about their importance. As José Quiroga writes: "Paz rejected the 'pure art' of the Contemporáneos" (3). It is important to emphasize that Paz's criticism of the Contemporáneos, unlike that of Monterde and Jiménez Rueda, was based on his evaluation of their esthetics and was not a rejection of their sexual preferences.

Despite Halperin's assessment, Paz's early years were dedicated to activism.[35] The Paz of the thirties who wrote socially committed poems does not act or think in the same way as the Paz of the eighties onward (the period of the newspaper *Vuelta*)—that is, the Paz who became famous (and reviled) for criticizing Fidel Castro and for seeming to approve of the neoliberal policies of Mexican presidents such as the discredited Carlos Salinas de Gortari (see Dawes, "Octavio Paz"; Van Delden, "Polemical Paz"). Some misconceptions are expressed about his so-called Marxist phase of the thirties, which is read by his detractors as opportunist, but his interest in Marxism at that time is understandable given that so many of his acquaintances at that time had opted to join the Communist Party. Let us remember that being a Communist or expressing solidarity with the Communist Party was popular in the 1930s among many of the important writers of the period, both in the Americas and in Europe.[36]

This atmosphere no doubt influenced Paz, but I also suggest that the complexi-ties of his strong attachment to Republican Spain, which began early and lasted throughout his life, echo the sentiments expressed by his grandfather, Don Ireneo, who exercised a notably strong influence on him.[37] Paz characterized his paternal side as being "liberal and also in favor of the Indians: anti-Spanish on two accounts" (*Itinerary*, 24). Paz calls his mother, Josefina Lozano de Paz, the "Spanish" side. Nevertheless, Don Ireneo expressed admiration and sup-port for the First Spanish Republic (1873–1874) in his novel *Amor y suplicio* (1873).[38]

Although that novel deals with the Conquest period, Don Ireneo cannot refrain from including his comments about the (First) Spanish Republic and its progressive ideas, in contrast to the negative feelings that he might have for the Spanish conquistadors. His enthusiasm for a "Republican" Spain leads him to reconsider the importance of Spain for Mexico. For Don Ireneo, the first Spanish Republic could serve as a model for Mexico. His grandson also appreciated the values and ideology of Republican Spain, so he was quick to use his pen in support of the Second Republic at the time of its great need. In another way, too, Paz echoed the official policies of the Mexican government under Lázaro Cárdenas, as noted above. In terms of his reactions to the reali-ties of the war, the loss of life, and the violence, Paz's poems do not reflect any particular personal emotion but are more grandiose and traditional. He does not describe the trials and horrors of war as they affect families, women, and children, as Garro does. Even in "Elegía," as noted, his reworkings of the poem distanced the poetic voice from the dead soldier. Paz does not seem to re-create the horrors of the battles from within the war zone. He seems more ideo-logically involved with the cause of Republicanism than with the daily distress of conflict.

Just as Paz was echoing sentiments about Spain that reflected his familial and national contexts, Garro also had familial ties to Spain as well as a sense of herself as a Mexican national in Europe and also as a woman, as she de-scribes her experiences in her *Memorias de España 1937*. Garro was one of a small number of women who attended the congress, but she was not an official representative, as was María Teresa León (1903–1988), wife of the poet Rafael Alberti, who was a political activist as well as a writer. León was secretary of the Alianza de Escritores Antifascistas (Alliance of Antifascist Writers) and founded the journal *El Mono Azul* (The Blue Monkey) together with her hus-band. She also transformed her experiences in the war zone into two novels: *Contra viento y marea* (Against All Odds), published in 1941 and most likely written during the war period, and *Juego limpio* (Fair Play, 1959). Like Garro, León knew what it was like to be married to a writer while trying to become one herself; like Garro's, her reputation as a writer has been overshadowed by the attention paid to Alberti.[39]

A number of delegations to Spain did include women whose interventions were included in the program, as we learn in Luis Mario Schneider's account of the congress. Indeed, women exercised an important role on the Republican side: not only was La Pasionaria (Dolores Ibárruri Gómez) a key figure, but for the first time in Spain other women became actively involved in politics. The Republican government had introduced limited divorce and given women the vote and some limited maternity leave, benefits that they would soon lose when the Nationalists came to power (see Bunk; Mangini González; Pérez, "Behind the Lines"; and Vollendorf). Nevertheless, even during the war, women in Spain were not only fighting as the famous militias but writing poetry, novels, and plays about their own experiences. A large body of criticism has arisen to give testimony to their contributions (see Lines, "Female Combatants"; Mangini González; Nash; Pérez, "Behind the Lines"; and others). In Garro's chronicle, however, the few women mentioned are those whose spouses were "officially" attending the convention or more rarely, like María Teresa León, were invited in their own right.

Unlike León, who published one novelized autobiography early and is well known for *Memoria de la melancolía* (Memoir of Melancholy, 1970),[40] Garro did not make public her reflections until a much later period. *Memorias de España 1937* came out as a book in 1992, although she did publish a fragment in the journal *Cuadernos Hispanoamericanos* in April 1979 ("A mí me ha ocurrido todo al revés" [To Me, Everything Has Happened in Reverse]). Marked by a witty and sarcastic tone, *Memorias* is divided into eighteen chapters which loosely follow the events that both Paz and Garro experienced in the year 1937 in Spain during the Civil War. Garro may mention events as they occurred, but she also refers to past events that provide a context for the action being described. Also, she often projects to a future thought or experience related to the moment at hand. For example, in the final chapter Garro describes the sorry state of their stateroom on board the ship that is to take the Mexicans home from Spain after their journeys during the Second International Congress. She adds comments that also hint at the sorry state of the matrimonial relations between Paz and herself: "During my marriage, I always had the impression of being in a boarding school with strict rules and daily reprimands, which by the way did not help me at all, since I continued to be the same" (150).[41] The memoirs contain many revealing anecdotes, not just about Paz and Garro and their wartime experiences. They were surrounded by many of the major writers of the day, so Garro inevitably comments about them in a personal way (see the discussion below). The book has not received consistent attention and unfortunately has not been translated yet into English.

As Garro describes whatever hits her fancy, she projects the persona of an innocent—the young woman who was barely twenty-one in 1937 (or, as some continue to affirm, merely seventeen at the time).[42] Eladio Cortés, for example, reads her words at face value and remarks that "[h]er innocent comments cause the anger of Octavio Paz to rain down on her" (70).[43] It is true that Garro often describes anecdotes that make her appear ignorant, if not innocent. Her first comment that opens the book, for example, makes her seem almost uneducated: "I had never heard of Karl Marx" (5).[44] This statement may be taken by some readers as an admission of a lack of knowledge, but I would agree with Celina Manzoni that its apparent ignorance is undercut by the following statements proclaiming her sphere of knowledge. We remember that she had been raised in an intellectual home and herself had been studying at the university. She declares that she had learned about "the Greeks, the Romans, the French, the German Romantics, the Spanish classics, the Mexicans—but not Marx!" (5).[45] These statements have to be placed in context and read not as a sign of her innocence or ignorance but as an admission of a political stance. Her comments are replete with irony. After all, this book recounts her trip to an official, ideologically defined battleground in which her new husband and all his friends are clearly allied with the socialists, and many were openly Communist.

Paz would later say that, for all his associations with Communist journals and friends, he was perhaps a sympathizer but never a member of the party, as were Rafael Alberti, César Vallejo, and Pablo Neruda. As Grenier explores in "Socialism in One Person: Specter of Marxism in Octavio Paz's Political Thought," in his youth Paz was influenced by Marxist thought, although Grenier believes that "there is a tendency to exaggerate Marx's influence on Paz's thought, especially on the young Paz" (49). Nevertheless, I agree with Van Delden that from the sixties onward, "historical circumstances pushed Paz toward his increasingly hostile view of Marxism" (Van Delden and Grenier, *Gunshots at the Fiesta*, 122). So the Paz of the sixties and later renounces his younger self of the thirties, while Garro's later readers learn that she discovered many connections between life and politics during the thirties that she would incorporate into her texts.

While Paz was receptive to the popular sentiment among the intellectuals regarding Marxism, Garro expressed her rejection of this "popular" intellectual stance. She follows her dismissal of Marx with further specific references to the Mexicans who formed part of her circle (the Contemporáneos), calling Salvador Novo "un gran poeta ilustre" (a great and illustrious poet). She informs her readers that "[t]he Contemporáneos re-established culture in Mexico after the revolution and the bloody Cristero Revolt. The Contemporáneos were not politicians, only scholars" (5).[46] The members of the Contemporáneos were her friends, she informs us. For example, it was Villaurrutia himself who had asked her to work on André Gide's *Perséfona*, because he knew that she was a choreographer who had already worked successfully with Julio Bracho (6). This Elena Garro, before her marriage to Paz and before she is taken away to Spain, appears to be an intelligent, successful intellectual fully integrated into the contemporary art scene of Mexico. Her comments about the apolitical nature of the Contemporáneos and her own lack of knowledge about Marx should be read as a sign of her rejection of communism.

In addition, throughout the book of memories she continues to criticize the people who appear to be political ideologues, showing how arbitrary and insubstantial their own political foundations are; in contrast, she praises the figures who have been marginalized as part of "effeminate literature," such as the Contemporáneos; by extension, she attempts to reassess the marginalization of homosexuals and other disempowered figures she encounters. Acting as a naïf is part of the performance of her "self" that she seems to have needed to develop in relation to the well-known, very strong macho figures that she encounters in Spain, such as Neruda, Carpentier, and Guillén but also Spender and Malraux, among others.

I propose that Garro's seeming negation of Marx, or at least her denial of his importance to her and the Contemporáneos, is a subtly transgressive way of repudiating the values of the Marxist groups who were establishing their power bases in both Mexico and Spain at that time. Paz, we recall, was a young radical of Marxist sympathies in 1937, whose politics and poems led him to be selected as one of the writers to participate in the Second International Congress of Antifascist Writers for the Defense of Spanish Culture. As Paz's bride, Garro wound up in the company of Carlos Pellicer and José Mancisidor, who along with Paz were the official representatives. In addition she met those she called the "spontaneous ones," who were not officially selected to participate in the Second International Congress, although their political credentials were above reproach: the composer Silvestre Revueltas (1899–1940); the

Communist (since 1928) writer Juan de la Cabada (1901–1986), who had been president of LEAR; Fernando Gamboa; Chávez Morado; and María Luisa Vera.

Along with Garro and Vera, other women are occasionally mentioned as the *compañeras* of some of the men. Garro refers in a positive way to Gerda Taro (21), the ill-fated companion of the famed photographer Robert Capa. Garro calls her "Tarro" and remarks on the similarity of their last names. Taro was tragically killed at the Battle of Brunete (July 1937), trying to take photographs in the heat of combat. Also part of the circle of women was the celebrated photographer and political Italian activist Tina Modotti (1896–1942). Garro refers to Modotti as María, her pseudonym in Spain. She worked for the International Red Cross as a nurse, as Elena Poniatowska chronicles in her novel *Tinísima*.[47] While Garro showed little fondness for "María," she had great respect for Taro.

Garro presents a number of anecdotes that show how the men—whether from Mexico or Spain, whether Marxists of one faction or another—were all basically alike in their eagerness to go to war, to engage in violence without forethought. These are the people she criticizes and considers hypocritical. For example, when she first mentions all the Mexicans who were eager to fight in the Spanish Civil War, she does not show the idealism found in Paz's poem "¡No pasarán!" Rather, she portrays their ingenuousness:

In Mexico, the partisans of one group and the other were fighting each other in the streets. The Mexicans were rushing to the Spanish Embassy to enroll in the Spanish army. "Yes, yes, but on which side?" asked the functionaries. "On any side—what I want to do is kill gachupines," they answered.[48]

Compare this apolitical yet bellicose behavior with another anecdote that occurs in Spain while Garro and the Mexican contingent are traveling through a war zone. Garro describes a dramatic scene that takes place in the dark of night; their car, whose passengers include Paz and Garro along with Silvestre Revueltas and Juan de la Cabada, is approached by several soldiers with rifles pointed at them. The famous question is posed: "¿Quién vive?" (literally, "Who lives?") This is not a rhetorical question, because the wrong answer leads to death, while the right one allows them to continue their journey. No one in the car knows what the "correct," life-saving answer should be because the identity of the soldiers and which side they are on is not clear. Should the passengers profess their true affiliation or lie to save their lives? Finally, the soldier who accompanies the Mexican contingent yells out, "La República," which happily turns out to be the right answer at that time. They are allowed to continue, only to be met with similar incidents as they make their way along the road. As they traverse the embattled countryside, Garro is a witness to this repeated request for identification, as frightened as the men in the car. Finally, she is the one to ask the difficult question:

> There was something that I did not understand, and I asked the driver:
> "Why do the Nationalist soldiers and the Republicans dress the same?"
> Nobody could answer. There was a silence and suddenly the driver gave me the explanation:
> "Wait a minute, what a question, don't you see that we are all Spanish," he said, amazed. (61)[49]

Garro makes no further comment at this point regarding the unexpected answer and the surprise of the driver concerning her question, but elsewhere she does show how foolish she thinks it is to have brother fighting against brother. In fact, this anecdote is the essence of her attitude toward war and civil war in particular—it makes no sense. She is not indifferent to ideology, for she has already begun her memoirs by recalling the deeply divided ideological environment of the 1920s and 1930s. Many of her anecdotes show how conflicts are based on class and perceived power relations, despite common ideology that would ordinarily unite people.

Another informative anecdote reveals Garro's discovery that hierarchies are based on arbitrary distinctions concerning ideological positions:

> Juan [de la Cabada] had "an impeccable revolutionary trajectory." He had been in prison and had been the cellmate of Carlos Pellicer, who had been detained for being a follower of Vasconcelos,[50] not for being a Communist like Juan, which showed, as I learned in Spain, that Juan was superior in the revolutionary hierarchy. So that when Juan protested, the "opportunists" became quiet. (39)[51]

Thus, Garro learns, it was not enough to have been in prison: Juan de la Cabada had more "street creds" than Carlos Pellicer because of the *reason* that led him to be imprisoned.

Perhaps the most illuminating vignette deals with the sorrowful circumstances of José Bosch, an old friend of Paz, to whom he attributed his own initiation into Marxism and revolution as a tool for change (Garro, *Memorias*,

34). Bosch, organizer of one of the largest student strikes in Mexico in the 1920s, had been forced out of the country and went back to Spain. Paz had been told that he had been killed in a battle and was inspired to write "Elegía a un compañero muerto en el Frente de Aragón."[52] Such information proved erroneous when Bosch resurfaced in Barcelona in 1937 and attempted to explain his tragic situation to his friends. He was able to speak personally with Garro at a poetry reading given by Paz, explaining that he needed help because he was being persecuted by Communists, who had already killed many of his companions. His fear was so great that Garro had to talk to him while he hid behind a curtain. Her comments again point out the insidious fratricidal nature of the Spanish context:

> Now, with Juan [sic] Bosch hidden behind the curtain, I felt an inexplicable rage: why do the reds or the Communists pursue other Communists? Why was Juan Bosch in that deplorable condition? . . . From then on, the shadow of Juan Bosch followed us throughout Barcelona. (35)[53]

Bosch's fate represented a real situation that was taking place in Spain, as George Lambie explains:

> Beside the official Republican war effort in Spain supported by the Communists, there was also a popular revolution taking place mainly under the auspices of the Anarchists and the POUM, both of which had their power bases in Barcelona, but whose influence combined with that of trade unions spread throughout republican Spain. . . . The Communists did not recognize the popular uprising because it threatened their power. . . . Consequently in 1937, just before the Writer's Congress was held in Valencia, the Communists attacked and destroyed the leadership of the POUM and isolated the Anarchists, putting an end to the main thrust of the popular revolution in Spain. ("Vallejo," 132)

While Lambie's historical text gives a reader the factual context, Garro's encounter with Bosch personalizes the ideological struggle taking place within the Spanish Civil War. Just as she asks questions about the factions among the supposed Communist groups, she also points out that in the end all the political divisions are useless in protecting anyone from death.

Garro discovers these truths about factions one night when her residence is attacked. Earlier she had been seen speaking with a Spanish Franquista who was staying at the same ambassadorial residence as the Mexican Republicans.

A plane was about to bomb them all, so they all ran out for cover in the garden—Franquistas and Republicans. Juan de la Cabada, who had taken "Elenita" under his wing,[54] tries to help her out of her supposed disloyal act, by commenting to Paz on their common destiny: "'It is strange, my man. Here in this garden we can all die together,' he told Paz, as if to excuse the fact that I had spoken with a Reactionary" (47).[55] In general, however, Garro notes that "[t]he Mexicans also felt sorry for Paz for having married me. His choice was disastrous. I feel consoled knowing that he is alive and enjoying good health and a reputation and glory that he merits, in spite of the grave error of his youth" (48).[56] I would suggest that Garro knew full well even then that she was breaking rules and quite enjoying it.

Just as the Contemporáneos were marginalized by some critics in Mexico for belonging to the "effeminate literature," so Garro in Spain is marginalized for a performance of excess, a hyperfemininity in the eyes of the macho Communist group. When she is with the Communists in their sessions, she feels as if she has entered a strange world: "They thought the opposite of what I thought" (88).[57] Whereas Garro was taught by her father that "no one was worthy of condemnation and God was the only one who had the power to judge us" (88), in Spain "we were all being judged and we were committing meaningless crimes."[58] She brings up the theme of homosexuals to show how arbitrary and unfair these ideologues, no matter which group they professed their allegiance to, seem to her.

Garro confesses that at that time, when the evils of the "pequeños burgueses and capitalismo" (petty bourgeoisie and capitalism) were being explained to her, she also found out about homosexuals: "For example, I just found out that there were homosexuals. It was very strange but true! . . . and in the same breath they explained to me that Shakespeare, Plato, Homer, Michelangelo, Byron, Shelley, Oscar Wilde, Marcel Proust, André Gide, Botticelli, Sophocles, and García Lorca were also homosexuals. My goodness! Because the bourgeoisie hated culture, for that reason they assassinated artists" (88).[59] Garro goes on reproducing her dialogue with her interlocutors, trying to make sense of what they are telling her about the treatment of homosexuals by the bourgeoisie, of which she is considered a mere "pequeña burgesa" (petty bourgeois). When she asks whether "it is good or bad to be a homosexual," she is told that such a question is typical of her petty bourgeois spirit and that there are "no good or bad [aspects]" to the issue.[60] Until this point readers may be judging her snidely because of what appears to be a forced naïveté or an assumed ingenuousness. Garro's next statement, however, seems to be the theme of all the anecdotes that she presents when she describes the various divisions among the groups, sectors, and allies that she has observed as an outsider: "And so how could they condemn someone if it is not good or bad [to be homosexual]."[61] Garro's point seems to be that all along divisions were being made about who is good, who is evil, who is acceptable, who is offensive, who is friend or foe, for reasons that are not clear, rational, or justifiable.

Called a sophist by Paz for bringing up these issues, Garro is often told to be silent ("callada," 89) while the men of the group are permitted to talk, talk, talk. Yet her comments are perceptive and speak to the heart of the matter of discrimination. At a time when homosexuality was still a taboo topic, Garro proclaims unequivocally that her community consists of known homosexuals, but their sexual orientation is not her basis for categorizing them: it is their intellect and humanity that concerns her. She shows the defects in that age-old focus which correlates masculinity with domination, making men the political actors and the warriors, leaving women out of the equation, and certainly leaving out "effeminate men" as well.

The men around Garro were using their political savvy as a way to show their superiority over her; moreover, they created an ideological hierarchy which placed "their" ideology—Marxism—above her "petty bourgeois status." Garro rebels by trying to show that Communists were no more intelligent than she was. Commenting on the Communists who considered themselves superior because they had been to the Soviet Union, she remarks to the reader: "[T]hey irritated me and, besides, they were unpleasant. Their arguments were as valid or as arbitrary as my own" (91).[62] This statement is not mere egotism but addresses the way the men were competitive among each other to prove the "correctness" of their ideology over other partisans.

While the men professed such an eagerness to fight and rush to battle, Garro wanted to stress the hypocrisy of their bravado, the corruption of their politics, and their utter ignorance of the realities of war. Think of her comment when she sees the results of the shells on the homes of Madrid: "If the fragments were capable of harming the stones, what would it do to human skin? I looked at my hands. Men were too fragile to treat each other with such brutality" (92).[63]

These comments may appear to show Garro's assumed ingenuousness or a forced naïveté. We should remember that she is discussing homosexuality at a time when her friends in Mexico, members of the Contemporáneos, were being persecuted. The entrenchment of patriarchy and homophobia in Spain during the 1920s and 1930s was also notorious, no doubt contributing to

García Lorca's assassination by the fascists early in the war, in August 1936.[64] Garro includes García Lorca in the list of famous men from history along with Gide, who was also at the Antifascist Congress (and had been maligned for his critique of the evils of Stalinist Russia), which shows that she is being political and not so simple after all.

Garro is deeply critical of the discourses which have framed public discussion of war and weapons of destruction. Although she seems to oppose war making as a practice, she does not openly suggest ways to avoid it. Yet her discourse seems to be in tune with contemporary antiwar feminists (Carol Cohn, Cynthia Enloe) who seek to replace violence with practices of nonviolent contest and reconciliation. Garro shows an abiding suspicion of the use of violence and doubts that its stated aims are ever achieved, while its multiple costs are undercounted and overlooked (Carol Cohn).

Garro also makes it abundantly clear that she was treated as a "female" even among the august group of progressive writers. One anecdote is indicative and forcefully brings home the state of gender relations in the thirties and—alas— later. Garro relates that all of the writers who were journeying from Madrid to Valencia and Barcelona had been invited to stop in Minglanilla and attend a huge banquet once again ("otro banquetazo"); in view of all the food they were served, she had no idea that the villagers were suffering from "hambres severas" (severe hunger; 31). Her description of what they were served is presented in a phrase that combines "Mexican" with her universal knowledge: "La comilona fue, como siempre, pantagruélica" (30–31). Here Garro takes a word from the familiar register, "comida," a synonym for the more formal "banquete" (banquet), and selects a form of the word with an exaggerated augmentative suffix, "comilona," which would be closer to the English expression "blowout," although "comilona" gives one the added impression of "unattractiveness" associated with the Spanish augmentative. She then describes it with an adjective taken from the literary world: "pantagruélica" from François Rabelais's huge character with an enormous appetite. Her ironic juxtaposition of the familiar and the literary, calling the huge feast a "Pantagruelian blowout," reflects exactly the ironies of their situation—the intellectuals with their food and the peasants with their hunger.

Garro continues with her narration: the points she wants to make relate not to language use but primarily to gender relations and political philosophy. Stephen Spender was in their group, and after dinner they all went out to the balcony to look over the village. Garro saw a group of women, dressed in black—Civil War widows with their children who were begging for food. Her reaction was immediate: "I began to cry. I felt tired and longed to be in my home" (31).[65] The group of intellectuals was supposedly there in Spain to help the Republican cause, and what they were doing in actuality was taking sustenance from the Spanish people. Garro recognized the inequities involved in the upkeep of the intellectuals at the expense of the common folk, yet none of the men seemed to be so emotionally affected by this unfairness, despite their political ideology that preached equality, self-sacrifice, and social justice for all citizens. When Spender later wrote about having met Paz and his wife, his narration shows all the inherent masculinist tendencies of the period, despite his own leftist beliefs and his writings on themes of social injustice and class struggle. Garro cites from his book: "When Spender's book appeared, he dedicated a line to us, which Paz read triumphantly: 'The handsome poet Octavio Paz and his young and beautiful wife who in Minglanilla became hysterical.' . . . I never forgave him for that line. Spender forgot that during the banquet Nordal Grieg asked us all to donate to the people the splendid food that was on the table. To no avail" (31).[66]

Spender's comments show that Paz was the important figure: he is named and his wife, for all her beauty, is just "the wife of." He adds another attribute: she is "hysterical"—a characteristic long associated with women. After all, the root of the word is Latin *hystericus* (hysterical), from Greek *husterikos*, from *hustera* (womb; from the former idea that disturbances in the womb caused hysteria). Garro shows that some men could commiserate with the hunger of the poor women and children, since Grieg also wanted to give their leftovers to the people. But that was not the overwhelming sentiment of the congress attendees, who were more like Spender in their inattention to the marginalized women figures around them. How ironic it must have seemed to Garro to realize that these poets, who had come to war-torn Spain to fight fascists with their poems, were also being feted at banquets and sunning themselves at the beaches when they were not railing against fascism in the conference halls and writing poems about the horrors. In the land of Miguel de Cervantes, their gestures must have appeared more like Don Quixote tilting at windmills than El Cid conquering the enemy.

Garro tells us, however, that she learned a lesson from this experience: "Years later, when in Paris Aldous Huxley found me enchanting, I did not say a word. I had learned my lesson" (31).[67] How sad it sounds to think that the lesson she learned in Spain was to keep quiet. Of course, while she may have gained knowledge of what "traditional" female behavior should be, thankfully for her readers, she did not follow the dictum to be silent. Moreover, Garro used these experiences to critique the harsh patriarchal system in her many texts.[68] By the time the *Memorias* were finally published in 1992, she had already become famous for her writings, although she had also become infamous after 1968 for her political postures.

After reading Garro's memoirs, it is not hard to conclude that Octavio Paz and Elena Garro were entirely opposite in their ideology and behavior: she the supposedly apolitical "pequeña burguesa" and former dancer; he the radical Marxist poet. Ironically, it is Garro who seems to be ideologically independent despite Paz's later persona as an independent thinker.

The incidents that Garro selects to critique point out underlying assumptions about war and the response to war that are based on traditional masculinist perspectives that are expressed in "binary terms": not just men versus women but also strength versus weakness, us versus them, front versus home, for example. In this text whose context is the Spanish Civil War, Garro also examines ideas and expectations about gender that come to the surface as she interacts with the "intellectuals" who are part of the power system. Although always loath to use labels and ascribe to categories (a feeling we see developing in the *Memorias*), Garro nevertheless expresses ideas in concordance with such twenty-first-century feminist critics of war as Carol Cohn in studies of the gendered discourse attendant to war debates and notes the prevalence of "masculine thinking" (as defined by our Western culture). Cohn reminds us that the masculine system of meanings receives popular support while the "female position" is considered weak and delegitimized, silenced ("Wars, Wimps and Women," 231–232).

The persona that Garro creates in *Memorias* is far from the sophisticated, complicated, worldly woman that we envision a writer of her experiences to be. With Garro we gaze back at her young self, as she imagined she was (136), and search for the connections between that young person and the woman who would write the *Memorias* along with more than a dozen other novels, essays, and plays.

Although Paz, like almost all men at the time, did not seem sensitive to gender issues in the way he dealt with women, he nevertheless attempted to show his own political independence when he did not support the condemnation of André Gide for having criticized Stalin and Soviet communism. This ability to think independently of party lines continued throughout his life. Paz and his comrade from 1937, André Malraux, for example, became vigorous critics of Stalinism while others such as Pablo Neruda and Louis Aragon continued to defend the Moscow regime. In Paris, as part of the Mexican consulate in

1951, Paz wanted to publish a report on the death camps of the Soviet gulag. The French Communist Party, to which many French intellectuals belonged, exercised enormous power, so Paz was expressly told not to publish his report. It is relevant at this juncture to recall what was said of Paz in one of his obituaries: "Paz's personality was always dominated by a relentless curiosity and equally indomitable individualism. In a 1980 interview published in a San Francisco magazine, Paz said: 'When I was young I took as my own a motto of André Gide, "The writer must know how to swim against the current"'" (quoted in Schwartz, "Mexico Loses a Modern Revolutionary Thinker," A15). These words by both Schwartz and Paz, while not falsehoods, seem almost deconstructed in Garro's *Memorias*. The person who seems most independent in the recounting of events from their mutual past is Garro, not Paz. Paz is always part of the male group, always acting in solidarity with his *compañeros*, more often than not chagrined and embarrassed at the inappropriate and unexpected remarks of his young bride. "Paz was unfair in not defending me" (99),[69] comments Garro at one point; and by then the reader agrees with her. We have gone beyond our view of her as a ditsy blonde who is always in trouble for her unconventional remarks. The men she describes are not so thoughtful or brave. Though Garro does not present herself as a fighter or as a political figure, we see her as a serious pacifist and humanist who describes the tremendous ironies of the Civil War.

In 1987 Paz was invited back to Valencia, on the fiftieth anniversary of the congress. In his published remarks on the topic we have his observations in a more reflective mode. In his speech in 1987 Paz romanticizes the congress and calls all the participants his comrades. "We shared the same hopes and convictions, the same illusions and disappointments. We were united by a sense of moral outrage, and by solidarity with the oppressed. We were a brotherhood of indignation, also a brotherhood of violence" ("Who Won the Spanish Civil War?" 26). These words sound grand and eloquent, as does the entire speech given by Paz as the keynote speaker.

When invited to share his reflections on the Spanish Civil War, Paz asks whether they returned to Valencia "to commemorate a victory or a defeat?" ("Who Won the Spanish Civil War?" 26). His answer is surprising, he admits: neither the Francoists, the supposed victors, nor the Republicans can claim that their ideas and plans have relevance in contemporary Spain. The two institutions that now form the basis of political and social life are democracy and constitutional democracy ("Who Won the Spanish Civil War?" 26). Paz admits that in 1937 he never would have been able to predict the form of government that Spain would enjoy in 1987. He tells the audience that while "the victory of our enemy turned into ashes" it is also true that "many of our own ideas and plans did too" ("Who Won the Spanish Civil War?" 27). He refers in his talk to the disappointments about the failures of "revolutions to bring about a worldwide regime of universal harmony" ("Who Won the Spanish Civil War?" 27), but it is also true that the political revolutionary he tried to be in the 1930s did not survive much longer than the Spanish Civil War did. Greg Dawes, who has studied this aspect of Paz's work, concludes that "in the final analysis Paz's avant-gardist aesthetics clashes with his beliefs as fellow-traveler and that this leads him to embrace Trotskyism and, later in his life, social democracy" ("Octavio Paz," 242–243). He always believed that it was important to have tried to defeat the fascists, but he rejected outright the attempts to control cultural expressions by the Communist Party or any other of the factions, such as the POUM, to which his close friend Bosch had belonged (and later been persecuted for his membership). In the 1940s Paz goes so far in the other direction from the Communists' support of social realism as to embrace surrealism.[70] (Let us recall that his former mentor Neruda, who was also influenced by surrealism at one time, cultivated more his interest in realism or what Dawes calls "dialectical realism" ["Realism, Surrealism," paragraph 4].) Paz suggests that he is interested in surrealism because of the way it subverts moral and political codes and not for any political position. In fact, through the years Paz associated less with political parties and more with the idea of criticism as a way of life. "Freedom of expression is always in danger," he says in 1987, and "is threatened not merely by totalitarian regimes or military dictatorships, but also in capitalist democracies, by the impersonal forces of advertising and the marketplace" ("Who Won the Spanish Civil War?" 30). He hopes for a democracy not tied to a political ideology or an economic system.[71]

In admitting this, Paz in the 1980s and 1990s sounds more like the Garro of 1937. In fact, he ends his keynote address by stressing two points. First, what he remembers most about his experiences in 1937 is meeting the Spanish people and maintaining life-long friendships with so many poets. "I learned that the word 'fraternity' is no less precious than the word 'liberty.' It is the bread of men, the common bread" ("Who Won the Spanish Civil War?" 30). We can be stirred by his recognition of the importance of friendships, but it is his final anecdote that appears ironic when juxtaposed with the observations recorded by Garro.

Paz relates to all the members of his audience that one incident taught him a significant lesson. He was with a small group of poets visiting the University of

Madrid, which had been transformed into trenches with sandbags everywhere, signs that the university was a literal battlefield at that time. In one of the big lecture halls they heard noises, and their guide asked for silence.

> On the other side of the wall we could hear, clearly and distinctly, voices and laughter. Who are they? I asked in a whisper. They are *the others*, he replied. His words shocked me, and then left me with a great pain. I had discovered, suddenly and for always, that the enemy, too, has a human voice. ("Who Won the Spanish Civil War?" 30)

Precisely, Octavio—that is what "Elenita" had been saying during those stressful days and nights that you and your male companions all spent running from war zone to war zone, from banquet to battle front. Akin to the findings of Gilbert and Gubar, who write mostly about English-oriented women writers, we could suggest that the cataclysmic experiences of war had had very different meanings for Paz and Garro and reinforced their disparities and dissonances, preventing a true marriage of the minds.

During the years following the Spanish Civil War, Mexico welcomed many of the exiled Republicans, who arrived on boats similar to the one that Paz and Garro took to return home.[72] And just as the exiles had problems in adjusting to their new home, Paz and Garro experienced difficulties in attempting to readjust to life in Mexico. They were no longer the same; their experiences in Spain marked them quite differently, as noted from the comments made by Garro in her *Memorias*. They both continued to live among a circle of intellectuals that included Mexicans, other Latin Americans, and the Spanish writers with whom Paz collaborated in a number of literary ventures, yet their life together was by no means ordinary. Even the arrival of their only child, Helena Paz Garro, in 1939, did little to make them a traditional couple.[73]

Paz continued his literary activities and the associations he had made in Spain. He became one of the founders of the journal *Taller* (Workshop), a magazine which signaled the emergence of a new generation of writers in Mexico as well as a new literary sensibility. For a while Garro worked as a journalist, and some of her articles of that time have been collected and published by Patricia Rosas Lopátegui in *El asesinato de Elena Garro* (The Assassination of Elena Garro). In 1943 Paz traveled to the United States on a Guggenheim Fellowship and once again involved himself in the literary world of the country in which he lived. Garro worked at nonliterary jobs to make money to help support the family. Two years later Paz entered the Mexican diplomatic service and was first sent to France. It was at that time, with a sense of distance from his homeland, that he completed the essay that would solidify his fame—*The Labyrinth of Solitude* (1950). Together with André Breton and Benjamin Péret, he also enthusiastically participated in various activities and publications organized by the surrealists. (Garro would say in her letters to Gabriela Mora that she was the one who first became friends with the surrealists [see Mora, *Elena Garro*].)

In 1952 Paz traveled for the first time to India and to Tokyo as chargé d'affaires. According to Helena Paz Garro (b. 1939), life was very difficult in Japan; finally her father was transferred to Geneva, Switzerland. While Paz was engaged in advancing his career as a poet and essayist, Garro wrote secretly, keeping the materials in her trunk. This image of manuscripts hidden in a trunk reappears in her novel *Testimonios sobre Mariana* and also in a book of critical essays about Garro's work, *Baúl de recuerdos* (Trunk of Memories). Garro said that she wrote *Recollections of Things to Come* when she was ill in Bern in 1953, although it was not published until 1963, with the support of Paz, who by then was living apart from Garro and his daughter. Paz and family returned to Mexico City in 1954, where he wrote his celebrated poem "Piedra de sol" (Sunstone) in 1957 and published *Libertad bajo palabra* (Liberty under Oath, 1957), a compilation of his poetry up to that time.[74] Garro also continued to write. In 1957 three of her theatrical pieces were produced on the stage: *Andarse por las ramas* (Beat about the Bush), *Los pilares de doña Blanca* (The Pillars of Doña Blanca), and *Un hogar sólido* (*A Solid Home*, all published in 1958), again with the help of Paz and his production group, Poesía en Voz Alta (Unger).

Paz was sent again to Paris in 1959.[75] In 1962 Paz was appointed Mexican ambassador to India, while Garro stayed on in Mexico with their daughter. While there, he was able to complete various books, including the collection of essays *El mono gramático* (1974; translated as *The Monkey Grammarian*, 1990) and the poems collected in *Ladera este* (*East Slope*, 1969). In India he married Marie-José Tramini, a Frenchwoman with whom he would share the rest of his life.

While Paz was solidifying his reputation as the great poet, essayist, and diplomat, Garro became increasingly involved in political life of Mexico in the sixties. As noted, she had had some literary successes, receiving the Villaurrutia Prize for *Recollections of Things to Come* and publishing both a collection of plays, *Un hogar sólido*, and a collection of short stories, *La semana de colores* (The Week of Colors, 1964). But at the same time when Paz was an official of the Mexican government, his ex-wife was actively involved with political issues that went against the official policies of the government. Whether it was regarding agrarian issues, mistreatment of the indigenous population, or the railway workers on strike, Garro wrote articles in various journals that were critical of the Mexican political system. When events in the sixties caused intellectuals across the globe to become involved wholeheartedly in protests, it is no wonder that Octavio Paz and Elena Garro were also drawn directly into the events, changing their lives once again in dramatically different ways (see Chapter 5).

"I commit many foolish acts, but I never regret them."
VERONICA
in *Socrates and the Cats* by Elena Garro

TLATELOLCO
THE UNDECLARED WAR

THE YEAR 1968 MARKED A TURNING POINT in Mexican history. Events that preceded or followed are often seen in relation to the occurrences of that year, especially its most important moment: October 2. What happened on that day had an impact in Mexico analogous to the effect of the assassinations of Martin Luther King, Jr., and Robert Kennedy in 1968, which initiated immediate and long-term political and social transformations in the United States. While most of official Mexico was focused on the preparations for the Olympic Games, to begin on October 12, untold numbers of university students gathered in the Plaza of Three Cultures for a peaceful protest regarding a number of their concerns.[1] Although the students planned a nonviolent protest, that day will always be marked by the massacre that took place at the plaza or, as it is most often called, "Tlatelolco." No Mexican or student of Latin American studies can remain indifferent to its evocation and significance. To this day, official government documents are inadequate and unreliable, so readers turn to the literary texts to find out the actual story of that period.

At present, the events at Tlatelolco have generated a diverse body of literature that includes many different genres and many perspectives. It is not unexpected that writers so involved with Mexico as Paz and Garro would also react in a literary mode to this cataclysmic event. Both respond in a way unique to their individual modus operandi (see the discussion below). It is important to situate the event in a historical context as well as in a literary tradition.

As a sign, Tlatelolco has a long and varied history in Mexico that has affected the lives of its inhabitants on both the national and individual level, from the pre-Conquest period to the contemporary moment. The place-name Tlatelolco, derived from the Nahuatl words *tlali* and *telulli*, meaning *cerro de tierra amontonada* (hill of the mountainous land), refers to an area of Mexico City that was eminent even before the tragic events of 1968. Tlatelolco was the second capital of the Mexicas or Aztecs, founded on an island in Lake Metztliapan around the year 1338. During the period of Mexica rule (fourteenth through sixteenth centuries), thousands of people visited the great market at Tlatelolco every day. When the Spanish reached what is now Mexico City, however, one of the final battles in their combat against the Mexica capital took place at this market area (1521). Cuauhtémoc, a nephew of the emperor Moctezuma II, and his young wife, who was a daughter of Moctezuma, had taken power just as the city came under siege by the Spanish. The Mexicas made their last stand at Tlatelolco and were defeated by the conquistadors led by Pedro de Alvarado. Over forty thousand Mexica men, women, and children perished at Tlatelolco on August 13, 1521.

Only fifteen years after the Mexica defeat, the Colegio Imperial de Santa Cruz de Tlatelolco (Imperial College of Santa Cruz of Tlatelolco), a school of translation and indigenous culture, was erected from the ruins of war by the Catholic priests who came to work with the Indians.[2] One of the central figures in the reformulation of this landmark was Father Bernardino de Sahagún, known for his proselytizing and early ethnographic endeavors among the Mexicas. According to Miguel León-Portilla, the noted Mexican anthropologist:[3]

> And there an encounter of two worlds in its best version takes place. On one side are Olmos, Sahagún, Gaona; and on the other side, a series of wise Indians, doctors, experts in the codices, people versed in the pre-Hispanic tradition, and young indigenous students. Imagine that in 1536 only 15 years had passed since the fall of the city. (Krause, "Entrevista con Miguel León-Portilla")[4]

This school of translation, one of the colonial period's contributions to positive relations between the Spanish and the Indians, marks one of the exceptions to the negative connotations of Tlatelolco. Another positive connotation related to the site occurred centuries after the colonial period—in 1967. Meeting in Mexico, the governments of Latin America and the Caribbean entered into an agreement called popularly the Treaty of Tlatelolco or the Treaty for the Prohibition of Nuclear Weapons in Latin America and the Caribbean. Signed on February 14, 1967, this treaty made Latin America the first denuclearized zone in the world. Ironically, despite this attempt to promote peace in the area, Tlatelolco once more became the site of brutal confrontation. On October 2, 1968, the Mexican government surprised student protesters by firing on the peaceful demonstration organized at Tlatelolco. Many hundreds (or more) were killed and thousands wounded,[5] staining the record of contemporary Mexican history with bloodshed and violence once again. Although much has been written in Spanish about that event and a growing collection of materials in English has also developed, the significance of Tlatelolco for most non-Mexicans is tempered by a lack of contextualization and cultural knowledge. Yet it represents as momentous and influential a cultural event as the protests against the Vietnam War in the United States, the Prague Spring of 1968, the battles of "Bloody Monday" in Paris on May 6, 1968 (one of the most violent days of the Parisian student revolt), and the Kent State shootings of 1970.[6]

As Kate Doyle, head of the U.S.-Mexico Documentation Project, comments, "Thirty years later [1998], the Tlatelolco massacre has grown large in Mexican memory, and lingers still. It is Mexico's Tiananmen Square, Mexico's Kent State: when the pact between the government and the people began to come apart and Mexico's extended political crisis began" ("Tlatelolco Massacre"). While for the United States, the assassination of students on a college campus was a decisive moment, Kent State cannot compare in scope with the violence, destruction, and significance to Mexico of Tlatelolco 1968. In contrast to events at Kent State, where Ohio National Guardsmen fired on campus during an anti–Vietnam War protest, leaving four students dead, one permanently paralyzed, and eight others wounded, the Tlatelolco Massacre destroyed many more lives, causing countless deaths and imprisonment and torture for the captured students. Numbers are not necessary for an event to be defined as tragic, but clearly the magnitude of devastation encompassed by the massacre at Tlatelolco marks it as a lamentable and brutal act, almost incomprehensible in its magnitude of destruction. While the events at Kent State can be seen as part of a national demonstration against the war in Vietnam, the protests at Tlatelolco had to do with wide-ranging national issues and only in part with foreign policy. Ironically, they were stimulated to some degree by the entrance of the "outside" into Mexico.

According to some critics, the Olympic Games that were to take place in Mexico City beginning on October 12 served as the catalyst for the student demonstrations. From the student perspective, the young people were appalled that so much money was being spent on the sporting event to entertain foreigners when so many Mexicans were without proper housing and food. In addition, they hoped to use their demonstration as a way to pressure the government into accepting their demands for educational reform and greater political freedom.[7]

President Gustavo Díaz Ordaz ignored the validity of the students' demands and concerns. His main consideration was to maintain order in his country at a time when the whole world would be focused on events there because of the Olympics. The Olympic Games were to commence on October 12, with 112 participating countries; the governing party, the PRI, did not want to be embarrassed by student protests. Mexico wished to present to the world community the image of a civilized, advanced society, worthy of being host to the Olympics. Ironically, in order to maintain that image, the president reverted to political techniques to which the people unfortunately had become inured in the political system: the use of illegal repression as a way to suppress opposition. Although student protests were occurring in other parts of the world, according to Mexican historians, the government's reaction was influenced by a national behavior pattern. In his study of the PRI and the student movement, Rogelio Hernández Rodríguez points out that the systematic use of repression in political conflicts dates from the Mexican Revolution (15).[8] Paz would later say that the government's reactions reflected a "regression to pre-Hispanic ways, to a past that contemporary Mexico considers dead and buried" (Leal, "Tlatelolco, Tlatelolco," 9).

On the surface, Mexico was a democratic country with political parties, the rule of law, and civil authority. The reactions to the student-led demonstrations proved that in reality a rule of fear, governmental violence, authoritarianism, and military intervention marked civic life. The people had no organized outlet to express their disagreement with governmental policies (González Casanova, 144–145). In summary, Mexicans were suffering a time of great instability and a liminal moment of change that outsiders might not have been able to detect from afar.

For the idealists among students and workers, it was a crime to witness hungry Mexicans being shunted aside once again, while well-toned athletes were invited to glory in folkloric Mexican riches with a generous budget. Billions of pesos had been spent in preparation for the Olympics, while the average

Mexican peasant could barely survive or find a job. As Leal notes, in the end, "the Olympic games were held on time and turned out to be an international success. But at what price? The nation's trend toward an open, more democratic and just society was aborted at Tlatelolco on October 2, 1968" ("Tlatelolco, Tlatelolco," 7). Indeed, this political success was read as an ideological failure by the students and their supporters, mostly a group of intellectuals whose writings after the event have kept alive the students' desires for a just and open society, a Mexico able to face its problems rather than attempting to suppress all dissent.

The tragedy of Tlatelolco and the betrayal of the students by their government created a major point of change in Mexican literature as well as in Mexican political life. "In literature, we can now speak of authors writing before or after Tlatelolco," says Leal ("Tlatelolco, Tlatelolco," 4). He concludes:

> The most important consequence of Tlatelolco, in literature, is the deep impression it left in the minds of the intellectuals and creative writers. All of them agree that the year 1968 marks a break with the past, a break with the period characterized by changes brought about by the Revolution of 1910–1917. . . . The literature of Tlatelolco revealed that the ideals of the Revolution so strongly defended by the party in power had become empty. ("Tlatelolco, Tlatelolco," 13)

Almost all major Mexican writers of the time have participated in creating the "literature of Tlatelolco," much as a subgenre exists with the theme of the Mexican Revolution. In the absence of official governmental documents, readers can consult a long list of essays and analyses by Octavio Paz, Carlos Fuentes (*Tiempo mexicano*, 1971; translated as *A New Time for Mexico*, 1996), Luis Leal, Carlos Monsiváis (*Días de guardar* [Days to Keep], 1970), Jorge Volpi (*La imaginación y el poder* [Imagination and Power]); Gilberto Balam (*Tlatelolco*); and Roberto Blanco Moheno (*Tlatelolco*)—mostly accusatory texts that help to explain the disillusionment and frustration of the intellectuals at their government's blatant disregard of civilian rights. In fact, Armando Bartra has suggested that there were and "are many '68s" (quoted in Frazier and Cohen, 620), depending on who is narrating.

One of the first essays to describe the outpouring of texts about Tlatelolco published in the United States was Luis Leal's "Tlatelolco, Tlatelolco" (1979). Leal offers a review of the literary works that deal with the theme, pointing out that some Mexican writers "had the wisdom to foresee what was to happen" even before the event (4). Leal names Carlos Fuentes, whose *La región más transparente* (1959; translated as *Where the Air Is Clear*, 1960) brought to light underlying causes of what became the Tlatelolco conflict and even went so far as to predict a confrontation. Fernando del Paso's *José Trigo* (1966) offers an almost uncanny anticipation of the events in the way it recounts the story of the railway strike of 1959 and the tribulations of the railway workers of the neighborhood Nonoalco-Tlatelolco. This conflict also forms the subtext for Garro's *Y Matarazo no llamó* (And Matarazo Did Not Call, 1991; see the discussion below).

The fundamental text, however, is Elena Poniatowska's collage *La noche de Tlatelolco* (1971) translated, with a preface by Octavio Paz, as *Massacre in Mexico* (1975); it has become synonymous with the event as the testimonial that mirrors the multivocal reaction in Mexico, with photos and firsthand reports that belie the government's official statement that few deaths occurred. Poniatowska bravely visited the Lecumberri prison, at great personal risk, to interview imprisoned students and record their testimonies.

Poniatowska chose to write not a personal memoir but rather a testimonial, documenting the actual voices of the varied and numerous distinct individuals who compose the body politic.[9] She includes eyewitness accounts of surviving students, parents, journalists, professors, police, soldiers, and bystanders. After the publication of *La noche de Tlatelolco*, Poniatowska continued to gain fame for her testimonial narratives, including *Nada, nadie* (Nothing, No One, 1988), about the 1985 earthquake. Her first testimonial, however, has been forever identified as the prime text of all the narratives of Tlatelolco. It is impossible to investigate the history of that confrontation without consulting it.[10] This multifaceted book includes the testimonies of many Mexican men and women, some in support of the students, others critical of their motives. Speeches and government statements share space with eyewitness accounts and creative reaction pieces written by key writers of the older generation, including Rosario Castellanos ("Memorial de Tlatelolco," 163–164), and José Emilio Pacheco ("Lectura de los 'Cantares mexicanos,'" 200), who was twenty-nine years old at the time. Moreover, readers who consult the English translation of Poniatowska's compendium are given an additional vantage point on Tlatelolco by Octavio Paz's introductory essay. His observations are important not only for his comments on the significance of Poniatowska's work but for the points he makes about the historical event after his initial personal and powerful response. Just as Paz had written "¡No pasarán!" to record his immediate response to the Spanish Civil War, he first wrote a poetic reaction to Tlatelolco in "México: Olimpiada de 1968" (Mexico: Olympics of 1968). In addition, he went on to write important essays that reflect his position as one of the premier social critics of contemporary Mexican culture.

Poniatowska herself mentions in the "Acknowledgements" that her work follows the protests already registered in print by poets such as José Emilio Pacheco, José Carlos Becerra, Juan Bañuelos, Eduardo Santos, and Octavio Paz. Thus she begins her own documentary by bringing to the fore the written work that Paz contributed as his strong response against the government's violent repression of the students and their supporters among the intellectuals and the middle class. In contrast, few critics include Garro's novel *Y Matarazo no llamó* as part of the Tlatelolco tradition. This compelling novel, ostensibly about the railway strike of 1959, anticipates the events of Tlatelolco and deserves to be included as part of that literary tradition of the Tlatelolco subgenre.[11]

Octavio Paz's essay "Olimpiada y Tlatelolco" (Olympics and Tlatelolco) included in *Posdata* (1970), in contrast, is deemed a fundamental text regarding the events of Tlatelolco. Leal notes that Paz's essay is "the first that thoroughly analyzes the significance of the tragedy of October 2, pointing out the causes and examining its consequences" ("Tlatelolco, Tlatelolco," 8). Consistent with their differing responses to the Spanish Civil War, Paz and Garro offer different symbolic approaches to the narrativization of Tlatelolco: what might be called the master narrative version of Paz and the private, emotional position in Garro's novel.

Before Paz penned his renowned essay, he had already responded to the government's actions in the form of the poem "México: Olimpiada 1968" (Mexico: 1968 Olympics), which he sent to "La Cultura en México," a cultural supplement of the magazine *Siempre!* It was translated into English by Mark Strand and published in the *New York Review of Books* (November 7, 1968), a month after it was written; the text included the letter that Paz wrote to the Mexican authorities as well as stanzas of the poem itself.

Paz wrote the poem in a moment of anger and shame for his government as a message showing his controlled anger at the Mexican government's brutal response to the peaceful protest by the students. It is interesting to compare the Paz poem with two others that Poniatowska included in her book, Rosario Castellanos's "Memorial de Tlatelolco" (In Memory of Tlatelolco) and lines from Pacheco's "Manuscrito de Tlatelolco" (Tlatelolco Manuscript).[12]

In contrast to Paz's brief, pungent poem (twenty-three short lines, with many spaces), Castellanos's poem is longer and more open in its emotions. Paz transmits a sense of controlled anger by utilizing the technique of short verses, which create open spaces on the page. The spaces almost seem like cries that are being silenced by the poet as he writes. Aside from the title, however, no concrete details indicate to the reader that the poetic voice is indeed describing the massacre of Tlatelolco. Perhaps not unexpectedly, the poem follows the style that Paz uses in "Blanco," which dates from 1966, when he was ambassador to India. "Blanco" also shows off the white spaces of the page and contains many short, charged phrases, some of which could also relate to the anecdotal description of what took place at the "Plaza of the Sacrificed."

For example, as in "Mexico City: The 1968 Olympiad," "Blanco" also includes many empty spaces and highlights the word "lucidity":

Lucidity.
> mouth of truths,
(*Selected Poems*, 88, trans. Eliot Weinberger)

The appeal to "lucidity," in particular, the abstract concept with which Paz starts his Tlatelolco response, recalls aspects of the thematics in "Blanco." What is this call to lucidity that seems to preoccupy Paz? Is it a reference to clarity—or the lack thereof—in the government's reaction to the student protests? The word invokes a reference to splendor, the light of expression, fluency—characteristics glaringly absent from the measures that led to the massacre. Lucidity is also defined as "a presumed capacity to perceive the truth directly and instantaneously."[13] Given that the poem was sent to the Mexican government on October 7, 1968, the poet was struck with "lucidity" directly and at the moment—a capacity to perceive the truth of his government's nature and its utter opposition to his own values of justice and freedom. His resignation from his post as ambassador to India marks the onset of his distance from the government and his stance as a gadfly of Mexican politics, which he maintained until his death.

Paz's poem only indirectly describes the deaths that took place at the plaza—he uses the word "sacrifice" to describe the location of the fateful encounter and refers to the blood that was spilled. For an uninformed reader, the lack of specific details might cause the poem to be read in a manner detached from the Tlatelolco context; yet once the facts of its genesis are known, the reader can link the lines to the extratextual reality. Castellanos's poem, in contrast, does not conceal its relation to the tragic historical reality. As a side note, one theory about her tragic death suggests that her "eloquent poem" so angered Díaz Ordaz that he might have had something to do with her death—so influential and pervasive in Mexico is the idea of government abuses of power![14]

Poniatowska uses the Castellanos poem to begin the final section of her testimonial, "Night of Tlatelolco." This section is followed in the English edition by many photographs of the student strikers; the soldiers and their attack on the students; family members going to the hospitals and jails to view the bodies; and more. The poem is an authentic link to the actuality that the photographs capture. Called "In Memory of Tlatelolco," its lines refer clearly, with lucidity we might say, to the very details of the massacre. She starts from the moment of October 2, when "they" killed—she does not name the killers for us or identify those who were killed that bloody night. Rather, and in this detail Castellanos echoes Paz and Pacheco, she calls upon the entire country to remember what took place under the cover of "la oscuridad" (darkness, night, obscurity). Like Paz, she also plays with images of light and darkness: the massacre was clearly a deed of darkness, while the literary record is an attempt to bring light and focus:

Recuerdo, recordemos
hasta que la justicia se siente entre nosotros.
(*La noche de Tlatelolco*, 164)

I remember, let us all remember
Until justice comes to sit among us.
(*Massacre in Mexico*, 172)

Castellanos projects her poem as a ray of light that would focus on all the wrongdoings of that night. She does not ask for explanations of why such violence took place; she is struck by the official attempts to hide the deed, to obscure justice, as she writes about the awful details. The plaza had been swept clean by the next day and the newspapers mentioned only the weather—nothing about the events that had taken place there.

Castellanos uses the passive voice in describing the "clean up," while in a brief nod to reality Paz names the "municipal workers" who "sweep the Plaza clean." Here the two poets register their dismay that other human beings actively ordered workers to clean the plaza and the streets to remove the evidence of the murders. As one of the voices collected by Poniatowska notes, in the rest of the country it seemed as if no one had noticed what took place at the Plaza de Tlatelolco that night. The writers accepted the obligation to announce the killings to the world, to denounce any cover-ups, and to bear witness for the future. As verified by a review of the various journals in Mexico the following day, the massacre that Castellanos openly proclaims was all but ignored.

Castellanos's poem is a personal and all-encompassing message to all the people of Mexico, sympathetic to both sides—those who dared to wreak havoc on the plaza and the defenseless citizens who were brutalized by the guns. Certain signifiers—such as "archives," "blood," "Goddess of Excrement"—recall the pre-Hispanic tradition in Mexico and another world of violence and bloodshed. Like Pacheco and Paz, Castellanos brings into focus the continuity of the cycles of violence that have marked the history of Mexico and the tragedy of the Mexican people who have lived under such political practices.

Pacheco's poem in particular, with his selection of words such as "Manuscrito de Tlatelolco," his reference to the "Lectura de los *Cantares mexicanos*" (Reading *Mexican Songs*) as his title, and the note referring to *Visión de los vencidos* (Vision of the Conquered),[15] explicitly invokes the past and the way the present invidiously repeats the events of a violent earlier period. Poniatowska includes lines from Pacheco's work in her own testimonial, and Pacheco published it in his collection *No me preguntes cómo pasa el tiempo* (1969; translated as *Don't Ask Me How the Time Goes By*, 1978). As Leal notes, three poems deal with the theme of Tlatelolco, "the most important of them being 'Lectura de los "Cantares mexicanos": manuscrito de Tlatelolco (octubre 1968),' in which Pacheco uses the same technique he had utilized in the novel *You Will Die in a Distant Land* [*Morirás lejos*, 1967], the juxtaposition of two actions separated in time which repeat the theme of assault and slaughter of innocent and defenseless people" ("Tlatelolco, Tlatelolco," 7; see also Cypess, "Tlatelolco: From Ruins to Poetry"). Pacheco first instructs his readers that the poem called "Manuscrito de Tlatelolco" may have as its subtitle "Octubre 1968," but it appears to paraphrase the *Cantares mexicanos*, poems from the Nahuatl that Father Ángel María Garibay and Miguel León-Portilla translated that were included in *Visión de los vencidos*.

The three brief stanzas of this first poem, totaling eleven lines, reach the reader in two temporal zones; as Leal observes, Pacheco "very skillfully makes use of an incident recorded in pre-Hispanic Mexico as a metaphor for a contemporary event occurring in the same place but separated by centuries" ("Tlatelolco, Tlatelolco," 8). Like Castellanos and Paz, Pacheco alternates the impersonal form of verbs ("todos se hallaban," "se alzaron los gritos") with the infrequent use of the first person pronoun, making the appearance of the personal all the more startling. Paz injects a personal subject for the first time in his poem when he uses the imperative form in his final stanza: "Look now." Castellanos also makes use of the imperative form, but to dispense negative commands; when she invokes the first person singular, it goes to the heart of her theme: "mi memoria" and "recuerdo, recordamos." The "I" and "we" remember, actively engaged in erasing the impersonal actions of an unfeeling governmental force that kills its citizens, innocent students, and family members. Paz summons the "nación entera" (entire nation), and Pacheco appeals to "nuestra herencia" (our inheritance)—a call to a patriotism that has been marred by the false images of the government forces.

On the one hand, the government presented the forced image of a progressive Mexico, Mexico of the Olympiad, Mexico as a member of the democratic nations of the world. On the other, to use the image of another of Pacheco's poems, "Las voces de Tlatelolco," the "mano cubierta por un guante blanco" (hand covered by a white glove) spilled blood on the Plaza of Three Cultures. Pacheco's poem depicts the utter disregard of the Mexican authorities for their people. Pacheco and Castellanos both appeal to their fellow citizens not only to remember what happened but also to empathize with all those who lost companions during the chaos of that night.

While Pacheco alludes to censorship in the rhetorically allusive way he chose to write about the event, Castellanos's poem and Paz's essay speak openly of government control of the media. While the Castellanos poem is powerful and articulate, it has not been as widely discussed and analyzed as Paz's essay (or his own poem, for that matter). There is something to be said for genre choice with regard to the weight that readers and critics place on the seriousness of content. Indeed, the essay is the form par excellence to analyze and illuminate an idea or theme. Paz certainly is a major figure in this genre, having written numerous serious essays on fields as varied as Mexican psychosocial history, surrealism, and esthetics in general as well as on many contemporary international writers. Undeniably, as José Miguel Oviedo remarks in "The Modern Essay in Spanish America," Paz's "essays are a compendium of all that can interest a modern man of universal aspirations: hermetic poetry, erotic customs, Hinduism, criticism of the totalitarian state, avant-garde art, magic, drugs, translation, myths, history" (405).

All of Paz's reactions to Tlatelolco were played out in the public arena. Indeed, for the most part, all of Paz's actions since 1937—the year he went off to Spain to show solidarity with the Republicans—were public, in contrast to the secrecy surrounding Garro's movements and motives. In 1968 Paz was far more engaged in the public sphere than was Garro, although she was deeply involved in the intense political debates taking place in Mexico, especially those related to the Mexican workers and issues of ethnicity and class as they affected cultural politics. Conversely, Garro was not openly active in feminist debates;

the idea of "feminism" was hardly a topic of open discussion in Mexico in the 1960s, much less critical inquiry (see Marcos).

Paz is described as a "rigorous thinker" and a "witness of his time" (Oviedo, 405); his seriousness and weight as a conscientious intellectual go unquestioned. Garro, however, would rarely have been considered a serious intellectual or rigorous thinker. For one thing, her gender certainly predisposed critical studies to disregard her material and also helped to relegate her work to the figurative locked trunk—to use the image she herself employed in describing where her many manuscripts were left abandoned.[16] Her behavior during the time of Tlatelolco, before and then immediately afterward, sharply contrasts with the grand gestures of Octavio Paz. In terms of the stereotypical judgments that have marked the evaluation of male-female behavior, the differences between the two might be seen as the typical polarity. Paz is the "informed," "intelligent" one, trained to base his decisions on "reason," as the historians Lessie Jo Frazier and Deborah Cohen note: "all traits commonly associated with middle-class masculinity . . . intelligence and reasoned sentiment [disregard] the unruly feminine emotion and uncontrolled spontaneity of the masses" (618). In reviewing both the "performances" and the texts that Paz and Garro have contributed to the literary tradition on Tlatelolco, I have found it useful to contextualize their work within the frame presented by Frazier and Cohen. They have analyzed the documentation surrounding the event and offer a review that takes gender into consideration.

The historiographies, memoirs, and testimonials written by ex-student male activists have reduced the multiplicity of responses to Tlatelolco to conform to "the version that puts at the center of this conflict the action, lives, and political visions of its male leaders" (Frazier and Cohen, 620). Not surprisingly, Frazier and Cohen note that the principal elite protagonists—overwhelmingly male—have by and large written or influenced the historiography of '68 (620–622). In applying their work to this study, it is perhaps important to view the occurrence on two levels, political and personal, by following the way in which each of these major cultural figures reacted to the tragic event. The response by Paz is similar to what Frazier and Cohen observed regarding the masculine response and discourse attendant upon the masculine reaction.[17] The view put forth is the "heroic masculinity of the youthful male body defying the patriarchal state" (Frazier and Cohen, 1). Octavio Paz was middle-aged (fifty-four), not young like the students of 1968, but in one way he was rejuvenated. Paz returned from the East after having been stationed there in the diplomatic corps, in that sense repeating the steps of the traditional archetypal hero described by Joseph Campbell, who reappears from the East after having suffered his trials and proven himself. He also had acquired a new spouse, Marie José, so he was reentering Mexico in a "youthful" way, as a newly married man.

Paz's gesture of renouncing his governmental position is also clearly an act of defiance against the patriarchal state and in that way akin to the response of the university students. Paz was hailed as a hero for his act; soon after the events of October 2, 1968, he returned from his post in India and accepted invitations to lecture in various universities in the United States. At the University of Texas, Austin, in October 1969, he gave the speech that has become known as "Olimpiada y Tlatelolco," in which he commemorated what the students had been trying to do at Tlatelolco and expressed what the government's violent act represented to him. In his essay, Paz begins with a general consideration of the student movement, relating the Mexican uprising to youth protests internationally; he attempts to show that the Mexican event is part of the phenomenon of youth rebellion in 1968 but that, more importantly, the official response to the student demonstrations reflects a fatal flaw in the Mexican political system. He does not ask "who is the killer," as Castellanos did, but says clearly that the army moved into the Plaza and "the killing began" (235).[18] He also states openly that none of the Mexican periodicals dared to publish an accurate number of how many people had been killed or how many were injured or imprisoned (38). According to Paz, "the second of October, 1968, put an end to the student movement. It also ended an epoch in the history of Mexico" (235).[19]

In the following two chapters, Paz elaborates further on this idea and links the current political structure to systems and procedures in place during Aztec times and under colonial Spanish rule. He then moves to an analysis of the power relations of the party in control of Mexico, the PRI.

"Olimpiada y Tlatelolco" became celebrated for its denunciatory tone that reiterated Paz's defiant act of renunciation of his governmental ties. This essay with its very open response to the Mexican government was then published in *Posdata*, which is composed of three essays in all: "Olimpiada y Tlatelolco" (Olympics and Tlatelolco), "El desarrollo y otros espejismos" (Development and Other Mirages), and "Crítica de la pirámide" (Critique of the Pyramid, a chapter heading used for the English translation: *The Other Mexico: Critique of the Pyramid*, 1972). The title recalls for Paz's readers his previous influential essay on Mexican culture, *The Labyrinth of Solitude*, tying this new set of essays to his previous work and offering the opportunity for him to respond to and refine the earlier exploration of Mexican national identity.

In consonance with my view that Paz's gesture in *Posdata* is similar to "heroic masculinity," Diana Sorensen categorizes Paz's work as a representation of a privileged gaze. Paz occupies an honored position as a "representative of high culture whose voice conveys authority" (Sorensen, 305). Sorensen also notes the circularity of the work itself and of Paz's view of Mexican history. He had been criticized for his "dooming, deterministic nature" visible in *The Labyrinth of Solitude*, and once again he sees the events of Tlatelolco 1968 as a repetition and reflection of the culture's Aztec roots: "The massacre at Tlatelolco shows us that the past which we thought was buried is still alive and has burst among us" (236).[20] For Paz, the repetition of not only the violence that marked Aztec life and marks the current government but also the geographic "doubling-up," as it were, of bloodshed recurring in the same space (236, 351) appears to prove that the past still dictates the present. This idea is echoed in a number of the pieces on Tlatelolco, most notably in the Pacheco poems.

Despite this devastating pronouncement of repetitive fatality with which Paz concludes the first chapter of *Posdata*, "Olimpiada y Tlatelolco," the next two chapters in effect attempt to show that he does not describe the events only to prove their inevitability. Rather, his watchword is that "without criticism, above all without self-criticism, there is no possibility of change" (236).[21] In the next two chapters Paz reviews the Aztec roots of his culture then analyzes the political development of modern Mexico, the institutionalization of the PRI after the Mexican Revolution of 1910–1920, and the relationship between Mexico and the United States. Finally, he suggests that the way official Mexico has produced its discourse about cultural identity is an example of an ideology of dictatorship. That is, the PRI government presents to the world a definition of Mexico in its own image, but that is not necessarily the only image of Mexico. Paz exhorts his compatriots to be critical enough to examine what really occurs: "criticism is not what we dream of, but it teaches us to distinguish between the specters out of our nightmares and our true visions" (325).[22] Paz seems to be suggesting that by being critical we can avoid repeating the errors of the past.

Throughout *Posdata* Paz emphasized metaphors and images of flux, yet at the same time the monumental pyramid is the pervasive trope. As Eduardo G. González noted, the text is "a particularly imaginative example of the 'psychohistorical' mode of writing"—especially noticeable in the third part, "Critique of the Pyramid" ("Octavio Paz," 30). In all, this is a grand gesture by an imposing voice. It is interesting that Paz initiates his formal critique of the government by resigning then begins his written attack while in the United States as a "voluntary political exile" (Leal, "Tlatelolco, Tlatelolco," 9). As noted by the historian Jim Tuck: "The Tlatelolco massacre was obviously a source of tremendous spiritual agony for Paz. He compares it to the Aztec rituals of mass sacrifice designed to keep the people in line and comments on the irony that the pyramid at Tlatelolco was a place where 'rivers of Indian blood' flowed in the heyday of Aztec dominance" ("Octavio Paz"). It was also the scene of the final stages of the Spanish Conquest and foreshadowed further bloodshed as the Spanish government dominated its Indian and mestizo subjects during the colonial period.

Paz and Garro reacted quite differently to the Tlatelolco Massacre. After Tlatelolco, Paz went into a three-year period of self-imposed exile. He taught at Cambridge in 1969 and in 1971–1972 held the Charles Eliot Norton Chair of Poetry at Harvard. Then he returned to Mexico and became an independent critic of one-party domination over Mexico's political system. He founded a magazine called *Plural*, a supplement to the well-known daily *Excélsior*. *Plural* became a highly regarded intellectual gadfly publication, but Paz suffered a setback when Julio Scherer García, the editor of *Excélsior*, was forced from his post by Mexican president Luis Echeverría because of the paper's attacks on Echeverría's leadership. In 1976 Paz founded another literary and cultural monthly, *Vuelta*, which lost no time in acquiring the sort of prestige that *Plural* had enjoyed.

From the 1970s onward, Paz refused to accept any official government positions, preferring to maintain his role as an independent critic of the government through his many different literary efforts. To the dismay of political activists on all sides of the fence, Paz was never affiliated with any political movement. With his punctilious execution of thought, Paz was indeed radical in the truest sense of the word (which derives from the Latin word for "root"). Therefore, "to get to the root of anything you must be radical," as Gore Vidal once pointed out (408). Paz painstakingly explored all levels of the Mexican psyche both personally and nationally. He thought that a true artist and philosopher must understand the roots and the whole of reality, without adhering to the viewpoint of any partisan organization. It is perhaps for this reason, among others, that Paz's writing has superseded that of any other writer or group of writers in Mexican history.

For Elena Garro, too, Tlatelolco would become a watershed, a liminal period in which she would be transformed from a member of the literati to a despised exile, a *desarraigada* (rootless one), and a Llorona figure.[23] She lamented that 1968 was "the year of the student movement and the year of my misfortune" (quoted by Poniatowska, *Las siete cabritas*, 112).[24]

Just as the meaning of "Tlatelolco" among Mexican and non-Mexican writers is diverse and complex, so are the interpretations of Garro's role in the events. How did a woman whose own writings have been called a "very sustained condemnation of violence in all aspects" (Muncy, "Encuentro" 70) come to be so negatively associated with the massacre at Tlatelolco?[25]

The public event of Tlatelolco had a devastating impact on Elena Garro's personal life and consequently on her creative life as well. From 1963, the date of publication of her much lauded novel *Los recuerdos del porvenir*, to 1968, Garro experienced a slow "decline" in critical and public acceptance. How much of this decline or rejection had to do with her divorce from Octavio Paz, her own strange behavior, or a previously hidden story in her life? This challenging question needs to be addressed in order to clarify aspects of her response to the events of 1968 and their long-term effect on her professional career and personal life.

In 1963, after having published the short story collection *La semana de colores* and some plays in *El hogar sólido*, Garro came out with *Los recuerdos del porvenir*. As noted, despite the failure of their marriage, Paz praised the novel and acknowledged its merits. As Emanuel Carballo notes, "although their matrimonial relationship was very bad, Octavio was more a friend of literary truth and exerted all his weight so that the work would be published" (quoted by Ramírez, 44).[26]

Within the next five years, however, their marriage was dissolved by divorce. Paz returned to Mexico in 1968 with a new wife. While Paz was abroad, Garro had become actively involved in political events in the 1960s, but from a very personal perspective. She had a reputation for acting impetuously, as some of the anecdotes associated with her public behavior suggest. Her actions usually championed indigenous peoples or the poor, belying her own class and ethnic affiliations. For example, in a conversation between Mexican literary critic Emmanuel Carballo and Huberto Batis, the editor of *unomásuno*, a cultural supplement to *Excélsior*, the two men recall some of the more infamous encounters between Garro and the establishment. Batis brings up an incident in which Garro was reputed to have slapped the governor of the Mexican state of Morelos because of the assassination of the agrarian leader Rubén Jaramillo by government forces.[27] The vicious assault against Jaramillo, his young children, and his pregnant wife was rumored to have been orchestrated by government forces in Xochicalco, in the state of Morelos, so the strike on the governor's person was a brave gesture of blame and accusation on Garro's part. No one was ever indicted for the murders. Carballo mentions another telling confrontation that is equally daring and indicative of Garro's collaboration with the poor and defenseless; in describing these anecdotes, Carballo adds that they are not fictional, for he was an eyewitness.

Again the incident has to do with the peasants of Morelos. Garro brought Archibald Burns, a wealthy businessman who was also purported to be her lover, and around two to three hundred peasants to a celebration hosted by the Fondo de Cultura Económica, the prestigious Mexican publishing house. The ensuing scene recalls what she had related in her memoir about her behavior in Spain in 1937—she had little tolerance for hypocritical intellectuals. The Garro of the sixties also disdained the intellectuals who were always talking about helping the poor and defenseless of Mexico but never did anything concrete and never even knew the peasants. The intellectuals who were at the party refused to meet with the peasants, so Garro decided to teach them a lesson. Organizing those who had been refused entrance, she directed them to deflate the tires of all the cars of the intellectuals who had been at the party, including Carballo (Carballo and Batis, 57). Both gestures are indicative of Garro's rich imagination and can be read symbolically. By striking the governor physically, Garro showed that a personal gesture could be a synecdoche for the public indictment that would not come in an autocratic society such as Mexico. By choosing to puncture the tires, Garro sent a message that the intellectuals perhaps had egos too pumped up and deserved to have their self-image deflated.

While the anecdotes recounted by Carballo and Batis in their conversation reveal the more audacious and physically demonstrative aspect of Garro's political action, she also published political commentary for journals, just as Paz is famous for doing. As early as 1964 she became a follower of one of the reform-minded leaders associated with the PRI, Carlos A. Madrazo, who was elected president of the PRI in December 1964, soon after Díaz Ordaz became president.[28] Madrazo's support of agrarian reform as well as political changes in the PRI led Garro to associate with him. Madrazo proposed structural changes in the way the PRI should elect its leaders and also considered the problem of land distribution (an issue that has always brought its supporters much grief, and often death, as in the case of Emiliano Zapata and possibly Madrazo himself) (Hernández Rodríguez, *El caso de Carlos A. Madrazo*, 140–144). The title of one of the articles that Garro had written and published in the journal *Siempre!* in particular shows that she clearly supported Madrazo: "El problema agrario sigue en pie después de cincuenta años de revolución" (The Agrarian Problem Continues Unabated Fifty Years after the Mexican Revolution). Her article is not an impetuous or thoughtless piece but carefully states facts: 2 million peasants have no land, and 115 million hectares are in the hands of a few large landowners. It is indicative of the lacunae in scholarship about Garro and the biases in her treatment in the Mexican press that she has not been sufficiently credited for her political pieces, some of which received serious analysis only after her death.

The situation in which Garro found herself in 1968—or rather, as some insinuate, the situation in which she placed herself—has been documented in the journals of that time and in detail by Volpi, Ramírez, Melgar, and Rosas Lopátegui. Ramírez and Rosas Lopátegui speak more as friends of Garro, while Volpi and Melgar attempt objectivity; they all agree, however, that immediately after the massacre of 1968 Garro was singled out in the newspapers as one of the instigators of the student movement and then, worse, as a key informer against the intellectuals who had supported the student movement. Ironically, she was damned first for having been part of the student movement and then for having betrayed it.[29] Leading figures in the press and in intellectual circles were quick to denounce Garro: José Luis Cuevas called her "loca" (crazy) and in *Siempre!* Monsiváis called her, colloquially, the "cantante del año" (singer of the year), pointing out in no uncertain terms that she had told all, betrayed the cause (Ramírez, 49).

The various documents and commentaries indicate that the student activist Sócrates Amado Campos Lemus, accused of possibly being an agent of the government (Volpi, 344), first named Garro as one of the financial supporters of the student movement, along with Carlos Madrazo.[30] Ramírez mentions that both Garro and her daughter, Helena, told him that they had been visited in September 1968 by one of the peasants she had befriended, who brought the news that she was being kept under observation by the government because of her controversial ideas (Ramírez, 80). After this accusation connecting her with Madrazo, a persona non grata among the PRI, Garro became afraid for her life. She left her home to hide as early as September 23; Ramírez says that from then on both she and Helena were on the run, never to return to that home again, as she recounts in her play *Sócrates y los gatos* (82). According to the summary offered by Ramírez, she was quoted by *La Prensa*:

Hidden in a guest house along with her daughter, Elena Garro accepted in part her participation in the student movement, but said that she only was a mediator, although she was ready to unmask all the professors and intellectuals who were indoctrinating the Mexican students to try to overthrow the government. (50)[31]

Garro also admitted that her home had been broken into and that furniture and other objects of value had been destroyed once the perpetrators saw that she was not home, and she was distraught because they wanted to kill her. She asked for protection from the state and also revealed that she had received several telephone threats against her person (Ramírez, 50). Garro said that some members of the Consejo Nacional de Huelga (National Strike Council) had informed her that they had received an invitation by Genaro Vázquez, who was a revolutionary hiding out in the mountains, to unite with his forces in order to fight against the government but that she had advised the students not to continue further opposition to the government (Ramírez, 51). Garro lost the support of her circle of intellectuals when she was quoted as saying that the student movement began in the Universidad Nacional Autónoma de México (UNAM) but that the intellectuals of UNAM were all "cobardes y farsantes" (cowards and phoneys) who had abandoned the students:

> [T]he young students are not to blame. The professors and leftist intellectuals are the ones who led them in this dangerous mission and then they betrayed them. Let them show themselves now. They don't dare. They are cowards, she commented sadly. (Ramírez, 50)[32]

Garro's attitude toward other members of the intellectual class was shocking and brought instant reaction. The important Mexico City newspapers, *La Prensa*, *Excélsior*, and *El Heraldo*, reprinted the names of the intellectuals Garro was supposed to have said were responsible for inciting the students, including the philosophers and UNAM professors Luis Villoro and Ricardo Guerra, the well-recognized writer Rosario Castellanos, Professor José Luis Ceceña, the journalist and poet/writer Sergio Mondragón, the painters José Luis Cuevas and Leonora Carrington, and the young and promising journalist Carlos Monsiváis. Garro is quoted as making many different accusations, including a plan that Madrazo was to be included in the movement only to be assassinated in order to convert him into a "Martin Luther King" (Ramírez, 53). She accused the president of UNAM, Javier Barros Sierra, of being "an accomplice and primary person responsible for the whole conspiracy that originated in University City" (Ramírez, 53).[33] The various newspapers also confirmed that Garro had disappeared soon after being singled out by Campos Lemus and had continued to hide out after making her initial accusations against the intellectuals.[34]

Not only did Garro herself behave in this unexpected manner in response to the democratic demonstrations of the students and the unprecedented violent reactions of the government; her daughter, Helena Paz, also functioned in a most astonishing way. It was well known in Mexico that the daughter was estranged from her father and took her mother's side in interpreting her father's actions. Helena had never felt comfortable with her father's remarriage, feeling as Elena did that the marriage between Paz and Garro was still a reality (against all common sense). Thus, soon after Paz renounced his ambassadorship and criticized the government for its repressive actions, when Garro herself was experiencing harassment from "unknown" sources (see above), Helena Paz published an open letter in *El Universal* on October 23, 1968, that condemned her father's stance. In his book *La imaginación y el poder*, Volpi includes long excerpts of the letter that reveal how similar Helena's ideas are to her mother's; indeed, Helena Paz's letter appears indicative of the thoughts and perspective of Garro as well. For example, Helena offers the same inventory of names that her mother had mentioned (Ceceña, Barros Sierra, Guerra, Villoro, Castellanos, Monsiváis), calling them Marxists and blaming them for inciting the students. She also rebukes her father publicly for not having been in Mexico during the months before October 2 (he had been in India as ambassador) and in that way tries to discredit him as a reliable narrator. More telling is the way Helena brings up old grievances and reuses them to reprimand her father. She reminds him of what he would tell her as a child when trying to discipline her: "the reason is that I am stronger than you are" (Volpi, 374).[35] Helena hastens to tell her father that the philosophy of "might makes right" also had motivated the government actions, so his resignation because of it reveals his hypocrisy. Moreover, in contradiction to all the major writers save her mother, Helena describes the students not as peaceful—Paz's portrayal of them--but as "violentísimos jóvenes" (extremely violent youths) who lacked a just cause (Volpi, 375). Perhaps to show her solidarity with her mother, Helena wanted all of Mexico to know that father and daughter were on opposite poles regarding this event of decisive political and cultural importance.

After responding in this surprising and reactionary manner to a situation that was tragic for the country and an apparent personal collapse/failure for the writer and her daughter, the two left Mexico. Rhina Toruño calls it a "self-exile" (*Tiempo destino y opresión*, 23), but in a way Garro could not come back because of the reactions against her both by Paz personally and by the other writers whose names she so undiplomatically bandied about and whose lives she put in danger. The injustice of her exile, in her opinion, is clearly expressed in a number of her texts published after 1980; in the first of these, *Andamos huyendo Lola* (We Are Fleeing Lola, 1980), the woman narrator confesses: "We are fleeing, Lola! Of course, we don't know who we are fleeing from, Lola, nor why, but in these times of the Rights of Man and the Decrees, it is necessary to flee and flee without stopping" (quoted by Ramírez, 55).[36]

All the newspaper reports note Garro's extreme nervousness and her declarations about receiving verbal threats and being menaced by assassins and that others also were being marked for assassination, notably Madrazo. Garro felt the necessity to disappear from public view, but she took the decisive step of leaving Mexico with Helena after she was ridiculed for her statements against the intellectuals, living first in Madrid and then in Paris for many years. Not until 1991 did she allow herself to accept an invitation to return to Mexico for a series of testimonial conferences.

What I find fascinating about the periodicals' reports on Garro's behavior is how much of the anecdotal material can also be found in two key fictive texts: Garro's novel *Y Matarazo no llamó* and her play *Sócrates y los gatos*. Garro dated the novel as having been written in 1960; but after reading the text I arrived independently at the same conclusion reached by Melgar ("Silencio y represión"), Toruño (*Tiempo, destino y opresión*, 80), and Rosas Lopátegui (*Testimonios*, 271–272): even if the novel had been started as early as 1960, it had also been reworked after the events of 1968. As for the play, its title refers to one of the main student protagonists, Sócrates Campos Lemus, who was one of Garro's opponents at the time. He named her as well as Madrazo among the important intellectual provocateurs of the student movement (Carey, 143), which Garro denied. In the play, Garro re-creates the scenes of her attempts to hide from the police as a result of being named a collaborator. The play was written in 1969, but it remained unpublished until 2003, when Océano finally brought it out. Many of the incidents, especially those having to do with the mistreatment of her cats by government officials, repeat the details that Helena Paz recalls from those alarming months when she and her mother were forced to hide in the home of a former servant, María Callado. The play deals with their lives in a direct way and is perhaps one of the most autobiographically explicit texts produced by Garro. What happened to Garro and her daughter during the events of the summer and fall of 1968 can be learned by reading the memoirs of Helena Paz, the various interviews given by Garro, or this play. The text highlights what Garro felt was the "Communist threat" and the persecution of the government—an unusual combination, given that the Mexican government was anti-Communist at the time. Nevertheless, whatever the political ideology of those who are cast as the oppressors, Garro's play depicts the sense of persecution and helplessness that the two women experienced. At one point Verónica, the alter ego of Elena Garro, expresses her disdain for the Communists: "The Communist revolution is the seizure of power by the petit bourgeoisie and by the minor intellectual. It is a question of getting rid of not only the wealthy bourgeoisie but also the great creators and thinkers" (54).[37]

More telling is another comment by Verónica, which has been also attributed to the real-life Garro: "I commit many foolish acts [tonterías], but I never regret them" (59).[38]

Most of the physical torture involves the cats owned by Verónica and her daughter, but the two women suffer mental stress. At the end of the play, they manage to escape from María's house, where they had gone in hopes of finding refuge. María betrayed them, as did many of their friends in real life. While the play itself is traditional in structure, its value lies more in its bluntness in re-creating Garro's sense of historical reality at that time. I suggest that *Y Matarazo no llamó* creates the same emotional and dramatic gamut, the same critique of the government and the co-conspirators, but does it all more subtly and more gracefully. It is a text that transcends the historical as it re-creates the sensations of the past.

According to a comment made by Garro [to Toruño], part of *Y Matarazo no llamó* is also autobiographical:

The date of the manuscript is 1960, prior to the events of October 2, 1968. However, based on certain dates, it would seem that before giving the manuscript to print [1991] Garro revised it and added new facts related to the happenings of '68. For example, based on the events of '68, they brought a seriously wounded man to Garro, leaving him abandoned at her door, just as she describes it in the novel. (Toruño, *Tiempo, destino y opresión*, 86)[39]

Whether or not a wounded man was brought to Garro's house, the idea of a moribund person in her home works well with her state of mind at the time of the Tlatelolco Massacre. Garro above all always maintained her vocation as a writer and found more "reality" in her fiction than in her own personal memory. After reading Garro's many texts and the interviews that she gave in her lifetime, and her reported personal reminiscences, I can only conclude that it is safest to look at her narratives in order to determine her ideas on a given event or problem of Mexican cultural reality.

The following two comments by Garro may help us to understand her approach to the reality of life and history and how she transformed her own personal history into fiction. First, "I believe that the imagination is a force that leads us to the truth, because lying is very boring, while on the other hand the imagination is exact and very beautiful" (Rosas Lopátegui and Toruño, "Entrevista," 55).[40] She also wrote: "People believe a lie more easily than a truth" (*Testimonios sobre Mariana*, 164).[41] These observations enable us to understand in part how Garro as an individual might have reacted in extreme and irrational ways in response to her personal fears in the aftermath of the Tlatelolco Massacre but at the same time was able to transform the emotions and psychological angst that she suffered into a highly charged and dramatic work of fiction and an autobiographical play. If no one would listen to her side of the events, then she would use her imaginative powers and prowess to fabricate stories that could be read and studied and analyzed. When critics inventory the many texts that belong to the Tlatelolco subgenre, however, very few thus far have suggested that this novel be considered part of the field; the play has also been largely ignored.

Some of the many poems, novels, and plays by other writers that deal with Tlatelolco include direct historical referents, while others make use of allegory and displacement strategies to represent their perspective. Cynthia Steele, who is knowledgeable in the field, mentions that "the two best fictional representations of Tlatelolco are relatively brief segments of two novels published a decade after 1968, both of them written in Europe: *Palinuro de México* (*Palinurus of Mexico*, 1977) by Fernando del Paso and *Si muero lejos de ti* (*If I Die Far from You*, 1979), by Jorge Aguilar Mora (*Politics, Gender and the Mexican Novel*, 9). She also notes that it would take twenty years after the student-government clashes before "women writers would continue Poniatowska's early attempt to interpret this turning point in history from a woman's perspective" (*Politics, Gender, and the Mexican Novel*, 9). Steele mentions Emma Prieto's *Los testigos* (The Witnesses, 1985) and Vilma Fuentes's *Ayer es nunca jamás* (Yesterday Is No More, 1988).

While few critics have incorporated references to the theatrical pieces into their surveys of the Tlatelolco literary phenomenon, one of the earliest plays to treat the subject on the stage was by a woman, Pilar Campesino, whose *Octubre terminó hace mucho tiempo* (October Ended Long Ago) was written in 1970.[42] Chronologically, it is the third play to be written but the first by a woman and the most direct in its historical referents, as the title shows. In 1999 Felipe Galván published it as one of the thirteen plays in his *Antología Teatro del 68*. Novels, plays, and poems continue to be written about the historic cataclysm, flooding the void in the documentation offered by official government policy; the government's silence and distortions of what took place were soon subverted by the writers of Mexico. While lists have been compiled, anthologies assembled, and writers selected, Garro does not appear in relation to the Tlatelolco Massacre except as one of the hypocritical government apologists, at best, or as an unbalanced and inappropriate victim. Perhaps it is too ironic for some critics that the very event which caused her self-exile and so many individual problems and personal sufferings should have been transformed into a chilling novel of suspense. Her play *Sócrates y los gatos* should also be incorporated into the list of Tlatelolco-inspired works, for it appears to be based closely on the experiences of Garro and her daughter during the days after the October 2 massacre. Helena Paz's autobiography recalls many of the same events, emotions, and reactions that are also re-created in her mother's play.[43]

While *Sócrates y los gatos* is obviously based on historical events and figures, *Y Matarazo no llamó* offers greater flexibility of interpretation. It may be considered prophetic, if written in the sixties, or part of post-Tlatelolco literature, if reworked after 1968. In either case, in ways that might rival Franz Kafka, the novel re-creates the atmosphere of fear, violence, injustice, and absurdity that enables a reader to experience what it must have been like to live through the days and nights of the Tlatelolco turmoil.

One reason why the novel has not been read as part of Tlatelolco literature is that Garro ostensibly includes no obvious historical referents in the novel and creates a male character as her chief protagonist. In this regard *Y Matarazo no llamó* recalls *Los recuerdos del porvenir* in the way it functions on multiple historical levels. On an obvious level, *Los recuerdos* deals with the Cristero Rebellion and its effect on small-town Mexicans, yet it offers polysemous messages with regard to cultural memory. Studies have shown that the novel includes what I have called the Malinche subtext (Cypess, *La Malinche*). Without an overt reference to La Malinche or the Conquest, Garro nevertheless was able to interweave enough referents that could lead a reader to discern the pattern of La Malinche and Cortés in the relationships between the female characters and General Rosas, the conquistador figure.

Y Matarazo no llamó also makes no overt references to a student strike or to the particulars of the event. But certain clues embedded in the narrative could lead the discerning reader to relate it to the events surrounding October 2, 1968. More than the anecdotal similarities, the emotional and psychological atmosphere that Garro creates in the narrative world parallels that of the upheavals attending to the massacre. While *La noche de Tlatelolco* (1971), in which

Poniatowska collected the testimonies and documents of others, is the epitome of testimonial literature, *Y Matarazo no llamó*, with its very personal story, is also the emotional history as recorded by an eyewitness protagonist. Garro has transformed the political into the personal story of her protagonist; and by means of narrative displacement, the personal tragedy of her life has been transformed into a political novel.[44]

Outwardly it is the story of how a nondescript office worker, Eugenio Yáñez, a solitary man of fifty, inadvertently involves himself with a group of striking workers and eventually gets caught up in the maelstrom. It is interesting that Garro chose a middle-aged male figure as her protagonist and alter ego. In his essays, of course, Paz spoke in his own voice, as did the lyrical poets Castellanos and Pacheco. Poniatowska in *La noche de Tlatelolco* plays down her own personal commentary in her choice of the testimonial genre with its polyphony of voices. Poniatowska's major works have been generally dialogic; perhaps she finds comfort in the polyphony, knowing in this case that the intensity of her sorrow at the deaths of the young is reflected in countless cases of the people whose voices fill her book. Garro creates even more displacement of her emotions and personal loss by crafting a main character whose gender differs from hers as the implied author but whose age would have been similar (around fifty).

Interestingly, almost all of the many other narrative texts that are part of the Tlatelolco tradition have been written by men and have male protagonists.[45] Ironically, male writers have often used women as the mirrors in which they see themselves reflected; as Virginia Woolf observes in *A Room of One's Own*: "Women have served all these centuries as looking-glasses possessing the magic and delicious power of reflecting the figure of man at twice its natural size" (Chapter 2, 34–35). In contrast, rather than speaking "like a woman," Garro makes use of a male figure as her "looking-glass" to reflect what her experiences were in 1968, when she became a "figura maldita" (accursed figure), as Ramírez notes (49). In facing the repercussions of this crisis in her life, a time that she calls colloquially and graphically "un desmadre" (a bitch of a year) (Ramírez, 80), Garro followed her usual modus operandi: creating a fictional character to explain her side of the story.

In *Y Matarazo no llamó*, Eugenio Yáñez's age as the story begins is not far from Garro's own age in 1968: if we take her to have been born in 1917, then she was fifty-one in 1968. Just as Garro was forced to give up her old way of life and wander about feeling persecuted, Yáñez in effect becomes the "miserable dried leaf carried away by the storm" that Azuela describes in *Los de abajo* (63).[46] I do not think that the reference to Azuela and the novels of the Mexican Revolution is unwarranted, for Garro seems to be offering clues that can lead the reader to that subgenre and its great practitioners, Mariano Azuela (1873–1952) and Agustín Yáñez (1904–1980). While Azuela used "Cervantes" as the name for the antihero in his classic novel on the Mexican Revolution, *Los de abajo* (first serialized in 1915), Garro uses the surname of Yáñez, a respected Mexican novelist, for her innocent antihero. Like Azuela's real hero, Demetrio Macías, the name of her protagonist is derived from the Greek (Eugenio, meaning "well born"); as we ought to remember, the name of the jailed union leader of the railroad workers is Demetrio Vallejo.

Garro, however, seems to be creating an ironic parody of *Los de abajo*: her hero is not a strong fighter like Azuela's Demetrio but an indecisive, anxious character. Another ironic aspect of this name also relates to the historical context: during the presidency of Gustavo Díaz Ordaz, when the massacre took place, Agustín Yáñez was secretary of Public Education and one of the few members of the literary establishment supporting the government's position. By using his surname for her tragic hero, Garro offers the informed reader another way to link this novel with Tlatelolco. Both Demetrio Macías and Eugenio Yáñez end up dead, of course, which shows that the destiny of Mexican protesters is similar for Garro and for her precursor Azuela.

Garro is showing the connection between Mexico during the Revolution and in the Tlatelolco period. Paz had already drawn correspondences between the brutality of the Conquest period and contemporary Mexican circumstances, as did the Pacheco poem discussed above as well as a play by Carlos Fuentes, *Todos los gatos son pardos* (All Cats Are Gray, 1970), in which the Mexico of the Conquest period and Mexico of 1968 are related. For Garro, the railway strike of 1959 and the student protests at Tlatelolco are considered a continuation of the quest for social justice that the Revolution of 1910 embodied but did not deliver. It is not surprising to distinguish these intertextual referents, for many of the Tlatelolco texts are marked by what Lanin Gyurko has called a "skillful utilization of intertextuality" in the way they cite each other's works (57).[47] For Gyurko, "an important characteristic of almost all of the literary responses to Nonalco-Tlatelolco [is that] they seem to form part of a single, immense text" (57).

Eugenio Yáñez begins as a Good Samaritan, offering cigarettes to the strikers as a simple gesture of solidarity, without realizing the consequences of his sympathetic act. Thinking that he can be trusted, the strikers bring Yáñez one of their dying companions, whose moribund body then becomes the responsibility of this outsider. While he is an innocent, those around him, whether in the union or in the government, turn out to be untrustworthy and opportunists. The only other person who seems to accompany Yáñez in his new predicament is a mysterious figure called Matarazo. As the title suggests, however, Matarazo did not call; even Matarazo finally proves incapable of helping Yáñez out of his impasse. A review of Garro's interactions with the students and the strike shows that she also attempted at first to be a Good Samaritan, offering her help, without realizing the consequences of her actions. Similarly, as Toruño mentions ("Protesta contra la opresión," 94), a dying man was brought to her door, left there under her care despite her inability to do much good. Garro's relationship with Carlos Madrazo, of the PRI, was of little use to her in this confusion, just as Matarazo (whose name echoes that of Madrazo) offers scant support to Eugenio.

Paralleling the way in which Garro changed from well-connected intellectual to pariah, the narrative action of her novel moves slowly but inexorably from Eugenio's state of innocence to his anguished descent into a hell from which he finds no escape. Yáñez converts from a mere supplier of cigarettes to a caretaker of one of the wounded protesters, to a hunted man, and finally to a prisoner of government forces who identify him as a dangerous revolutionary killer. While there are no overt references to the specifics of time and place regarding Tlatelolco in 1968, the astute reader nevertheless can identify clues that Garro has imbedded in the text. The situation she describes, however, is also unfortunately too common to be associated only with the massacre at Tlatelolco and also bears similarities with other possible authoritarian episodes in Mexican history.

I want to highlight additional significant aspects of the text that appear to be clues to Tlatelolco or at any rate serve as elements of the text that can be associated with the students' rebellion. For example, although the strike described in the novel is supposed to be organized by "los obreros" (the workers; 15), Eugenio calls them the "muchachos" (young men; 16), allowing us to relate them not only to the railway workers of 1959 but to the youths who participated in the student strike of Tlatelolco.

In the novel, the workers appear to have been incited to rebel only to be abandoned by their leaders. Garro had complained publicly that the student leaders of Tlatelolco were also encouraged by the intellectuals who then did nothing to help them face the government forces. Garro includes in the text a series of dialogues that refer to the right to strike but that also show how the innocent can be misled. At one point, Eugenio is so taken with the rights of the workers and their sad plight that he exclaims that "his heart is pounding with pride because he was walking in their company" (18).[48] When Eulalio, one of the leaders of the strike, asks if he is "new to the struggle," Eugenio responds much as Garro might have: "Yes, that is, not really new, but spontaneous, confessed Eugenio, suddenly embarrassed" (18).[49] Garro the humanitarian may have been carried away by her emotions in her expression of solidarity with the student protests, but Garro the writer sees how dangerous it can be to persist as a naïf, an impulsive actor. The novel is a long nightmare of what can happen, what has happened, to activists, to dissenters, to her friends, to herself. It outlines step by step all the Kafkaesque horrors of the innocent who falls into the lion's den. What happens is almost crueler than what Kafka had imagined. Garro infuses her protagonist with a deep anxiety that permeates the text, overflows into the reader's own psyche, and pressures us with its disturbing power of evocation.

Remember that the comments of the various participants relate to the workers' strike that is "ostensibly" the fictional element of Garro's story. One of the men reports to Eugenio, who at this moment in the narrative is still an innocent observer of events: "'Imagine, comrade! . . . They fell upon us with all their force. What a barrage of bullets! They say there are many dead bodies . . . and also many wounded,' shouted Ignacio, excited, almost with happiness" (27).[50] The almost strange presence of the descriptive phrase "almost with happiness" may perturb the conscientious reader, but at this point early in the narrative we may be curious but have no further clues as to what this tells us about Ignacio and his role in the armed attack; he turns out later to be one of the leaders of the strike who had been co-opted by the government cause.

In contrast to Ignacio's perplexing reactions, another strike leader, who also was at the assault, is described as being fully distressed: "'They fired on us,' . . . said Tito as if he were about to cry. He was emotional; he did not expect such a violent reaction on the part of the government, he felt betrayed" (29).[51] Tito, unlike the more sanguine and dishonest Ignacio, turns out to be one of the more trustworthy leaders and representative of the uncorrupted workers. These confessions in the novel by the people involved in the strike reproduce quite literally the events of the night of the Tlatelolco Massacre. The surprise of the protesters when they were fired upon, the many youths who were wounded or killed, and the covert contentment of some—those who duped their companions into such an imprudent move—echo some of the reports reproduced by Poniatowska. For example, one of the student leaders of the Consejo Nacional de Huelga (CNH: National Strike Council) comments:

It never occurred to us that the government might attack us on October 2, because a few days before there had been a meeting at Tlatelolco . . . and we thought that a sort of tacit truce had been arranged. . . . But then they started shooting—and got their own asses shot off. (*Massacre in Mexico*, 238)

Other comments reproduced in *Massacre in Mexico* also resonate with Garro's novel:

In a few minutes the whole thing became a scene straight out of hell. The gunfire was deafening. The bullets were shattering the windows of the apartments and shards of glass were flying all over. (*Massacre in Mexico*, 226)

The Plaza de las Tres Culturas was a living hell. Every so often we could hear gunfire and the bullets from the machine guns and high-powered rifles were whizzing in every direction. (*Massacre in Mexico*, 237)

The behavior of Ignacio and Tito serves as a synecdoche of the different reactions of the people involved in Tlatelolco. While most often we read of the Titos and their shock at being overwhelmed by the government, the Ignacios are the ones that Garro blames for leading the gullible into the morass of the collective trauma of that shameful moment in Mexican history. She returns to the fate of Tito and Ignacio at the end of the novel and contrasts their paths with that of the main protagonist, Eugenio.

Just as the brief dialogic disparity between Tito and Ignacio is significant, so are the details that Garro chooses to include as events in her protagonist's life or his feelings about how these actions are unfolding. She describes how an individual reacts when caught in a "larger than life" deed over which he has no control. For those of us who may want to know how it must have been for those actually caught up in the horror of the moment, the various eyewitness expressions captured by Poniatowska offer one important perspective. Yet these are fragments, often statements caught in medias res, that leave us feeling incomplete or frustrated at not finding a whole narrative. The plaintive cry of one of the sisters of an innocent victim of the debacle, "Why don't you answer me, *hermanito?*" (227), reaches us after a number of previous interpolations describing Diana Salmerón de Contreras's steady involvement and final realization of her brother's death. Intellectually, we may appreciate her anguish and decry the brutality suffered by the innocents caught against their will in the government's harsh repressive acts. By means of her controlled and carefully constructed text, however, Garro re-creates in the reader not only the intellectual call to action but also the strong emotional and dramatic state that parallels in the vicarious way of great literature what it was to be part of Tlatelolco '68.

The details ascribed to the life of Yáñez are telling, especially when we know what Garro underwent in the weeks from September 23 through her years of exile. Just as she always felt that she was being spied upon, Yáñez experiences the anxiety of doubt, the fearfulness that he is being stalked. For example, when Yáñez attempts to go to the office after the few days of his involvement with the strikers, he interprets every act in a more suspicious way. His companions at work are no longer necessarily to be trusted. When they attempt to joke with him about his worried demeanor, trying to attribute his sleepless and agitated look to being involved in some immorality, Yáñez reacts as Garro did: "And how could he tell if they were teasing him or were just hired to spy on his words?" (*Y Matarazo no llamó*, 61).[52] Just as Yáñez acts as if he can trust no one, Garro and Helena began to suspect anyone entering their home in September 1968.

As recounted by Ramírez, their electricity suddenly went out, strange people came to the door, and some of their cats were killed (Ramírez, 80). Once all the servants had left one by one because of the strange events, they were able to find only one person who would work for them: José, a man sent by Garro's mother-in-law, Josefa de Paz. As Ramírez recounts their version of events (*La ingobernable*, 80–82), the two women began to suspect José of duplicity as well. In a scene that could well have been incorporated into *Y Matarazo no llamó*, Helena confronted José with the idea that he had been spying on them. When he would not confess, she searched for a gun that Madrazo had left with them and threatened to kill José if he did not admit his culpability (81). Garro and her daughter finally decided to leave their house and hide elsewhere any papers that could possibly incriminate them (having to do with Garro's involvement in agrarian issues), but first they tied José up with wire and locked him in a room. When they returned, José had disappeared. Josefa de Paz, who had sent them José, after all, called them to complain about the disconcerting way they had treated him, as if poor José was only an innocuous servant. While some aspects of this incident reappear in the novel, the role of the meddling mother-in-law, who is also unbearable and offensive, recurs in the fiction of Garro, first in "La culpa es de los tlaxcaltecas" but most notably in *Mi hermanita Magdalena* (My Little Sister Magdalena, 1998) (see Chapter 6).

Garro and her daughter indicate in interviews and in Helena's autobiography that the presence of a dying man who becomes a responsibility happened in Garro's own life. Re-created in the narrative of *Y Matarazo no llamó*, the body also can be read in a metaphorical manner for what it tells us about compassion and commitment on both the personal and national level. On a realistic plane, Yáñez becomes obsessed with this stranger in his home, showing a compassion and consideration for others that he had been unable to express in his marriage and his profession. His feeling of solidarity with the man is expressed not only by all he does for him—feeding him, finding medication—but by addressing him as "compañero." This body could well serve as the objective correlative of Garro's own fears and unhealthy relationship with Mexico at the time. T. S. Eliot had written in his essay "Hamlet and His Problems" (1919) about the objective correlative:

> The only way of expressing emotion in the form of art is by finding an "objective correlative"; in other words, a set of objects, a situation, a chain of events which shall be the formula of that particular emotion; such that when the external facts, which must terminate in sensory experience, are given, the emotion is immediately evoked. (100)

We can see the description of the decaying body in Eugenio Yáñez's home as an objective correlative signifying the loneliness, desolation, and despair of Garro/Yáñez's life. Although the body lies inert in bed in Eugenio's apartment, unable to move or react, its image contaminates Eugenio's well-being wherever he is. Concern and suspicion are normal reactions, but obsession marks the way Yáñez acts and reacts to all the events that follow his initial gesture of goodwill; it is the exaggeration that so closely parallels what others have described in Garro's actions during the fateful months of 1968. Excessive fear of José, people watching her home and spying on her, her name on a list of subversives—these may have occurred, but clearly the imprint of these events wreaked havoc on Garro's sense of well-being, and no amount of outside help was able to come to her rescue. Garro/Yáñez leaves the decaying body behind in an attempt to escape, but when the body dies, there is still no escape from the frightful fortune of the outcast or pariah. It is as if s/he is suffering from the plague and must be shunned by all. This image is used by Garro in a letter quoted by Mario Velázquez, writing a review of Lucía Melgar and Gabriela Mora's *Elena Garro: Lectura múltiple de una personalidad compleja* in *La crónica de hoy*. He includes this telling anecdote:

In a letter signed September 25, 1974, Elena Garro writes to Gabriela Mora what could probably be considered an objective synthesis of her life and work: "Dear Gabriela, if you consider that I have been living for six years without speaking to anyone, as if I were an annoyance and with the anguish of not having money, or hope of work, perhaps you would understand me. I don't understand what has happened to me. You tell me that I should write my personal biography; that is very easy. My downfall is not because of my education or my tendency to depend on my husband, but exactly the opposite!"[53]

Here we note her anguish at her "sick" condition ("apestada"—translated idiomatically as "nuisance"—gives the sense of being infected with plague, and she is treated as a pariah). This nameless moribund body may well be an alter ego for Garro and at the same time a symbol of the Mexican body politic, shown by the events of Tlatelolco to be decaying and corrupt. Whether it represents Garro or the Mexican people, the treatment of this defenseless, decomposing body shows that the innocent and law-abiding have little hope to survive.

Injustice and arbitrary violence are always alarming, and Eugenio's life becomes a nightmare of perplexity and persecution as he suddenly abandons his home and the dying man in order to escape being attacked by ominous strangers who appear to be searching for him. He waits for a call from Matarazo, but Matarazo never calls: Eugenio never receives the call of salvation. Before anyone can invade his home again, Eugenio escapes, hails a taxi, and, like the "dried leaf" (Azuela's "hoja seca") that he has become, begins his final trajectory that leads to his own capture and identification as a fugitive and government rebel: "he was escaping without knowing where or why he was fleeing" (95).[54] These lines, it should be noted, echo similar ones found in *Andamos huyendo Lola*. Clearly, Garro's protagonists, if not Garro herself, are obsessed by the need to escape their homes, haunted as they are by persecuting figures. Garro sends her protagonist off in a northerly direction, the same direction she chose when she began her exile in 1972.

Eugenio becomes a wanderer, hunted despite his innocence, consumed by anxiety. Garro shows her readers that one simple step of unselfishness can result in a concatenation of events that can lead to more than the loss of friends, material goods, peace of mind, physical health, and a homeland—it can bring upon one the ultimate sacrifice: loss of one's own life. In the northern city (still in Mexico) Eugenio continues to suffer from confusion and forebodings that he will not be able to escape this nightmare. He finally attempts a positive act by going to a church and asking for the priest's help, an age-old practice that ironically enough probably brings about his capture by government forces.

Once again, Eugenio appears to be an innocent, trusting in the priest when it appears to the reader that the priest might well be an accomplice of the police. Some men attack the car in which the priest and Eugenio presume to be making their escape (118). At first the reader concludes either that the priest is as naïve as Yáñez and did not realize that they were being followed or that he agreed to betray Yáñez. At any rate, Garro implies that no one can be trusted to help the innocent—and worse, being blameless is no protection against false arrest and torture.

The police accuse Eugenio of being a rebel, assassin, and traitor to the country, using colorful idiomatic expressions such as "tumbagobiernos" (someone willing to overthrow the government), "cabrón asesino" (son of a bitch assassin), and "cabrón traidor de la patria" (son of a bitch traitor to the fatherland) (119). He is savagely beaten, stripped, blindfolded, threatened with imminent death, only to be taken to Mexico City and imprisoned in the same cell with another man whose voice he finally recognizes—it is Matarazo! The two are at last reunited only to realize that neither of them has understood the tempest into which they have been hurled. Eugenio simply wanted to be of use to the strikers, giving cigarettes in exchange for companionship; he only wanted to assist the wounded man who had been left on his doorstep. He winds up being accused of beating to death the man he had tried to save. Ironically, he becomes identified with the strikers and is himself transformed into the tortured and dying man. Instead of finding a "Eugenio" to help him and make his final hours more comfortable, he is paired in jail with Matarazo, whose name recalls the verb *matar* (to kill) and reminds us of "death blow" in Spanish, symbolic of his meaning for Eugenio. Both Eugenio and Matarazo receive the death blow: the two of them are killed in cold blood by the police, who make it appear as if they had attempted to escape.[55]

The novel does not end with the scene of their assassination but with the commentaries of all those whose lives had been touched by Eugenio. As readers, we are privy to the "truth" of his activities and can judge with impunity the reactions of his co-workers, his boss, various people from the city of Torreón, the priest, and, finally, the striking workers whose intervention in his life had started him down the fatal path toward his death. We learn that some, like the boss, are shallow and stupid and willingly believe the newspaper accounts that call Eugenio an assassin. The priest ultimately is depicted as a naïve character, who did not realize how the police would behave toward Eugenio. He insists that "Yáñez was a just man" (132) and that the newspaper reports are false.[56]

Yáñez and Matarazo find out too late that the leaders of the strike had turned their records over to the police and then escaped to Acapulco. They led their followers into a massacre only to escape from harm themselves, which certainly matches Garro's own attitude about the intellectuals who had served as counselors to the students: "The professors and the leftist leaders were the ones who led them in the dangerous enterprise and then betrayed them."[57]

From Pedro and Tito the reader learns that Ignacio and Eulalio, the supposed leaders of the strike, had been working with the police all along and had probably tortured the man left at Eugenio's home, selected by chance: "'They chose Yáñez because they saw him with us and they had to hide something. ... Sold out,' ... repeated Pedro in a low voice" (235).[58] We are encouraged to believe Pedro and Tito because, of all the characters, they alone remain loyal to their revolutionary ideals and express at the end what appears to be the author's voice. They explain the craftiness of Eulalio and Ignacio, who betray the rest to save themselves. Worse, Ignacio and Eulalio give false statements to the newspapers suggesting that the workers' movement was being infiltrated by petit bourgeois types like Matarazo and Eugenio—fabrications meant to place the blame on others and exculpate themselves for their own treachery. Garro seems to suggest parallels with the student rebellions that preceded the Tlatelolco Massacre. One telling point is that Yáñez inexorably finds death once he leaves the safety of his home and flees to northern Mexico. In contrast, though she shares so many experiences with Yáñez, including his sense of helplessness and frustration, Garro did not end up dying physically. She managed to eke out an existence (see Chapter 6).

We learn from the details and descriptions included in *Y Matarazo no llamó* how duplicitous, unreliable, and corrupt the Mexican government is—ideas that were also clearly articulated by Paz in *The Critique of the Pyramid*. Certainly, if we wish to understand the historical context for the violent reaction of the state against its own citizens—mostly the young generation of students— we can opt to read his essay. The reader receives a historical overview of the Mexican political system and the way the PRI evolved from the Aztec rulers (Tlatoani), through the viceroys of the colonial period, up to the twentieth century and the aftermath of the 1910 Mexican Revolution. Reading Paz's essay in the twenty-first century, we can still appreciate his historical observations. But many more essays and studies have documented and enlarged upon the historical context of the Tlatelolco Massacre. A far more personalized and human perspective is found in Garro's novel *Y Matarazo no llamó* and in her play *Sócrates y los gatos*. Ongoing governmental oppression, official corruption, and unreliable officials (not to mention unreliable narrators) are some of the topics found in these texts. But Garro has been able to re-create with graphic details and unforgettable actions the emotions that will forever be associated with Tlatelolco: the fear, the surprise, the terror, and the final disillusionment and despair. These same emotions are associated with the disturbing events that took place in Nicaragua under the Somozas (1937–1979), in Argentina during the Proceso de Reorganización (National Reorganization Process or Dirty War, 1976–1983), and in Chile under Augusto Pinochet (1973–1990), to cite some examples. Garro's work will find resonance within readers from other countries and in other historical contexts, because the emotions she engenders in her readers unfortunately can be applied to many contemporary political systems. Independently of how history may judge their actions during the events as they unfolded, Paz's essay becomes quite particular and circumscribed, while Garro's text pertains to a wider and more all-inclusive audience.

"I believe that in this world love is very difficult."
ELENA GARRO
in Rosas Lopátegui and Toruño, "Entrevista"

"It is not for nothing that love has been compared to war."
OCTAVIO PAZ
The Double Flame

FROM CIVIL WAR TO GENDER WAR
THE BATTLE OF THE SEXES

AS THE PREVIOUS CHAPTERS HAVE SHOWN, wars between nations as well as civil wars and conflicts between races and tribes and even within families have inspired notable works of literature. Indeed, as John Limon reminds us in his study of American (meaning U.S.) war fiction, *Writing after War*, the pedigree of traditional literary history begins with Homer (194).[1] Moreover, as Jean Bethke Elshtain's *Women and War* illustrates, conflicts have traditionally been represented in highly gendered ways. The great canonical Latin American novels of the early twentieth century often dealt with wars between man and nature, where "man" refers not to "humankind" but in effect to the exploits of men (think of José Eustasio Rivera's *La vorágine* [The Whirlpool, 1924], about one man's battle with the Colombian jungle). Later novels focused on "man" (now more or less humankind) and inner human conflicts (think of the Argentine Ernesto Sábato's *El túnel* [The Tunnel, 1948] or Chilean María Luisa Bombal's *La última niebla* [1935; translated as *House of Mist*, 1947]). In this chapter I want to focus on a fundamental category of war that has been ongoing from time immemorial: the battle of the sexes. Based on military imagery, the expression "war between the sexes" conjures up the idea of a relationship marked by intrigue, treachery, power struggles, displacements, violence, injury, victimization, and death. Elena Garro and Octavio Paz enter into the fray of the battle of the sexes from very different perspectives—and different positions of power.

The ongoing hostilities between Garro and Paz and the contrast in their professional personas become most evident nationally and internationally in the post-Tlatelolco period. From 1968 to 1970 Paz served as a visiting professor of Spanish American literature at the University of Texas at Austin, the University of Pittsburgh, and the University of Pennsylvania. He was honored as the Simón Bolívar Professor of Latin American Studies (1970) and Fellow of Churchill College (1970–1971) and Charles Eliot Norton Professor of Poetry at Harvard University (1971–1972). On returning to Mexico, he founded and was editor of *Plural,* the literary supplement to the well-known daily *Excélsior* from 1971 to 1976. With the demise of *Plural* because of government pressure, he then became editor of *Vuelta,* which enjoyed a reputation as one of the foremost literary journals in the Hispanic world and which provided him with the means to function as an independent critic of Mexico's political system and the PRI.[2] From the seventies onward, Paz increasingly became known in international literary, academic, and cultural circles; his books were published and translated into many languages. After his divorce from Garro in 1959 (or 1963, according to other sources),[3] he enjoyed a happy marriage to Marie-José Tramini, whom he had met in India and married in 1964. In addition, he was recognized with important literary prizes, culminating in the Nobel Award for Literature in 1990. Clearly, by all objective criteria, the post-Tlatelolco period was productive and positive for Paz.

Garro, who had been living apart from Paz since before the divorce, continued to live in Mexico City with their daughter, Helena, during the 1960s. She had won the prestigious Villaurrutia Prize in 1963 for *Los recuerdos del porvenir* and brought out the short story collection *La semana de colores* in 1964. From 1964 to 1968 she was a combative journalist, expressing an independent, confrontational perspective on the important political issues of the day in the newspapers and journals of Mexico—including forthright support of controversial figures like Rubén Jaramillo (1900–1962), the leader of the campesinos, and Carlos Madrazo (1915–1969), the outspoken critic of the PRI. Patricia Rosas Lopátegui compiled and published these articles, which deserve careful study and analysis; but Garro did not publish (or was prevented from publishing) her creative fiction until 1980, when her next collection of short stories came out—*Andamos huyendo Lola* (We Are Fleeing Lola), followed in 1981 by the novel *Testimonios sobre Mariana,* which was awarded the Juan Grijalbo Prize despite uneven reviews. Garro received no further distinctions until 1996, when *Busca mi esquela* (translated as *First Love*, 1997) received the Sor Juana Inés de la Cruz Prize. How can we explain this long period of silence or lack of publication? Was it inertia, idleness, inactivity? In the case of Garro we cannot attribute the absence of publications to the absence of texts to be published.[4] She often said that she wrote many of the later novels and short stories during those years of exile; but it was only after 1980, when the "curtain" or "ban" was lifted, that she was able to bring to light the works she had already created.

In consideration of this publishing silence, it is evident that the discursive warfare between these two cultural icons was weighted heavily in favor of Paz for a while, until some feminist readers, more partisan than others, joined in on Garro's side and accepted all that she confessed as gospel. Clearly, we should be cautious in evaluating Garro's interpretation with regard to Paz and the intellectual establishment, since she was always inventive in her comments, in real life as in her literary texts (all is fair in love and war).

We learn from Elena Garro's letters and interviews, as well as the books published subsequently, that she reacted after 1968 as if under constant siege— as if under attack by forces that she identified not only with the government but with her ex-husband, Octavio Paz.[5] Based on her own fictive world of creation and her personal behavior, Garro seems to have felt that she was engaged in yet another battle, not for the rights of workers or for the indigenous minorities of Mexico but for women's rights—in particular, her rights and those of her daughter. She did not call herself a feminist, because for Mexican women in her generation that word often meant being "anti-men" or lesbian; nevertheless, Garro's narratives did protest against the minority status of women and their inferior position vis-à-vis the masculine world.[6] Considering the way she portrays relations between men and women in her texts, we could easily use the conventional phrase "war between the sexes" to describe gender relations in Garro's work. Octavio Paz's depictions of gender relations vary, depending on genre. For example, in his essays he rarely thinks of women as part of the "we" of national identity, considering them as the "other" (see Chapter 1). In his poetry and drama, women are objects as well as metaphors for art (see the articles by Biron and others). Did he ever acknowledge the real issues dealing with women's role in Mexican society?

When critics analyze the oeuvre of Octavio Paz, their focus is rarely on the representation of the women in his life—or on the women described in his texts. The two exceptions include Paz's dedication to the Tenth Muse, the major woman writer of Mexican letters—Sor Juana Inés de la Cruz (1648– 1695). His massive (over 600 pages) magnum opus, *Sor Juana Inés de la Cruz o las trampas de la fe* (1983; translated as *Sor Juana or the Traps of Faith*, 1988), is a "biography, critical study and historical treatise" (Santí, "Sor Juana," 102). At the opposite pole, Paz is continually associated with the other historical woman who is the "first female" of the Conquest, La Malinche, about whom Paz wrote perhaps two full pages in *The Labyrinth of Solitude*. Ironically, this limited discourse nevertheless has projected him as the recognized expert on male-female relations in Mexico. His brief "portrait" of La Malinche, we recall, is found in "The Sons of La Malinche," a chapter that has more to do with machismo than with Malinche lore.

Perhaps I should clarify that Paz does not ignore all aspects of "gender" issues—in fact, his writings in *The Labyrinth* are often the starting point for critics who wish to discuss machismo in Mexico. Debra Castillo, for example, suggests that Paz's work has to do with "masculinist studies" (20). The many essays and books on masculinities in Mexico and Latin America in general that have become popular in the twenty-first century begin with reference to Paz's ideas on machismo and his discussion of the role of the *chingón* in Mexican culture.[7] It is de rigueur for most commentators on Mexican culture to begin with Paz, just as it is with regard to anything to do with La Malinche.

Paz's love poems as well as his essay collection *La llama doble* (The Double Flame, 1993) are relevant in discussing the theme of love. His published ideas about women reflect a traditional patriarchal view and in one sense represent what feminists would react against: why are women the Other or the submissive ones in a relationship? Why must women be talked about, instead of being subjects of their own discourse?

For Mexican women—and for women globally—Paz does not offer a discursive space of agency, except for his acclaimed study of the woman who is considered perhaps the greatest writer of colonial America and Mexican letters: Sor Juana Inés de la Cruz. As Margo Glantz notes, "Sor Juana can easily be called the founder of the literary tree, the primeval mother of his genealogy, and the only one who is as great as himself" (Glantz, "Octavio Paz and Sor Juana," 130). She adds: "Sor Juana cannot be spoken of now without thinking of Octavio Paz. And even if some of his concepts about her could be disputed, his authority is so great that one thinks one is transgressing the law when one tries to contest his words. He has become the guardian of her door" (130). His interest in Sor Juana can be traced as far back as his publication of "Homenaje a Sor Juana Inés de la Cruz en su tercer centenario (1651 [sic]–1695)" (Homage to Sor Juana on the Third Centenary of Her Birth) in the Argentine literary journal *Sur* (December 1951) and then his fifth chapter of *El laberinto de la soledad*. For Paz, Sor Juana was both "transgressor and victim" (Santí, "Sor Juana," 102), having been co-opted in her last days by the orthodox bureaucracy of the Catholic Church in Counter-Reformation New Spain, just as so many Latin American intellectuals in the twentieth century were co-opted by their governments. He sees her as embodying "the situation of the twentieth-century intellectual, especially in totalitarian countries. Also, of course, the Latin American intellectual, understood as the one who struggles with constituted powers and with society but who is stripped of all weapons, except his or her pen" (Santí, "Sor Juana," 103). According to Santí, Paz attempts to restore "the work of this woman poet to its rightful place within the canon of Hispanic Golden Age literature alongside better known male peers like Calderón de la Barca, Góngora and Quevedo" ("Sor Juana," 102).

In a broad sense, Paz might be seen as engaged in feminist politics, enlarging the canon to include an important Baroque woman poet. But Sor Juana had not been neglected or ignored before Paz's book. The critical materials focusing on her were certainly numerous, especially as the feminist movement gained strength in the twentieth century (see Merrim); some key feminist readings of her work were even published prior to 1983. An important essay by Dorothy Schons in *Modern Philology* in 1926, for example, was the first feminist reading of Sor Juana; as Georgina Sabat de Rivers points out, Schons attributes a certain amount of agency to Sor Juana with regard to her decisions about withdrawing from the social world ("Octavio Paz ante Sor Juana," 422).

Schons's perspective is very different from that of earlier reviewers, especially Father Diego Calleja and the critic Ludwig Pfandl, whom Paz critiques but never goes so far as to suggest they were sexists. Perhaps within the sphere of the sexual politics of literary reception, particularly for patriarchal critics outside Mexico, Paz's dedication of his critical time to Sor Juana would indicate that she was worthy of their perusal as well. While Santí claims that Paz's book is "far and away the culmination of that canon" ("Sor Juana," 103), he also suggests that Paz's reading of Sor Juana casts her variously as a New Spanish intellectual suffering from "double loneliness as a woman and intellectual" (112) and as a "melancholy loner" (116).

For Paz she was neither a pious exemplar nor a martyred dissident but a "betrayed accomplice" and an "active agent" (Santí, "Sor Juana," 116). Unlike those who read Sor Juana's actions within religious terms, Paz saw her actions in political terms. He has been criticized for his comparison of the church's treatment of Sor Juana to the Russian dissident Nikolai Bukharin's treatment by Joseph Stalin (Sabat de Rivers, quoted by Santí, "Sor Juana,"

118). For Paz the two cases are similar examples of intellectuals who are forced to change their behavior or be faced with death. He suggests that Sor Juana was "terrorized into submission because she was a woman intellectual" (Santí, "Sor Juana," 119), while more traditional feminists claim that she refused to be intimidated, because she acted out of religious conviction. Here we see Paz in the middle of a debate about the "first" Mexican feminist—whether she was terrorized into accepting the dictates of a harsh bureaucracy or whether she preferred eternal salvation of her soul, capitulated to the dictates of the Catholic Church, and therefore gave up writing at the end of her life. What is intriguing in Paz's arguments about Sor Juana is that her case may have foreshadowed not only the victims of Stalinist purges but also Paz's sense of his own status within Mexican cultural life as it was dictated by the PRI. Subsequently he formally rebelled by renouncing his ambassadorship to India in 1968 as a result of the Tlatelolco Massacre. In a telling phrase he admits that he identifies personally with Sor Juana, so that he could say, "un poco como Flaubert: 'Madame Bovary, c'est moi'" (a bit like Flaubert: "Madame Bovary it's me"; *Obras completas*, 16:547). Sheridan calls Sor Juana Paz's "semblable" (likeness) and says that many times when Paz talks about Sor Juana "es sobre sí mismo" (it's about himself; *Poeta con paisaje*, 54, 45).

Despite his strong literary and personal identification with the Mexican colonial poet, Paz is not the writer I would most consider an avatar of Sor Juana. Rather, it is Garro herself who is identified as the most important woman writer since Sor Juana and whose life bears similarities to the persecution suffered by the nun.[8]

In spite of his sense of persecution, Paz was not prevented from publishing in 1968, as was Sor Juana in the 1690s. On the contrary, his poems, essays, and books were always in print and were consistently translated throughout the world. Earlier in his career, when his fellow intellectuals were mostly practicing and strident Communists, he felt some constraints concerning his political position vis-à-vis communism. He was horrified in the thirties with the way the doctrinaire Communists treated André Gide when the French writer tried to alert them to the deficiencies in the Stalinist system. Nevertheless, Paz was not ostracized but rather was able to initiate his own journals with a group of confreres, publish with the top Mexican publishers, and find translators for his texts even after leaving government service.

Elena Garro is the one who was apparently restrained for the most part from 1968 until 1980 because of her anti-institutional stance and her complaints about the "bishops" in power. Like Sor Juana, Garro was silenced as a published writer. Ironically, then, of the two Mexican iconic figures with whom he is associated as a critic, Paz is less like Sor Juana but can be considered a *malinchista*, using his own definition from *The Labyrinth of Solitude*. Paz always appreciated outside influences, married a foreigner after rejecting a Mexican, and became alienated from his child. Garro is the woman intellectual who suffered the "double loneliness as a woman and intellectual" that Paz attributed to Sor Juana (Santí, "Sor Juana," 112).

While Paz may be the keeper of Sor Juana's legacy, he actively "decoupled" himself from one of Sor Juana's major successors, on a personal and professional level. Few people outside Mexico who are not literary specialists actually know that Paz was first married to Elena Garro. Ironically, as Elena Poniatowska has commented, too often critics invoke Paz when discussing Garro, as if it is impossible to understand her without him. Although it is rarely discussed, there was a time when Paz's work acknowledged Garro's presence in his life. The young Garro was his inspiration in the love poetry he wrote in the 1930s that formed part of *Raíz del hombre* and the sonnets in *Bajo tu clara sombra* (Under Your Clear Shadow), some of which were later expunged from his oeuvre or, as Guillermo Sheridan notes, "no guardada" (not kept; *Poeta con paisaje*, 152). In commenting on the love poems of *Bajo tu clara sombra*, Sheridan further notes that some of the descriptors relating to the beloved's characteristics prevailed as a consistent yet paradoxical part of Garro's relationship to Paz: "su carácter a la vez fugitivo y perdurable" (her character at once elusive and everlasting; 155).

Luis Enrique Ramírez suggests that references to Garro can also be discerned in two other poems: the masterful "Piedra de sol" (Sunstone) and "Pasado en claro" (A Draft of Shadows) (*La ingobernable*, 100). In his conversations with Garro, Ramírez discussed the possibility that the beautiful, enigmatic, and destructive wave in Paz's short story "Mi vida con la ola" (My Life with the Wave) might be a reference to her (*La ingobernable*, 100). Such a reading of this highly metaphoric piece is possible; but as capricious and enticing as the wave may be, it is not obvious that Garro might be a subtext.[9] Most of the critical or biographical materials about Paz, especially those written outside of Mexico, rarely even mention that he had been married to Garro.

Ironically, Paz later served as Garro's muse, motivating the negative portraits of male figures in her later novels (*Testimonios sobre Mariana, Inés, Mi hermanita Magdalena*), an issue I develop below.

The relationship between Paz and Garro from the outset was characterized by conflicts and differing perspectives regarding gender roles as well as ideologies, a true battle of the sexes. Their problematic marriage, on the personal level, mirrors many of the male-female relations depicted in representative Mexican texts (whether *Los de abajo* or *La muerte de Artemio Cruz*, *Balún-Canán* or *Los recuerdos del porvenir*). Rumors about the difficult marriage between Paz and Garro always circulated among the Mexican intellectual community. Letters between the young Paz and his *novia*, archived at the Princeton Library collection, attest that he was quite traditional in his attitude toward his wife.[10] In the post-'68 years Paz almost never openly wrote about his relationship with Garro and erased her name from his official biography and most interviews, so we learn much more about the conflicts marking their union from the pen of Garro as well as from the memoirs of their daughter, Helena Paz Garro.

In *Memorias de España 1937*, which documents Garro's version of their first year of marriage and their experiences during the Spanish Civil War, disagreements in their attitudes are immediately discernible. She was not hesitant to admit that Paz was frequently critical of her actions, her "bourgeois" behavior, and what he saw as her lack of political awareness or commitment to the Republican cause (20). Readers can easily identify Garro's attack on Paz and the patriarchy in her many comments regarding her treatment by Paz and his new acquaintances (see Chapter 4). Despite having had her own creative voice before marriage, she lost her independence as well as her birth name (Garro) as soon as she married Paz and became known as his wife, "Elena de Paz." She suffered by being deprived of her individual identity but did not always express her rebellion until she began to write in her own voice.[11] Treated as a typical Mexican wife, she needed her husband's permission to travel, to take her own child out of the country, and to deal with her finances.

Garro's reaction to this societal structure is expressed strongly and repeatedly in her work. The aggrieved wife as a voiceless, powerless victim is a constant image in her texts. The novels she was able to publish after her extended period of professional silence (1968–1980) are read as romans à clef that describe her life with Paz and her bellicose attitude toward him. *Testimonios sobre Mariana* and to a lesser degree *Mi hermanita Magdalena* are cited as examples of Garro's use of her literary voice to attack Paz. I argue, however, that Garro is criticizing Mexican *machista* society in toto rather than merely her own experiences.

Unfortunately, the literary representation of the battle of the sexes has been hampered from the women's perspective by the many religious, political, and cultural prohibitions regarding woman's role in many societies. For example,

Shirley Nelson Garner brings these problems to the surface in her study of the difficulties of the Chinese American writer Maxine Hong Kingston. Garner reminds us of the proverb "Mulierem ornat silentium" (Silence garnisheth a woman) by the cleric Richard Taverner, who adds that "the Apostle Paul requireth, while he forbiddeth Women in the Church or congregation to speak, but willeth them to ask their husbands at home, if they be in doubt of anything" (quoted by Garner, 117). The Christian cultural heritage not only esteemed chastity in women but also placed a value on silence, whereas men were praised for their oratory in the public sphere and for bravery on the field of battle. Garner's observations are also valid in the Hispanic world: silence is considered a virtue for women, so that "speaking itself becomes an act of assertion. Speaking in public becomes a radical act—a movement away from woman's role, a vast impropriety" (Garner, 118). Feminist artists "talk about 'breaking silence' as a crucial experience." Garner names Adrienne Rich, Audre Lorde, and Tillie Olsen as writers for whom silence is a central theme.[12] For Garro, too, silence is one of the themes she shares with these Anglo women as well as with other Mexican feminists. Rosario Castellanos, a contemporary, clearly represents in her work the negative consequences for women and for Mexican culture when women are constrained to silence.[13]

Garro explores the dictum against female talk in a number of texts, most notably *Los recuerdos del porvenir* and *Testimonios sobre Mariana*;[14] but with regard to her own life experiences, breaking her silence as a writer was not always in her control. According to many of the interviews she gave, Garro openly blamed Paz first for her inability to become a writer and then for her inability to publish in the post-1968 years.[15] When she did speak out on political issues, however, she suffered great personal anguish, especially during the time of the Tlatelolco Massacre (see Chapter 5). Evidently forces beyond Paz account for Garro's marginalization and exile. At the same time, Paz enjoyed greater freedom related to his growing stature as a renowned intellectual and was more insulated from repercussions than Garro was. Garro truly feared for her life, as she and Helena Paz claimed.[16]

As noted, Garro had always been concerned with the theme of silence from her earliest texts (including *Los recuerdos del porvenir* and plays such as *Los perros* [The Dogs], 1965; *Andarse por las ramas* [Beat about the Bush], 1957; and *La mudanza* [The Move], 1959), but she becomes more focused on the issue in the post-1980 narratives (*Testimonios sobre Mariana*, *Reencuentro de personajes* [Reunion of Characters], 1982; *Inés*, 1995). Garro explores the nature of "cultural silence," portraying how the social milieu influences her women characters.[17]

Many of the women are silent, as Lucía Melgar has illustrated, or unexpressive, so that they are labeled insane. Melgar has also shown that Garro's texts depict a wide range of silences: "Garro's texts augment the gamut of silences and show not only that the 'muteness' of subordinate groups is a product of a sociohistorical process in great measure institutionalized, but also that the silence of 'mute' groups or individuals can be in fact a chosen silence, an expressive option" ("Violencia y silencio," 13).[18]

It is easy to assume that the women protagonists of Garro's novels are her alter egos because they are characterized as living in exile, often with a lone daughter, and suffering in extreme poverty because of the evil machinations of a husband. The assumption is that Garro is "just" reflecting on her own familiar life experiences, the same patterns of behavior that she has suffered, and the identical relationships with men, with no subtlety, only "exposé." Garro, as a woman, is said to have written thinly veiled "autobiography," while Octavio Paz's publications are categorized as essays, philosophical explorations of major issues of the day (for example, *El laberinto, Posdata*, and *El ogro filantrópico*). He wrote "major texts" on the culture and history of his native Mexico, on world politics, and on many other topics. *Itinerary*, his foray into biography, was described as "an intellectual autobiography," with the adjective bearing the weight of what defines him—his ideas, his commitment to work for freedom, publicly and politically. Paz's observations and opinions were printed as essays, and his interviews were also published in profusion in many languages. Garro's portrayal of gender relations and their impact on society offers a powerful message that transcends Mexican national identity and temporal constraints.

Instead of viewing Garro's work as veiled autobiography, I believe that her women characters are not reflections of the author "Garro" alone but are her representation of the distortions she had come to signify in the war between the sexes. These fictive women, moreover, are attracted to men who are victimizers, and in their uncommunicative state they eventually trigger their own death (think of Mariana in particular or Inés).

Despite these autobiographical "echoes," I still would not want to identify these characters as avatars of Garro but as portraits of women she critiques, examines, and holds up for scrutiny and criticism. None of these women are positive role models; nor are they likable, assertive, or productive. Mariana (*Testimonios sobre Mariana*), Lola (*Andamos huyendo Lola*), and Verónica (*Reencuentro de personajes*) may be as attractive to men as Garro was and may enjoy wearing fine fur coats and eating in elegant restaurants, as she did, but that is as far as the resemblance should be carried. On the superficial level, they are women with needs that are not met by their male companions. As for their inner life, these women are all unassertive and fearful, led around by the males in their lives. It may well be that Garro the woman often felt overwhelmed by her circumstances: the economic difficulties, the political ostracism, her literary marginalization for so many years. One wishes that her characters would have been able to overcome their circumstances, but the society that would have enabled them to do so had not yet been so structured. As a writer, however, she wielded a powerful pen that illustrated how women had been and still could be crushed by the patriarchy.

For all of Garro's complaints about Paz and her documented fears and anxieties, she was able to write and produce a great many narratives in which she re-created the kinds of women that we would find as vulnerable and weak as the persona she often projected in her own letters to friends. Was Garro the writer also vulnerable and weak? Was she haunted by men so that she was unable to speak, unable to produce her work? Did she remain a victim?[19] Clearly, whatever the "real Garro" felt, the writer Garro cannot be considered a victim of silence or madness; the many novels she was finally able to publish testify to her successful expression and her courage as a warrior in the battle of the sexes. Of course, some readers may find the texts unsuccessful or perhaps, worst of all, not consider them literary accomplishments. If we expect to read them as romans à clef alone, as a way to find out the gossip and scandals of the Mexican and Latin American literati, then we discern only one side of the story. It seems more probable that Garro, like other women writers, used her texts to uncover the history distorted or ignored by the hegemonic structure. As Jean Franco (*Plotting Women*, 230) and Josefina Ludmer remind us, many Latin American women writers have had to make use of subversive techniques in order to bring to the surface their forgotten/denied stories.

I suggest, moreover, that Garro is not above playing with her readers and taking advantage of the sensationalism that surrounds romans à clef, encouraging the associations between her own life and her narratives. For example, naming the repellent husband of Mariana "Augusto" would clearly associate him with "Octavio"; is this a literary device that acknowledges the rumors and encourages more people to buy the book to learn about the inner torments of their life together? *Testimonios* serves as a manipulation by Garro—a way for her to influence the view of her previous relationship with Paz. In the battle of the sexes, we may say that Garro is using subterfuge, a stratagem to "get even" for the supposed poor treatment she first suffered at the hands of Paz and his mother.[20] But just as Mariana, the wife who has been equated with

Elena, is never present as a first person narrator, Elena is not really Mariana, and Octavio is Augusto only in the way many Mexican men are authoritarian, patriarchal, and oppressive to their wives.

Clearly, for most of her life, Garro was neither a slave nor a wife. In the strength of her voice and the power of her passion, she has shown herself to be a woman warrior engaged in one of the great battles of the sexes: to express herself freely.

With regard to gender issues, it is easy to place Paz the human being on the traditionalist side, especially after reading his letters to Garro when they were first engaged. According to Melgar, Paz treated Garro as a traditional Mexican male would ("Octavio Paz y Helena Garro"), notwithstanding the few positive comments that he did publish about *Recollections* ("Novela y provincia," 143–144). Yet, overshadowing any encouraging comments is the dialogue often repeated by Helena Paz, in which Paz is fearfully, tearfully, reproaching Garro for her talent. The daughter recounts that after reading her work, Paz would weep and say, "You are a genius . . . You are a better writer than I am" (*Memorias*, 80).[21] He would plead with Garro to burn the work, which she somehow would agree to do; then, Helena Paz comments, "my father would become happy" (*Memorias*, 81).[22]

It is not my purpose to engage in fruitless evaluations of which of the two is the "better" writer or whose story is more credible as it relates to their marriage. But it is important to remember that Paz's place in the Latin American and international canon is secure, while Garro only relatively recently has entered a more widespread critical arena. Most of her plays and novels still have not been translated into many languages, while Paz is certainly one of the most translated and recognized writers of Latin America. Garro was not considered a canonical writer and was not part of U.S. academic reading lists during the 1970s and 1980s.[23] As a reflection of critical neglect (as is true about women writers in general: see Cypess, "¿Quién ha oído hablar de ellas?"), a review of the MLA bibliographic entries shows that perhaps only about a dozen essays on Garro's work were published from 1964 until 1980.[24] From 1964 to 1980 over 300 entries deal with aspects of Paz's work. From 1980 to 2009 I found 304 on Garro and 1,063 on Paz.[25]

For all the years of their marriage, by Garro's own admission as well as in comments found in letters by Paz or others, she apparently never did behave as a proper wife who would fit into the traditional idea of a spouse for a Mexican diplomat. In the 1950s and 1960s Garro spoke out in favor of indigenist rights and supported the cause of the antigovernment worker Rubén Jaramillo. Paz, who was a low-level government functionary at the time, was told by Mexican president Adolfo López Mateos: "[Y]our wife bothers me a lot, send her out of Mexico" (quoted by Vega, 127). Garro was criticized not only for her outspoken behavior and her support of causes directly opposed to government policies, such as indigenist problems and the rights of railroad workers. She was also rather openly associated with men other than her husband, from the internationally famous Argentine writer Adolfo Bioy Casares to the politically controversial Mexican political reformer Carlos Madrazo.

Garro must have been a fascinating woman indeed, as intellectual as Sor Juana. She certainly was the belle of the court if we are to believe the letters of her admirers like José Bianco, the Argentine writer she first met in Paris in 1946. Bianco describes her as almost perfect: he is a friend who, "when compar[ing] you to the rest of the women (all, without exception), finds them boring, banal, vain, unintelligent" (quoted by Melgar, "Correspondencias literarias," 426).[26]

Just as Garro included a portrait of Bianco in *Testimonios sobre Mariana*, in the guise of Pepe, Bianco offers a portrait of Garro in his novel *La pérdida del reino* (Lost Paradise, 1972). Their correspondence has been archived at Princeton University; it reveals how Bianco, in supposed contrast to Paz at the time, encouraged Garro to write and idolized her above other women, unlike the way Paz supposedly treated her during their years in Paris.

More controversial was Garro's relationship with the renowned Argentine writer Adolfo Bioy Casares (1914–1999), whose letters to Garro from the forties through the sixties have also been preserved in the archives at Princeton University. Readers of the memoirs of Helena Paz learn that their relationship was not quite the way it was described in Garro's novel *Testimonios sobre Mariana*. Garro and Bioy Casares first became lovers in 1949, when they both were married—she to Paz and he to the poet Silvina Ocampo (1903–1993).[27] Some readers find a depiction of Garro in Bioy's novel *El sueño de los héroes* (The Dream of Heroes, 1954) (Ramírez, 100).

Garro has also been linked to Archibald Burns, the impresario who befriended her in real life and who also appears transformed into a character of *Testimonios sobre Mariana*. Helena Paz openly discusses various details about their relationship, and their love affair is also alluded to by other writers. Interestingly, the daughter mentions (but without much elaboration) the various women in Paz's life during the time of their marriage, as does Sheridan in *Poeta con paisaje*. Garro evidently was enchanting, as Carballo describes her in the 1950s, when he would frequent their "salon," along with other young writers:

Elena was a beautiful woman, but when she would speak she became transformed and something made her the most beautiful, most intelligent, most
ethereal woman, the one who would pronounce the last words of a gathering. Together, Paz and Garro, the talent was on the side of Garro. (quoted in
Ramírez, 43)[28]

Perhaps most meaningful in regard to her own political profile is her relationship with Carlos Madrazo, who had been national president of the PRI (Partido
Revolucionario Institucional) between 1964 and 1965.[29] In the fifties Garro
had already been involved with the struggle for human rights for farmwork-
ers, who came from mostly indigenous and mestizo populations. She had been
friends with Rubén Jaramillo, the campesino leader, who was assassinated by
government forces in May 1962. Through her work as a journalist for *La Cultura en México* and with the leftist newspapers *Sucesos* and *¿Por Qué?* Garro
befriended politicians like Carlos Madrazo, Javier Rojo Gómez, and Norberto
Aguirre Palancares. Madrazo had a major role in the PRI, but his disillusionment with the ruling faction led him to consider forming his own party, the
Patria Nueva (New Homeland) (Melgar-Palacios and Mora, 317). Garro wrote
a series of essays in Mexican journals in 1965 through 1968 that discussed the
political ideas of Madrazo as well as her own critique of the Mexican government, especially what she considered its racism and mistreatment of its indigenous population.[30] Madrazo and Garro were involved in a number of political
plans, which were cut short when he died in a plane accident in June 1969.
Rumors suggest that the crash was really an assassination, in view of Madrazo's
anti-PRI stance (Hernández Rodríguez, *El caso de Carlos A. Madrazo*, 19). This
claim has never been proven but is unofficially considered reliable.

While Garro's personal life might be described as the life of a liberated
woman, this is only true in some ways. She was able to act on some of her
beliefs about women's rights, but she was chastised for this by her peers. Although she always had a few important supporters among Mexican intellectuals
after 1968—especially the renowned dramatist Emilio Carballido—she became
associated with the wrong side of intellectual life in Mexican culture. Rightly
or mistakenly, Garro began to feel more and more persecuted and finally went
into self-imposed exile, not for three years (like Paz) but for decades. Garro
left Mexico—or made her escape, as she might have put it—with her daughter
in 1972, under pressure from Mexican president Luis Echeverría, who had
been minister of the interior during the Tlatelolco Massacre. For twenty years
mother and daughter moved about, from New York (1972–1974), to Madrid

(1974–1981), and then to Paris (1981–1993), feeling hunted and aggrieved. Their lives were penurious; Garro claims that they had to subsist on her earnings as a writer, and she had great difficulty in publishing her work.

Obviously the "word" is everything for writers, and the ability to get their words into the public arena is even more important. Not being able to publish was a burden for Garro. According to those in whom she confided, she began to blame Paz more and more, for in her mind he was the guilty party responsible for her inability to publish her work. This topic of who was responsible for her long silence in publishing is discussed by a number of critics. According to Toruño and Rosas Lopátegui, Garro was persecuted by Paz. Other critics, such as Christopher Domínguez and Elena Poniatowska, have been quick to suggest that perhaps it was Garro herself and her "paranoia" that caused the silence surrounding her work. Gabriela Mora, who maintained a long correspondence with Garro and shows her objectivity in dealing with the writer, suggests that Garro's personal behavior was not the only reason for this prolonged silence.[31]

Garro's ongoing struggles in favor of political and human rights for the disenfranchised workers and indigenous peoples of Mexico and her use of her imagination and esthetic prowess to "redeem" the plight of women become even more poignant in light of Paz's agenda in writing about Sor Juana. Paz was busy attempting to restore the work of Sor Juana "to its rightful place within the canon of Hispanic Golden Age literature" (Santí, "Sor Juana," 102) at the same time his first wife was finally coming out of the shadows of the literary void to which she had been relegated.

The first texts to appear in Garro's post-Tlatelolco period were read by many critics as an attack on Paz. Despite the critical dismay about her supposed negative portrait of "Paz" in *Testimonios*, we should also remember that she has a number of negative portraits of male figures in texts published prior to 1980. Her narratives and plays openly portrayed the difficulties for women who did not obey the patriarchy. While some critics have seen a sharp difference in the depiction of women in the texts published after 1968, in reality Garro had always shown the problems of women vis-à-vis male authority figures. Certainly, the plays of the fifties (*Andarse por las ramas, Los perros, La mudanza*), as feminist critics have shown, are highly critical of the negative treatment that women receive from their husbands, their lovers, and their peers. For many readers, Garro's novels and plays are key weapons in the war against the patriarchal oppression of women.

Thus, before Augusto in *Testimonios*, we have many earlier examples of negative male characters to choose from: General Rosas of *Recollections* is certainly a despotic man who abuses the women around him. And Don Fernando de los Siete y Cinco of the play *Andarse por las ramas* is also a typical blustering patriarch who does not understand his wife or his child. He realizes that he does not have a clue about women when he bleats out: "Las mujeres viven en otra dimensión. La dimensión lunar" (Women live in another dimension. The lunar dimension; 86). Being "lunar" (from the moon) equates women in Spanish with *lunáticas* (crazy people), as Garro herself was labeled in the period of her exile and poverty-stricken movements throughout Europe.

Garro's critique of the patriarchy and the conflicts between men and women in these early pieces is notable for the sense of humor with which she treats the topic and the occasional appearance of a real love relationship, as depicted in *Recollections*. Julia is renowned for having been able to escape with a kind and thoughtful lover, Felipe Hurtado, thus becoming one of the few women in the Garro cosmos who apparently was able to break away from the patriarchal oppressor and escape in a positive manner. Isabel, the woman who takes Julia's place in the life of General Rosas, disappears in a negative way—incredibly turned into stone to atone for her sins (such as having engaged in an illicit love affair and having caused the death of her brother). Moreover, neither Julia nor Isabel appears to be afraid of the general. As the narrator of *Recollections* tells us, "More than once the General lashed out with his whip at those who dared to look at her, and more than once he slapped Julia's face when she looked back at them, but Julia seemed unafraid and remained indifferent to his anger" (36). Isabel also follows the general instead of rejecting him or fearing his presence. In contrast, Mariana, married to Augusto, seems to have disappeared, like Julia, except that we as readers are not quite sure what her fate might really be. With Julia, we are led to think that her escape was a happy one, because she was accompanied by Felipe Hurtado. Mariana was accompanied by her daughter, another victim of the patriarchy. But each of the three testimonies that make up the novel suggests a different finish for her. This novel, one of the first which the public has openly identified as a roman à clef and the first that is said to include a portrait of Octavio Paz (negative, unflattering, or for some, accurate), deserves closer attention.

The journalist Patricia Vega laments that some readers could not separate truth from literary fiction and equated the descriptions of Augusto with a portrait of Octavio Paz's treatment of Garro (100).[32] On the one hand, Garro almost reveled in this association; on the other hand, she herself stated that real people are always transformed when they are made to pass into fiction (Melgar, "Elena Garro en París," 156). As she retorted to Carballo:

You say I harass Paz. Surely he told you this. Can you tell me how I harass him? Writing? The novel [*Testimonios sobre Mariana*] is not a private controversy—it is a novel! I'll tell you something. Do you remember that Mariana brings Vicente to visit a ballerina in New York? Well, she was a Russian friend, a ballerina of the Ballet de Montecarlo, who married a monster, who persecuted her and destroyed her. . . . I ignore the life and miracles of Paz. If I ignored them when I was married to him, well, now even more, and he and his friends envelop him with a thick veil of secrecy impossible to penetrate. (Ponce)[33]

By referring to *Testimonios sobre Mariana*, Garro appears to be answering the criticism that she was attacking Paz in that novel; she tells Carballo that the ballerina of the novel is not patterned after her relationship with Paz but is based on a real-life Russian dancer she knew. The important point is that we should read the novel as a symbolic representation of problems affecting all women and not one woman alone.

Furthermore, when *Testimonios sobre Mariana* is removed from the "autobiographical" category, it can be seen as an example of the "new novel" or postmodernist novel: it subverts chronology, has multiple narrators, and constantly questions the stability of "reality" by rejecting definite solutions (see Duncan, *Voices*). *Testimonios* is composed of three different monologues that are presented as testimonies according to the title: as the "truthful" evidence of the people who knew Mariana. In effect, however, not one of the narrators is equipped to know all of the truth—they do not know what has transpired between Mariana and Augusto or what the boundary is between memory and imagination, between private and public (Galván, "Multiplicidad de testigos," 65).

Vicente, a South American playboy, is crazily in love with Mariana and is the first to introduce her to the readers. He is considered to be a veiled portrait of one of Garro's lovers, the Argentine writer Adolfo Bioy Casares. Vicente maintains his devotion to Mariana, although at times her bad behavior toward him causes him to hate her. Nevertheless, he takes advantage of any opportunity to see her, even if it means openly leaving his wife alone or causing negative reactions in Augusto, Mariana's cuckolded husband. In Vicente's testimony, Augusto is shown to be cruel, abusive, and unbearably mean to Mariana. He finally tells Vicente that Mariana has escaped them both and gone to the Soviet Union—a political solution that is incongruous with Mariana's lifestyle. Vicente has a dream, however, that she and her daughter (named Natalia) are not in the "workers' paradise" but have departed for the heavenly paradise—they are dead. Vicente would rather consider Mariana dead than imagine her suffering the verbal missiles of Augusto or the bleak life of the Soviets.

Gabrielle, an old Frenchwoman who is poor and beholden to her employer, Augusto, is supposedly a good friend of Mariana, but she is compromised because she relies on Augusto economically for survival. She, too, paints a damaging portrait of Augusto and also of Mariana. While Augusto is domineering, false, and uncaring as well as cruel, Mariana appears weak, submissive, unsure of herself, and sometimes masochistic.

André, a young Parisian, narrates his great love for Mariana and his search for her and Natalia, Mariana's daughter with Augusto. Augusto is painted in an evil light in all the testimonies. For André, Mariana and Natalia have committed suicide, but they can still be recovered/remembered by his steadfast true love. It is noteworthy to contrast André, who remains alone, pining for Mariana, with Felipe Hurtado in *Recollections of Things to Come*, who was able to escape with his love, Julia.

Mariana is variously and antithetically described as deceitful and uncomplicated, healthy and ailing, youthful and infirm, beautiful and destructive/repulsive, innocent and harmful. She is the Other for Vicente, Gabrielle, and André, very much as Paz describes woman as the Other for man in the *Labyrinth of Solitude*. Interestingly, Mariana and Augusto do not offer their own testimonies and are always seen from the perspectives of others. Neither is given the discursive possibility to construct an individual memory in his/her own voice. Ironically, if Mariana does not have control over her own voice and representation, neither does Augusto. We read the testimonies of others in their lives, the supposedly marginal Gabrielle, the young André, and Vicente, the lover who helps Mariana to betray her husband. The mystery of why Augusto mistreats Mariana—and why Mariana accepts such abuse—remains throughout. In one way, this may be what Garro herself wondered vis-à-vis her relationship with Paz, except that Paz showed himself to be very much the typical Mexican macho even in his early correspondence with her.

In the text, Gabrielle claims to have the letters by Vicente to Mariana and Mariana's diary in her possession, but those sources are not used to clarify any of the mysteries. They are purported to be in the bottom of a trunk, which may remind readers of what Garro always said about her own creative work: she carried her manuscripts in her trunk.[34] I suggest that the association between the papers that Gabrielle has at the bottom of the trunk and the trunk identified with Garro's creative work could well be yet another clue that the text is *not* to be taken as autobiography but as fiction.

Mariana herself, the "subject" of the *Testimonies*, is really not a subject in the sense of being the thinking agent or principal: the ego. Rather, she is a subject in the sense of being "placed under the authority, dominion, control, or influence of something else," according to one dictionary definition. As a textual being/construct, Mariana is known to the reader by means of what the other narrators say about her—very much like that most famous of Mexican women, La Malinche/Doña Marina. A first-person narrative by La Malinche does not exist, yet she is always being described, discussed, and envisioned by others to this day. Mariana, whose name echoes Marina, the Spanish version of La Malinche's name, is the subject of all the testimonies that make up the novel. At the same time, she is a literary character who lives under the authority and control of her husband, Augusto, according to the three very different narrators who claim to have known her.

By using echoes of names that link their biographies (Augusto, Mariana), Garro is purposefully blending autobiography and the postmodern mode in her representation of lives in conflict. As Vicente says about Mariana, she appears simple but creates intricate labyrinths (34). The whole of *Testimonios* is a multifaceted labyrinth (pace Paz) that serves as a refutation of the commentary generated by her critics. In her creation of texts to show that stories are always being created about persons and "personas," Garro employed the only weapon at her disposal—the pen. Ironically, it was Paz who defined the Latin American intellectual as "one who struggles with constituted powers and with society but who is stripped of all weapons, except his or her pen" (quoted in Santí, "Sor Juana," 112).

In this battle of the sexes, Garro certainly is judged to be using her pen to attack Paz. But if these novels (*Testimonios*, *Mi hermanita Magdalena*, *La casa junto al río*, and *Inés*, for example) were only valid as veiled autobiographies or mere diatribes in a divorce case, then we would have little reason to consider their inclusion in the canon. The wronged woman who is Garro's typical "heroine" and supposedly her avatar is really an archetypal figure with long roots that go back to the classical Medea and Dido, if not postlapsarian Eve. Many novels have been published about aggrieved women, including those famously penned by the canonical male writers, such as *Anna Karenina*, *Madame Bovary*, and *Nadja*.[35] Unhappy women are all too common in popular fiction too. In fact, Garro's novels should be read more for their commentary about male-female relationships, sexual abuse, violence against the defenseless, and power relations in general than as mere veiled autobiographies. Moreover, she does not depict the unhappy woman only to have her find happiness by falling into the arms of a lover or another husband. Rarely and only in her early tales did she depict the possibility of men and women finding happiness together: again, Julia and Felipe in *Recollections* are the rare exceptions, along with Anselmo and his mysterious female muse in the play *El encanto, tendajón mixto* (Enchantment: Five and Dime, 1958).

In *Mi hermanita Magdalena*, Magdalena appears to find happiness in marriage, but it seems more a parody of the typical marriage than a faithful picture of marital accord. The roots of Garro's portrayal of Magdalena might conceivably be found in the depiction of the women in search of marriage in Sor Juana's play *Los empeños de una casa* (The Trials of a Noble House, 1683). Sor Juana also offers a satire on the *machista* attitudes about marriage in a text that is clearly a parody of *Los empeños de un acaso* (The Trials of Chance, 1639) by the canonical dramatist Calderón de la Barca.[36]

In addition to its focus on marriage rites, *Mi hermanita Magdalena* plays with the limits between real life and fiction. Garro sets up a narrative that people who know her will compare with her own life's story, as she did with *Testimonios*. In this novel the young Mexican woman Magdalena marries suddenly and leaves Mexico City with her husband, Enrique, only to wind up in a Paris fraught with unrest due to the Algerian crisis of the late 1950–1960s. Most of the narrative takes place in Paris (Chapters 2 and 4). Chapter 1 is set in Mexico City and Chapter 3 in Ascona, Switzerland, on the shores of Lake Maggiore.[37]

Paralleling the official Garro biography in many details, the main character—Magdalena, the youngest of her family, at seventeen—marries a friend on a lark, against her parents' wishes. He immediately takes her away from her family and homeland. Because of the legal nature of matrimony, Magdalena is dependent on Enrique and must obey his will. Her family is horrified by her disappearance. Her parents seem helpless to find her by official means, so her sisters, Estefanía and Rosa, begin their desperate search for their youngest sister. For Magdalena, her physical separation from her family and her spatial displacement from her home country are acts of violence that reflect the violence that she encounters in Europe. At the end of Chapter 1, her family discovers from a phone call from Magdalena that she has been abducted to Paris under duress by her husband. This physical separation from her family and native country, living during a time of political turmoil in which Algerians are fighting for self-rule, increases Magdalena's own desire for independence. She is rebelling not only against her own restricted familial upbringing but also against her husband's tyranny.

Garro informs her readers of two types of wars going on at the same time. The first, on the obviously referential level, is the Algerian Crisis that marked

French society most persistently from 1958 to 1962. Her young Mexican protagonists meet people involved with both the Front de Libération Nationale (FLN: National Liberation Front) and the Organisation de l'Armée Secrète (OAS: Organization of the Secret Army), the two opposing terrorist groups with whom Magdalena and her sister come into contact as they are navigating their way around the streets of Paris, trying to evade Enrique. On a personal level, the second conflict is between Enrique and Magdalena. The inequality between them is evident: the laws favor the husband in the relationship, and Magdalena is breaking the law when she hopes to be independent of Enrique.

It should be noted that divorce was finally permitted for Mexican women after the Revolution as part of the 1917 Constitution, but the de jure situation did not mean that it was easy for women to initiate divorce proceedings. As Garro shows, the husband had many legal rights and privileges to support his will and wishes over those of his wife. Enrique warns Estefanía, for example, that Magdalena should not continue with her plan for an annulment, threatening violence against both her and her family should she dare to divorce him.

Magdalena appears helpless in the face of Enrique's masculine power; instead of opposing him outright, she employs the military tactic of retreat. Rather than return to her Mexican home, however, where Enrique has influence, she escapes to Switzerland, a country known for its neutrality during wars. Magdalena does indeed find a safe haven there, a freedom that she did not enjoy before. She engages in a brief homosexual experience as well as several heterosexual liaisons. This kind of open sexuality is another way in which Garro destabilizes the sense of identity and of nationality as well. On the one hand, Magdalena is a married Mexican woman in the face of the law; on the other hand, she has no set identity in terms of her sentiment and affective life. Contemporary feminist critics like Gloria Anzaldúa and Teresa de Lauretis explore assumptions about privileged male space and nonheterosexual experiences to show that women who do explore lesbian experiences are challenging the "cultural assumptions and social practices attendant upon the categories of sex and gender" (de Lauretis, "Eccentric Subjects," 139).

Moreover, the idea of what "home" signifies for women is also being destabilized. Garro's wandering women are in a quandary as Mexican nationals, disobeying the cultural assumption of their nation and the traditional cultural memory held by the patriarchy. Although Magdalena does not follow through on the invitation by the character Helga to engage in a homosexual adventure, she does break stereotypes by engaging in sexual affairs with three men at the same time. Always thinking of her heterosexual relationships as a lark, the Magdalena who was disappointed in marriage by Enrique decides to become engaged to Helmut, Manfred, and Johnny. She spends different times of the day with each of them and wears the corresponding engagement ring. This gesture of changing rings is a key to the performative nature of Magdalena's actions. Her theatricality is a form of fiction making, albeit of a different sort than in *Testimonios sobre Mariana*. In *Testimonios* the fictionality of the main characters—both Mariana and Augusto—is put into play in each of the three sections, and each narrator is also cast as a fiction maker. In *Mi hermanita Magdalena* Estefanía is the narrator who tells us all about Magdalena and her journey through life, but it is Magdalena who is the supreme fiction maker. As such, she draws attention to the discrepancy between appearance and reality and interrogates stereotypical models of "proper" feminine behavior.

Although Enrique at first maintains the power of decisions and seems to be in control of Magdalena's life, she slowly increases her own ability to move about and interact with others. She fights against the enforced marriage imposed by Enrique; when he will not give her the divorce she wants, she acts as if she is already divorced. As noted, she accepts multiple lovers and becomes engaged not just to another man, which would make her a bigamist, but to three other men.

Garro provides her protagonist a way out of this legal dilemma by causing the death of Enrique in a car accident. Magdalena becomes a widow, that special state in Hispanic culture that the young Magdalena (in Chapter 1) sees as unique and useful: "widow's pain hurts a lot and lasts a little" (14).[38]

The sociopolitical context of these novels and their engagement with repressive systems and notions of exile give rise to some intriguing ideas in relation to the politics of identity. Moreover, Garro subverts the traditional gender roles upon which the institution of marriage is based. At the onset of the narrative, Enrique performs as a typical patriarchal male, almost kidnapping his woman and maintaining her in his thrall. This is a variation of a number of vignettes explored by Garro in her stories and plays. In *Recollections* Antonia was kidnapped from her father's home and taken to Col. Justo Corona, who had picked her out as his prize (39). In the play *Los perros* a young woman is brutally taken away from her mother by the man who wants her, repeating the history suffered by her own mother. The women appear to be objects in a performance over which they have no control.

"Autobiographical literature" is said to represent the individual aspects of the author's personal environment (such as family, education, and social position) as well as providing a historical image of actual events and persons that the author encountered. I cannot emphasize enough that these narratives, like

Garro's plays *Andarse por las ramas* and *Los perros*, are historical in their depiction of patriarchal behavior as well as fictional in their anecdotal details of place and character.

I suggest that Garro's narratives will be remembered in years to come not because she was "mistreated" by her ex-husband or thought she was injured by him and by the Mexican intellectual community but because the metafictionality and self-referentiality of her narratives comment on a false "otherness." As Amy Kaminsky posits, "It is, for example, possible to experience one's self as other, i.e., to hold self and other within one" ("Autobiographical Criticism," 101, n. 8). Unlike Paz and members of the patriarchy, who see women as the Other, Garro writes to see herself both as her "self" and as an Other whose existence illustrates the problems of living as a woman in twentieth-century Mexican or European society. That still fundamentally patriarchal society, with clear, differentiated roles and values for men and women, produced the daily difficulties and social problems suffered by Mariana, Magdalena, Consuelo, Lola, and Inés—and by Elena Garro.

Kristine Ibsen in her lucid article on *Testimonios* reminds us that the "integration of autobiographical elements in female authored texts violates cultural boundaries twice over: not merely by writing, but by making public details of a private life" (93). Indeed, Garro is "masterful"—to use a sexist adjective in a positive way for a woman—in bringing to the surface the inner life of her protagonists. The women's secrets that are usually hidden from males are examined in her narratives. Garro does not re-create only "true confessions of wronged women." On the contrary, she explores the process of representation of women in texts and by extension in reality. Like her characters, Garro also felt isolated and reduced to the perception of her behavior that Paz created. I would like to suggest that the "Paz" we are attributing these patterns of behavior to is also a creation of Garro, in her sense of fear and distrust of the power structure. If Augusto is "Paz," "Paz" is also a symbol of the male authority figure against whom Garro and countless other women have had to contend. The way Augusto describes Mariana as a "hysteric" conforms to the traditional understanding of hysterical women, as a disorder of excess among "thinking women."[39] As Ibsen observes: "To Augusto, her refusal to follow his rules is synonymous with insanity because it violates a hierarchy of discursive authority dependent upon female silence and submission" (98).[40]

Garro emphasizes an important lesson. As readers, certainly as writers, and as protagonists in our own life story we often say and remember not the facts but our perception of the facts—what we might like to have happened or even what we think took place, which may not coincide with what other participants in the same event accept as "true." Certainly Garro, like any young woman of Mexico (like any human throughout the ages), learned that what she assumed to be true was in fact only a perception, an observation based on her ideology as it was formed by her sex, class, and life experiences. Was she a talented choreographer who married a young poet because she wanted to "drink coffee," as she is quoted as once confessing?[41] Was her mother-in-law as strict and wicked as Garro indicates in her correspondence and then re-creates in *Un traje rojo para un duelo* (A Red Dress for Mourning, 1996) and *Mi hermanita Magdalena* (1998)? Was she really as antifeminist as she suggested in one of her quotations: "I am not a feminist. Nothing of the sort. Why? We women deal only with ideas that men have discovered. The day we deal with our own ideas then I will be a feminist"? Garro insisted in that interview that "there is no woman who has an idea."[42]

Nevertheless, my question remains: can we believe what Garro says to an interviewer? She is well known for comments that belie documents and the memories/perceptions of others, such as her insistence on a date of birth (1920) that contradicts the official record indicating that she was born in 1916. Her friends and enemies alike have pointed out that Garro's comments in letters and interviews were often contradictory (Beucker, 42). Perhaps she is a more reliable narrator of fiction than of her personal life.

Paz, in contrast, has not been caught in the sins of commission (creating fabrications) but was more liable for sins of omission. He did attempt to control his image by omitting documents that he did not want included in his official oeuvre (an example is his erasure of Garro from his authorized life record). As Lucía Melgar's *Writing Dark Times* clearly shows, it is also very possible that many members of the Mexican literary establishment serving on juries were loath to award any literary prizes to Garro because of their fear of consequences from the powerful members of the Paz circle, a "chilling effect" that seems to have lasted for decades.[43] Melgar's work detailing the "shunning effect," as she calls it, is convincingly researched and presented.[44]

Twentieth-century Mexican society was fundamentally patriarchal, with clear, differentiated roles and values for men and women. Daily difficulties and social problems continue to exist for women, especially those who want to act independently, beyond the parameters of the traditional roles for women. Some of Garro's women, like Verónica in *Reencuentro* or Consuelo in *La casa junto al río*, have to learn that to speak out is to begin to trust the system: silence is often a sign of a lack of trust in the culture and the government or the sociopolitical milieu. Garro had attempted to speak out when she was first married, as she chronicles in *Memorias de España 1937*, but she was met with derision, reprimands, and prohibition. According to Patricia Vega, Garro's description of her treatment by Paz and his mother was similar to a "guerra entre titanes" (war among Titans; 118). Paz purportedly prevented Garro from returning to her university studies after they came back from Spain; he and his mother supposedly blocked her every attempt at self-expression.

From the moment she married Paz and went off to the "theater of war" in Spain, Garro's life turned into a war (between the sexes) and a theater (performances of different roles). Paz's life became more and more public, but as a public man engaged in the events of a global stage. This reminds us of the vast difference in describing someone with the Spanish adjective for "public." It is perfectly acceptable for a man to be out in public. Calling a woman *pública* (public) means that she is a woman of the streets, a prostitute. Supposedly Paz and his family did everything they could to make sure that Garro would not become a "public woman" in all senses of the term. Nevertheless, Garro did express her opinions rather openly and also had lovers who were public figures (such as Bioy Casares and Archibald Burns).

What happens when we read these stories divorced from the historical accuracy of Garro's life's burdens? What is their import beyond the gossip level? Clearly, Garro has a great deal to say about some of her basic themes, including sexual abuse and violence against women that will not stop until society undergoes a spiritual transformation.

Paz has been connected to Sor Juana as a forerunner of "the situation of the twentieth-century intellectual, especially in totalitarian countries" (Santí, "Sor Juana," 103), as noted above. Garro, in contrast, seems to think of the condition not only of the intellectuals but of all marginalized peoples. She identifies with those who seem to stand alone to face the powerful and the privileged. Sor Juana was the one who introduced into literary discourse one of the key themes in the battle of the sexes: the inequality of women's treatment in a patriarchal society, as she bravely announces in "Hombres necios" (Foolish Men). Interestingly, when Paz reads this poem he appears to illuminate Sor Juana's female voice. Yet nowhere in the poem does the narrative voice identify as a woman (see Cypess, "¿Quién ha oído hablar de ellas?"). Sor Juana knew well that she could not directly address the men in her society as a woman. Indeed, as Josefina Ludmer reminds us, she often had to use the "tricks of the weak" ("Tretas del débil").

Garro's life mirrors aspects of Sor Juana, as noted, more than the life of Octavio Paz would. Indeed, it is an interesting exercise to look at the women in Paz's life in terms of three prototypes: the woman of his youth (Elena Garro);

the woman of his maturity (Marie-José Tramini); and his muse (Sor Juana). Yet two of them were not quite as he represented them—either in his mind or on paper. For example, despite his wishes (as we learn from his letters), Garro was not the typical obedient, submissive wife cast in the mold of the Virgin of Guadalupe. When writing to Gabriela Mora years later, Garro was quite negative about Paz's role in her life: "I want you to know once and for all . . . that I live in spite of him . . . I studied in spite of him, I spoke in spite of him, I had lovers in spite of him, I wrote in spite of him and I defended the Indians in spite of him, I wrote about politics in spite of him, in summary, *all, all, all* that I am is in spite of him. For that reason he harasses my friends and family" (Mora, "Elena cuenta su historia," 296).[45] For Garro, whether this was true or was her perception, Paz was her enemy (296). Just as Paz did not want her to work when they were first married, she contended that "[t]he [Nobel] Laureate did not want, does not want, and will never want us to work. It is his way of nullifying us, enslaving us, and making us schizophrenic" (296).[46]

Garro does not re-create merely the "true confessions of wronged women." On the contrary, she explores the process of representation of women in texts and, by extension, in reality. Nevertheless, because Paz is still considered "the most famous Mexican intellectual of the twentieth century" (Grenier, "Octavio Paz and the Changing Role of Intellectuals," 125), his views of iconic women—La Malinche and Sor Juana—continue to influence critical discussions of the representation of women in Mexican cultural history.

CONCLUDING REMARKS

In the preceding chapters I document how these two celebrated writers have had an important role in transmitting and reworking the legacy of Mexican culture in regard to major historical events, from the Conquest to modern times. Clearly, their views were conditioned by their gender and sociocultural background and education. In this concluding chapter I have examined the battle of the sexes between Paz and Garro in both their texts and their personal life. Their personal relationship was certainly reflective of traditional Mexican attitudes toward women and has been evaluated within that context by the critics dedicated to the work of Elena Garro. In contrast, Paz readers do not comment on the artistic relationship between Paz and Garro. After an examination of the nature of their personal relationship, especially as reflected in Garro's published comments, it is not difficult to describe/descry their relationship as a "war."[47] This is not unlike the situation that has been detailed in relation to Nellie Campobello and Martín Luis Guzmán, Antonieta Rivas

Mercado and José Vasconcelos, and Rosario Castellanos and Ricardo Guerra (see Unruh).

My argument has not been to continue but to negate the popular perspective that sees Garro as a by-product of Paz. Although they dealt with similar topics, my study shows that Garro clearly had her own voice, her own perspective. Her creativity was expressed in a variety of genres, from essays to novels, short stories, plays, and even poetry (which has yet to be fully analyzed).[48] Despite the dangers to her persona, Garro upheld her commitment to speak out against the inequities in regard to workers, Indians, and women throughout her lifetime. In this commitment to criticism and to social justice, she and Paz were similar. While his ideas about the Mexican Revolution and the sociopolitical implications of the Tlatelolco Massacre have contributed to the development of historical memory for the Mexican people, Garro's texts, although not as well known, also convey a version of Mexican cultural memory. But her version differs from that established by the patriarchy, to which Paz unquestionably belongs. Whereas Paz often ignores gender or even class issues, Garro decidedly does not. When it comes to the issue of the patriarchy itself, Paz does not comment so much as live it. As an example, his ideas about La Malinche (see Chapter 1) clearly show that he views women as the Other, as submissive beings who can be controlled by the dominant and dominating male figure. By reinforcing that aspect of Mexican cultural memory in which women continue to repeat the "root paradigm" of Malinche-Cortés, Paz suggests that change in gender relationships is impossible. In contrast, Garro challenges the inviolability of such gender relations and suggests that the Malinches of Mexico do have agency and can change the nature of the power structure in terms of both gender and ethnicity. Granted, Paz does admit in *The Labyrinth of Solitude*: "Women are imprisoned in the image masculine society has imposed on them" (198). Although he acknowledges the constraints of the social forces placed on women, he never goes so far as to propose social changes that would affect women's rights. His silence on women's issues contrasts with his vocal and consistent opposition to the corrosive effects of fascism, communism, and religious intolerance. Paz also does not problematize the issue of survival of women in wartime, which Garro addresses in several texts. Indeed, Garro is consistent in her critique of the inequalities of gender, ethnic, and class relations in contemporary society.

When it came to their personal relationship, both Paz and Garro tried to rewrite history, offering partial perspectives on their shared experiences. They both explored the social and political injustices that brought about the insurgency of the Mexican Revolution and would agree that the civil war was not successful in changing the Mexican social hierarchy. For Paz, the Revolution was "a rediscovery of the nation's identity, an immersion in its past, and a break with the falsehood and inauthenticity that had characterized all of Mexico's political endeavors since Independence" (Van Delden and Grenier, 126). While Garro was more skeptical of official political parties from the onset (as we see in their attitudes about the Spanish Civil War), Paz later came to the same conclusions as Garro regarding communism and its polarizing, antihumanist stance.

It is comprehensible, in a rather perverse way, that their own form of a "civil" war—discord, disagreements, controversies—would begin within their matrimony in the framework of the Spanish Civil War. Their interactions were often uncivil, public, and partisan, underpinned by strong differences in ideology, most evident in the way they each responded to the crisis brought on by the Tlatelolco Massacre. Although both Paz and Garro disagreed with the Mexican government's response to the students who clamored for more rights and greater democracy for their country, he took on the role of critic of the Mexican government, becoming a voice trusted by the international community. Garro, in contrast, became so alienated from Mexican life that she lived in exile; her voice was undermined as Paz's grew stronger. As changes in society made it possible to appreciate her perspective on gender and power relations and more readers and critics paid attention to her texts, Garro's literary reputation and cultural stature have grown dramatically. I agree with Carballo's observation regarding the black legend of her personal life: "She was able to convert it to gold in her literature" (Carballo and Batis, 65).[49] Whether it be the extraordinary narratives and dramas of Elena Garro or the prodigious poetry or illuminating essays of Octavio Paz, both Garro and Paz should be required reading.

NOTES

CHAPTER ONE

1. See my study of Garro's development of the Malinche paradigm in "The Figure of La Malinche in the Texts of Elena Garro" and *La Malinche*.
2. For further discussions of the tribulations of Garro vis à vis Paz, see Melgar, *Writing Dark Times*; Biron, "The Eccentric Elena Garro"; Domínguez Michael, "*El asesinato de Elena Garro*, de Patricia Rosas Lopátegui"; and Rhina Toruño, "Protesta contra la opresión." In one of her last published interviews Garro says that she could not publish because she was on a "black list," a detail she discovered many years after 1980, when *Andamos huyendo Lola* (We Are Fleeing Lola) was finally published (Bermúdez, 18–19).
3. In regard to the chronology of personal and literary events in the lives of both Garro and Paz, it is often difficult to ascertain accurate information. Both writers disputed dates and sometimes omitted pertinent information about life-cycle events and literary activity. For example, the date of their divorce is most often given as either 1959 or 1963. According to some reports, Octavio Paz initiated divorce proceedings in 1959, though the Mexican government did not acknowledge the divorce as legal until some years later. See Elena Garro Papers, 1930s–1994, Princeton University Library, Manuscripts Division, http://diglib.princeton.edu/ead/getEad?eadid=C0827&kw. Garro is quoted as having said that Paz sent her divorce papers from Ciudad Juárez in 1959 but that the divorce was declared "illegal" by the Mexican government (Muncy, "The Author Speaks . . . ," 35).

4. As Luis Enrique Ramírez reminds us in *La ingobernable* (The Ungovernable One), Elena always fascinated other writers. José Bianco paints a portrait of her in *La pérdida del reino* (The Loss of the Kingdom); Adolfo Bioy Casares also creates a character that is reminiscent of Garro in *El sueño de los héroes* (The Dream of Heroes), while Carlos Fuentes attempts to capture the intimate relationship between mother and daughter in the short story "Las dos Elenas" (The Two Elenas) (100). Ramírez also suggests that Paz refers to her in "Piedra de sol" (Sunstone) and "Pasado en claro" (A Draft of Shadows) as well as *Mi vida con la ola* (My Life with the Wave, a piece discussed in greater detail in Chapter 6).

5. Poesía en Voz Alta was initiated by Paz and collaborators Leonora Carrington, Juan Soriano, and Juan José Arreola. In 1957 Garro achieved fame for her three plays *Andarse por las ramas* (Beat about the Bush), *Los pilares de doña Blanca* (The Pillars of Doña Blanca), and *Un hogar sólido* (A Solid Home), which were staged by Poesía en Voz Alta and then appeared as part of the first edition of *Un hogar sólido* (1958). The Agrupación de Críticos de Teatro chose *Un hogar sólido* as the best Mexican play of 1957. For more information about the movement, see Unger.

6. See Chapter 6 for more information on this topic.

7. These events are developed in Chapter 5.

8. Translations of Garro's work, aside from the longer narratives *First Love & Look for My Obituary: Two Novellas* published by Curbstone Press and *Recollections of Things to Come* published by the University of Texas Press, appear in journals or anthologies that include many authors, so it is not easy to keep track of the translations.

9. As a point of comparison, both novels of Rosario Castellanos have been translated into English. Moreover, three of the novels by a younger writer, Carmen Boullosa (b. 1954), have already been translated into English: *Son vacas, somos puercos* (1991; translated as *They're Cows, We're Pigs*, 1997), *Treinta años* (1999; translated as *Leaving Tabasco*, 2001), and *De un salto descabalga la reina* (2002; translated as *Cleopatra Dismounts*, 2003).

10. "Elena Garro ha quedado tan confundida con Octavio Paz que muchas veces resulta difícil separar su obra y su vida del nombre del poeta. '¡Ah, la que fue mujer de Paz!' es una frase que parece formar parte de su identidad" (Poniatowska, *Las siete cabritas*, 111).

11. See "Women in the Culture of Belief": "Women are often seen as the guardians and are certainly the generational transmitters of culture. Because women care for children, women are the teachers of children" (no pagination).

12. I recognize that from the late twentieth century on the narratives of Nellie Campobello (*Cartucho* [Cartridge], 1931), Elena Poniatowska (*¡Hasta no verte, Jesús mío!* [Here's to You, Jesus!], 1969), Laura Esquivel (*Como agua para chocolate*, 1989 [translated as *Like Water for Chocolate*, 1992]), and Ángeles Mastretta (*Mal de amores*, 1996 [translated as *Lovesick*, 1997]) are sporadically included in lists of narratives of the Mexican Revolution.

13. For further discussion of Nellie Campobello's treatment by twentieth-century Mexican critics of the Revolution, see Nickel. See also Linhard.

14. This material develops the work presented in Cypess, *La Malinche*.

15. The concept of the "Malinche paradigm" is described fully in Cypess, *La Malinche*.

16. For further discussion of the influence of Paz on contemporary masculinist studies, see Chapter 6. Also consult the introduction and Chapter 4 of Irwin, *Mexican Masculinities*.

CHAPTER TWO

1. For a discussion of the *Lienzo de Tlaxcala* and other pictorial depictions of the Conquest from the indigenous perspective, see Kranz; and Wake.

2. For a discussion of the various names of La Malinche, see Cypess, *La Malinche*; and Karttunen, "Rethinking Malinche."

3. As noted, mestizo children were born within nine months after the first Spaniards arrived in the indigenous world. Martín Cortés is usually considered the first documented mestizo whose parents are identified by name (see Cypess, *La Malinche*; Lanyon). See also note 27 below.

4. See the bibliographies on La Malinche in Cypess, *La Malinche*; Karttunen, "Rethinking Malinche"; and Romero and Harris.

5. In order to clarify which of the Paz writers I am discussing, I refer to Ireneo Paz as "Don Ireneo" and to Octavio Paz as "Paz." For more information about Don Ireneo and his influence on both Mexican letters and his grandson, see Santí, "Octavio Paz."

6. As Teresa Hurley phrases it, Garro's "light was no doubt somewhat eclipsed by the fact that she was at one time married to Octavio Paz" (2). Throughout the chapters when appropriate I refer to aspects of their personal lives that help to contextualize why Garro has not received the international recognition garnered by Paz.

7. "[*El laberinto*] se ha convertido en un manual irrefutable" (26).

8. The translation is so readily available that henceforth I use the English version in citing Paz's essay. Page numbers refer to the 1985 Grove Press edition included in the Bibliography.

9. While the supremacy of the male child is one of the themes of many writers, see also *Recollections of Things to Come* by Garro and *Balún-Canán* by Rosario Castellanos for early twentieth-century Mexican feminist critiques in narrative form.

10. While it may be almost too well known, the word *chingada* and its variants, as Paz explains them, are among the most despicable curse words in Mexican culture. *La chingada*, as it is defined by Paz and used currently in Mexico, means the (fucked/fucked-over) woman. The *chingón* is the active male who perpetrates the violence or the conquest.

11. For some references on the changing status of women in modern Mexican culture and politics, see Castillo, *Easy Women*; and Rodríguez, *Women in Contemporary Mexican Politics*.

12. Phillips's "Marina/Malinche" and my *La Malinche* are among the rare studies that incorporate Ireneo Paz's work. I also refer to a number of late nineteenth-century novels in which the view of La Malinche is negative, including Eligio Ancona's *Los mártires de Anáhuac* (1870).

13. *Jicoténcal*, the eponymous novel about a Tlaxcalan warrior (also spelled Xicoténcatl), was published anonymously, although a number of critics have suggested possible identities for the writer. See Luis Leal's introduction to the Arte Público Press edition as well as his article "Jicoténcal."

14. For information about the Porfiriato and the man after whom it is named, Mexican president Porfirio Díaz, see among others Bryan; Thomas and Benjamin; and Ocasio-Meléndez.

15. "Y si tenemos una palabra de perdón y de olvido para los españoles de hace tres siglos que vinieron a martirizar a nuestros abuelos, ¿como no la hemos de tener fraternidad para los republicanos de ahora que nos instruyen con sus obras, que nos electrizan con su palabra y que se colocan a la cabeza de la civilización europea?" (157).

16. See Santí's "Octavio Paz" for a discussion of the complicated relationship between Don Ireneo and Porfirio Díaz.

17. Some scholars have suggested that at first Moctezuma and the other indigenous peoples thought that Cortés might be the returning god Quetzalcoatl and that the Spanish were somehow more divine than human. That theory has been questioned by more recent scholars. For example, see Carrasco.

18. Joseph-Arthur, Comte de Gobineau, was one of the most important promoters of racial ideology in Europe during the mid-nineteenth century and had a huge impact on late nineteenth-century social theory. Published in *Essay on the Inequality of Human Races* (1853–1855), his theory was widely read, embellished, and publicized by many different kinds of writers.

19. See Cypess, *La Malinche*; Kolodny; and Sommer.

20. For more on Ancona's views, see Skinner.

21. "[T]raigo a mi lado a una mujer honesta que sólo ha delinquido llevada por la fatalidad . . . y le ofrezco respetarla y amarla por todos los días que me queden de existencia" (*Doña Marina*, 2:455).

22. For a complete portrait of Marina in the texts of Don Ireneo, see Cypess, *La Malinche*; see also Harris.

23. I discuss this aspect of the legend of La Malinche in "Eve and the Serpent: The Nationalists' View" in *La Malinche*.

24. "No podía haber concluido más heroicamente esta entrevista de los dos antiguos amantes" (*Doña Marina*, 2:374).

25. For a discussion of the importance of existentialist thought in Paz, see Franco, *The Modern Culture of Latin America*; and Katra.

26. See the treatment of La Malinche in *Doña Marina* (1957) by Jesús Figueroa Torres and in *La dama de la conquista* (1942) by Federico Gómez de Orozco.

27. In addition to his Spanish wives and La Malinche, the historical Cortés had several more sexual liaisons and children with indigenous women, including three of Moctezuma's daughters, who were with him during the battles of conquest. Only one of the daughters survived the catastrophic events of the Noche Triste to live into the 1550s.

28. The mural by José Clemente Orozco in which Cortés and Malinche are depicted as Adam and Eve hangs in the National Preparatory School, which Paz attended in his youth; he refers to this depiction of the Mexican Eve in *The Labyrinth of Solitude* (86). I also discuss this mural in *La Malinche* (92, 97).

29. In "Malintzín Tenepal" Adelaida Del Castillo rejects Paz's view of the sexual act as an inherent violation for the woman: "I could have . . . chosen to describe Octavio's 'violation' as actually being that of the male, in the sense that a woman can be understood to 'engulf' the man, actually consuming him entirely in the act of loving; making him the overwhelmed! We can't say a woman is violated just because she participates in copulation, any more than we can say that we violate the mouth every time we eat, although there is a definite 'penetration' involved. Associations such as those given by Octavio Paz can only be attributed to an 'ego-testicle' world-view" (145).

30. For a historical discussion of the events that might have taken place in Cholula, see Schwartz, *Victors and Vanquished*; and Beckjord.

31. Ironically, notwithstanding disapproval by a number of critics of Paz's view of "the Mexican," most reviews of his essay were not negative. Aguilar Mora comments that until at least 1978, for almost twenty years, the great majority of the reviews were "apologia servil, desprovista del mínimo criterio lógico, al menos histórico" (servile apologies, lacking the minimal logical or historical criteria; *La divina pareja*, 26).

32. Rubén Salazar Mallén's essay on *malinchismo* appeared in *unomásuno* before *The Labyrinth* was published but has been all but forgotten under the shadow of Paz's book (see Ontiveros, 98). When Paz informs his readers that the phrase had become popular in newspapers (86), perhaps he is referring to Salazar Mallén without giving him credit, as suggested by José Luis Ontiveros in my interview with him in Mexico City in 1985.

33. See the commentary by Lucía Melgar in "Octavio Paz y Helena Garro."

34. In the translation published by Grove Press, which is the most popular, "The Sons of La Malinche" is on pages 65–88; the few pages dealing with La Malinche begin on page 86, at which point the translator added a note to explain that Doña Marina is "the name given to La Malinche by the Spaniards."

35. Chapter 5 provides a discussion of what happened at Tlatelolco and its impact on the lives and works of Paz and Garro.

36. In *La muerte de Artemio Cruz*, Fuentes includes an entire chapter that plays with the word *chingar*, so his novel naturally might be linked to the earlier essay by Paz, especially since the word had been used only sparingly in texts of high culture until Paz broke that taboo.

37. For different views on the exchange, see Díaz del Castillo, *The Conquest*; Cypess, *La Malinche*; and others. For information of a more general nature, see Rubin.

38. See Gyurko, "The Vindication of La Malinche," for further discussion of the various representations of La Malinche in Fuentes.

39. In private conversations with Don Luis (Santa Barbara, 2000), he offered the explanation that Martín Cortés is considered the first mestizo only because of his upper-class origin and because his life is documented, unlike that of the other children of these early Spanish-indigenous unions.

40. As further elaborated in Chapter 6, in his own relations with Garro, Paz acted within the typical macho stereotype that he outlines in "The Sons of La Malinche." In the battle of the sexes, Paz wants to be the *chingón*.

41. Paz "se ve sumamente 'contagiado por tendencias extranjerizanes'" (124).

42. Paz spent time as a young man in both the United States and Spain, where he was influenced by the modernist and surrealist movements. As an ambassador to India (1962–1968), he further developed his interest in Hindu philosophies.

43. "[E]s una obra de verdad extraordinaria, una de las creaciones más perfectas de la literatura hispanoamericana contemporánea" (Paz, "Novela y provincia," 143–144).

44. The Cristero Rebellion (also known as the Cristiada) is the name given to the struggle between the Catholic Church and the Mexican government that broke out in armed conflict from 1926 to 1929. See Meyer, *The Cristero Rebellion*; and Tuck, *The Holy War in Los Altos*.

45. This perspective (of men being guilty of doing one thing but saying another) was already evident in Sor Juana's celebrated poem "Hombres necios" (Foolish Men). In *Balún-Canán* by Castellanos the female child is also admonished for entering into discourse, with disastrous results.

46. In his essay "Malintzin, imagen y discurso de mujer," Baudot suggests that La Malinche was still alive in 1539 and possibly died in 1541 (73), while Martínez states that she died in 1527 (*Hernán Cortés*, 523).

47. See Cherríe Moraga's essay "A Long Line of Vendidas" for a Chicana's reaction to this theme.

48. "La ilusión, la voluntad y el amor recíproco"; "trágica petrificación, opacidad e inercia" (Anderson, "*La señora en su balcón* y *Los recuerdos del porvenir*," 134).

49. The line of different readings runs from recent essays such as those of Bowskill and Gladhart back to early pieces, such as Boschetto's "Romancing the Stone" and Balderston's "The New Historical Novel," which still resonate with meaning.

50. An English version of "La culpa es de los tlaxcaltecas" can be found on the web: "It's the Fault of the Tlaxcaltecas" by Elena Garro, translated by Patricia Wahl (texts distributed by RIF/T, e-poetry@ubvm, and the Electronic Poetry Center, Buffalo: http://wings.buffalo.edu/epc/rift/rift02/wahl0201.html).

51. Aspects of Garro's magic realism have been studied in Anderson, "La cuentística mágico-realista de Elena Garro"; and Pertusa.

52. The name "Pablo" resonates in Christian onomastics with St. Paul and his andro-centric views that subordinate women. In 1 Corinthians 11:3–16 he taught that women are inferior to men, primarily culpable for sin and the fall of humanity, and should be excluded from ordained ministry.

53. "[P]arecía que iba a convertirse en ese otro al cual se parecía. Pero no era verdad. Inmediatamente volvía a ser absurdo, sin memoria, y sólo repetía los gestos de todos los hombres de la ciudad de México. . . . ¿Cuántas veces arma pleitos en los cines y en los restaurantes? . . . En cambio mi primo marido, nunca, pero nunca, se enoja con la mujer" (10).

54. A good example of the importance of "white blood" vs. indigenous genes can be found in *Balún-Canán*; Castellanos explores gender relations and how ethnicity influences choices of mates.

55. See Cypess, "The Cultural Memory of Malinche in Mexico City."

56. "[Y]o soy como ellos, traidora"; "Sí yo también soy traicionera" ("La culpa es de los tlaxcaltecas," 10).

57. See Alegría and Elu de Leñero.

58. In her essay Adorno reviews the way in which the Spanish chroniclers imagined Amerindian peoples. She notes that the historian and court official Ginés de Sepúlveda first described the "Mexica warrior as cowardly as a woman" when he was attempting to denigrate the indigenous peoples as opponents (232). Trexler also discusses the Iberian attitude toward victims being described as "effeminized males" (65, 74, 169).

59. See Aparicio and Domínguez Miguela for discussions of the meaning of "tropicalization."

CHAPTER THREE

1. The bibliography is vast on all these topics, but for an introduction to these nineteenth-century events, see MacLachlan and Beezley. Many writers have focused on the figures of this century, Mexican and foreigners alike, and the bibliography dealing with Maximilian and Carlota alone grows each year. See Meyer; Sherman; and Deeds for a useful review of the Porfiriato and the causes of the Revolution.

2. The political naïveté of Madero, who was elected president in 1911, soon alienated many groups; he also was ousted from power. In what would become a tragic feature of Mexican politics, Madero was murdered in a revolt led by Félix Díaz, a son of Don Porfirio, and Gen. Victoriano Huerta, supported by U.S. ambassador Henry Lane Wilson, who had befriended Huerta in opposition to Madero.

3. Artistic giants such as Diego Rivera, José Clemente Orozco, and David Siqueiros and performers in the rich tradition of the *corrido* or ballad have offered varying depictions of the Revolution in art and song. For references to the *soldadera* figure, see Salas; and Arrizón.

4. Villa has turned into a folk hero for some, a bandit for others, and at times a caricature of the Mexican macho, as we see most famously in Sabina Berman's play *Entre*

Villa y una mujer desnuda. Although Madero's name does not resonate in the same way as do those of Zapata and Villa, he does become a hero for Garro (as shown in a later section of this chapter).

5. For more detailed descriptions of the Zapatista rebellion and its background, see Collier with Quaratiello; and Harvey.

6. Pratt adds the important comment that Campobello is the only woman of the twelve authors who were included in the canonical Aguilar edition of *La novela de la revolución mexicana* prepared by Berta Gamboa and completed by Antonio Castro Leal after her death. Pratt's essay notes that Gamboa's work was literally excised from the anthology despite her important role. See also Mata. Campobello's two novels have been translated as *Cartucho and My Mother's Hands* (1998) by Doris Meyer and Irene Matthews.

7. Garro often gave 1920 as her birth year, but it has been established by others that her birth certificate shows December 1916. In an interview with Rhina Toruño, published in *Cita con la memoria*, Garro freely admits to her birth date as December 11, 1916 (13).

8. "Apenas tenía unos meses de edad cuando los azares de la Revolución nos obligaron a dejar la ciudad de México; mi padre se unió en el sur al movimiento de Zapata mientras mi madre se refugió, conmigo, en Mixcoac, en la vieja casa de mi abuelo paterno, Ireneo Paz, patriarca de la familia. Cuando yo era niño visitaban mi casa muchos viejos líderes zapatistas y también muchos campesinos a los que mi padre, como abogado, defendía en sus pleitos y demandas de tierras. Participó en las actividades de la Convención Revolucionaria. Posteriormente fue representante de Zapata y de la Revolución del Sur en los Estados Unidos. Mi madre y yo lo alcanzamos en Los Angeles. Allá nos quedamos casi dos años" (Paz, "Octavio Paz por él mismo 1914–1924").

9. Interestingly, in *Los de abajo* (1915) Azuela uses the image of the hurricane to convey the idea of the Revolution's force in sweeping away the individual's will to act independently; Solís, a possible spokesperson for Azuela, says: "La revolución es el huracán y el hombre que se entrega a ella no es ya el hombre, es la miserable hoja seca arrebatada por el vendaval" (The revolution is the hurricane and the man who gives himself to it is no longer a man, but a miserable dry leaf blown about by the wind; Chapter 18 of Part 1). Some historians, if not literary critics, have read the metaphor of the "leaf caught in the storm" as a reference to the intellectuals who "played only a marginal role in Mexico's revolutionary process" (Hennessy, 78).

10. For example, the eminent Don Luis Leal states that Paz "is able to portray the Mexican people and their culture in a convincing manner" ("Octavio Paz," 310).

11. See Anthony Stanton's many essays, especially "Models of Discourse and Hermeneutics in Octavio Paz's *El Laberinto de la Soledad*."

12. It was Kemp who famously rendered the title as *The Labyrinth of Solitude* rather than the title that Stanton and others suggest as more accurate: *The Labyrinth of Loneliness* ("Models of Discourse," 210, n. 1).

13. See Chapter 5 on the Tlatelolco Massacre for a detailed discussion of Paz's role in this tragic occurrence in Mexican history.

14. First published in *Plural* 50 (November 1975), the interview was reprinted in *El ogro filantrópico* (1979). I quote from the English translation of the essay found in the Grove edition of 1985.

15. It is important to note the words that Paz uses in Spanish to refer to the return: *la devolución*: "La primera demanda de los zapatistas fue la *devolución* de la tierra y la segunda, que era subsidiara, la repartición. *La devolución*: la vuelta al origen" (Paz, *El ogro*, 25).

16. Paz's sympathetic portrait of Zapata is considered by many literary scholars to be an innovative aspect of his view of the revolutionary figures. Yet recent studies by historians view Zapata as an "apostle of agrarianism" (Gilbert, "Emiliano Zapata," 143), although Womack had not yet introduced a heroic Zapata to North American academics. See Gilbert, "Emiliano Zapata," for the changing narratives in Mexican historiography concerning Zapata; Womack's book appeared in 1969 and instantly became famous. See the review by Mancall, who notes that Zapata and Zapatistas are epic heroes for Womack (339).

17. Among the many articles and books that focus on Villa and Zapata are Parra's *Writing Pancho Villa's Revolution* and Gilbert's article "Emiliano Zapata." At the end of the twentieth century the name of Lázaro Cárdenas, the president with socialist leanings, was invoked frequently when his son, Cuauhtémoc Cárdenas, became involved in presidential politics. On Lázaro Cardenas, see Paz, *The Labyrinth of Solitude*, 240–242; see also Ashby; and Shirk.

18. Madero in particular but also the Flores Magón brothers are controversial figures to this day. See Wood.

19. In Chapter 5 on the Tlatelolco Massacre, I discuss in greater detail the position that Paz takes on the relationship between the Aztec sacrifices and violence as an influence on contemporary Mexican practices. See Paz, "Olympics and Tlatelolco," in *The Labyrinth of Solitude*, 236. Garro is writing about the corruption and violence of the revolutionary period during the fateful year of 1968, when the events were taking place that would lead to the student uprising and the government's bloody reprisals.

20. As is common with work by Garro, the date when she might originally have conceived and written a text is often contested and is frequently years earlier than the publication date. Antoine Rodríguez, for example, suggests that the play *Felipe Ángeles* was written in 1961 (1151).

21. See Stanton, "Models of Discourse": "What surprises the reader and certainly the historian is the virtual absence of Madero, the Liberal instigator of the Revolution" (230, n. 20).

22. "El primer gran socialista mexicano, mártir de la causa obrera" (45).

23. Garro's interest in the plight of workers can be seen in the novel *Y Matarazo no llamó* (discussed in Chapter 5). In addition, Garro also worked hard for the rights

of campesinos (peasants), as Elena Poniatowska describes in her profile of Garro in *Las siete cabritas* (111–132). Rosas Lopátegui reproduces Garro's essays on agrarian reform in *El asesinato de Elena Garro*.

24. "La legalidad, la lucha limpia por las ideas, el respeto profundo a la vida, el ejercicio del poder en el nombre de unos valores, habían muerto con el señor Madero. Trágicamente, el país retrocedió al punto desde el cual inició su lucha el Presidente Madero" (*Revolucionarios mexicanos*, 170–171).

25. For an academic history, see Slattery.

26. "El nombre del General Felipe Ángeles dice Garro que le era familiar desde niña, dado que uno de sus tíos, Benito Navarro, combatió a sus órdenes. . . . Los tíos de Elena por parte de su madre eran todos revolucionarios, villistas. El único que sobrevivió fue el que combatió con Ángeles" (Toruño, *Tiempo, destino y opresión*, 67).

27. A number of essays have focused on the plays of the Mexican Revolution and in particular on Garro's depiction of Felipe Ángeles. See Cypess, "Dramaturgia femenina"; Galván, "Felipe Ángeles"; Peña Doria; and Winkler, "Elena Garro ante la Revolución Mexicana"; for a more general study of the plays of the Revolution, see Del Río.

28. In an interview with Michelle Muncy, Garro confesses: "Empecé a investigar y vi que era una figura prohibida oficialmente. Como me gusta lo que no es official . . . " (I began to investigate and saw that he was a figure prohibited officially. Since I like what is not official . . . ; "The Author Speaks . . . ," 24).

29. The role of women in the Mexican Revolution is an area that has been steadily investigated since 1957, when Garro first attempted to offer her own perspective on the theme. See Montes de Oca Navas, who says, "En la novela de la Revolución Mexicana la mujer aparece como un ser sin nombre ni rostro, anónimo y secundario, aunque siempre presente: la compañera inseparable del soldado con quien comparte su destino; un 'artefacto masculino' que se toma y se abandona cuando ya no es útil ni necesario; un ser sin ubicación propia" (In the novel of the Mexican Revolution woman appears as a being without a name or a face, anonymous and secondary, although always present: the inseparable companion of the soldier with whom she shares her destiny; a "masculine artifact" who is taken and abandoned when no longer useful or necessary; a being without her own position; 136). Also, Linhard ("A Perpetual Trace") reminds us that Nellie Campobello had earlier documented the perspective of a young girl in her narratives *Cartucho* and *Las manos de mamá*. For Garro's presentation of positive roles for women in her plays, see Cypess, "Dramaturgia femenina." Moreover, in 1996 Ángeles Mastretta wrote a novel dealing with the period of the Mexican Revolution whose main character is a woman: *Mal de amores* (1985; translated as *Lovesick*, 1997).

30. "Gavira: Nosotros ganamos la partida. Los vencidos nunca tienen razón. La historia está con nosotros." "Diegues: La historia es una puta, general. No hay que fiarse de ella" (19).

31. "[Q]uizá podríamos inventar la historia que nos falta. La historia, como las matemáticas, es un acto de la imaginación" (52).

32. Del Río studies seventeen plays in detail. Her appendix lists over a hundred plays on the topic written by 1960. Of these, only nine are by women dramatists, not including Garro.

33. Were it not for the reference to the Revilla family in *Cartucho*, we would think that Garro had invented the character, because there is no record of her in the official documents that I have been able to investigate.

34. "¿La Revolución? ¿Llama usted la Revolución a una camarilla de ambiciosos que están sacrificando a todos los que se oponen a sus intereses personales?" (15).

35. See Leal's key article on the traditional representation of Mexican women: "Female Archetypes"; Buck is also useful.

36. Ángeles: "Él [Carranza] cree que la revolución es un medio para alcanzar el poder absoluto y yo creí que era un medio para exterminarlo" (26).

37. "Hay muchos años por venir. Muchos cruces de caminos. Muchos hombres por nacer, habrá alguno que busque sus huellas y las vuelva otra vez vivas en el tiempo" (33).

38. For further information, see Ramón Jrade, "Inquiries into the Cristero Insurrection against the Mexican Revolution," *Latin American Research Review* 20, no. 2 (1985): 53–69; and Jean Meyer, *The Cristero Rebellion: The Mexican People between Church and State, 1926–1929* (Cambridge: Cambridge University Press, 1976).

39. "[U]na de las creaciones más perfectas de la literatura hispanoamericana contemporánea" (Paz, "Novela y provincia," 143–144).

40. I base this number on the entries found in the Modern Language Association online bibliography (http://www.ebscohost.com/public/mla-international-bibliography), which is a conservative estimate of the essays dedicated to the novel; many more pieces probably refer to it tangentially.

41. One of the initial critics of Garro in English, Gabriela Mora, made this point as early as 1977 ("A Thematic Exploration," 95). Mora says in a note that the novel, written in Switzerland in 1950, was read by García Márquez before he published his novel (97). For other readings of the novel, see the Bibliography, which includes the many articles that address the myriad thematic and stylistic aspects of this provocative and rich narrative.

42. For a detailed reading of how the subtext develops in the novel, see Cypess, *La Malinche;* and Chapter 2.

43. I agree with Adam D. Morton, who suggests that Fuentes does not posit the possibility of breaking "the repetitive cycles of oppression" (43).

44. This affirmation of Garro's objectives in altering the state of Mexican society has also been noted by Cypess, Mora, and Rosas Lopátegui, among others; further discussion of this aspect of her work is found in Chapter 6.

45. "[M]ar azul bañado de soles amarillos" (173–174).

46. "—¿Has visto al gobierno?

"—Sí . . . lo vi una vez . . . Rutilo me dijo: el cabrón gobierno es muy matón . . .

"—El mató al general Rueda Quijano.

"—Lo mató para siempre—Eva dijo estas palabras con voz grave" (167).

47. For readers who wish to compare Rulfo's Spanish text with that of Garro, I include the original dialogue:

"—¿Dices que el gobierno nos ayudará, profesor? ¿Tú conoces al Gobierno?

"—Les dije que sí.

"—También nosotros lo conocemos. Da esa casualidad. De lo que no sabemos nada es de la madre del Gobierno" (102).

48. As discussed in Chapter 2, during the postrevolutionary period there was again a need to identify a father and mother for the Mexican nation; Orozco visualized it most clearly in his painting, selecting Hernán Cortés and La Malinche as the Adam and Eve of the Mexican mestizo nation.

49. As examples, see the essays of Aguilar Mora; Bidault de la Calle; Glantz; Nickel; and Pratt, as noted in the Bibliography.

50. See the information on the *soldadera* in note 3 above; see also Linhard, *Fearless Women*.

51. At the end of her feminist play *El eterno femenino* (The Eternal Feminine, 1975) Rosario Castellanos has her female character ask a "loaded" question: "Si hubiera triunfa [la Revolución] . . . ¿Existirían aún muchachas como [Lupita]?" (If [the Revolution] had succeeded . . . would there still be women like [Lupita]?; 137). That is, would there still be inequality in Mexico? Castellanos, like Garro, believed that Mexican society needed to address gender issues in order to deal with the machismo of Mexican culture.

CHAPTER FOUR

1. Some contemporary critics suggest that the ideology was not so clear cut as the general discussions seem to indicate. Moreover, Elena Garro also expressed a more nuanced perspective on the nature of the political ideology in her *Memorias* (see the discussion below in this chapter).

2. See Vaughan: "the Mexican Revolution was the first social revolution of the twentieth century, part of a much broader conflagration that devastated Europe in internecine warfare and, from the peripheries of Russia, China, India, Egypt, and Mexico, challenged empires, landlords, and capitalists" (21).

3. See Lambie for a nuanced description of the antifascist forces and the nationalists.

4. U.S. Marines had landed in Veracruz in 1914, occupying it for months. In 1916 Gen. John J. Pershing had entered northern Mexico in search of Pancho Villa, whose troops had raided the town of Columbus, New Mexico, in March 1916 and killed many citizens.

5. As Mackey explains, many were motivated by both ideology and economics: "The threat of fascism and the reality of economic crisis seemed great. Unemployment

was two- to three-million, with even more affected by wage and social-services cuts; the failure of capitalism seemed clear" (89).

6. This poem has had various titles, including "Elegía a un joven muerto en Aragón" (Elegy to a Young Man Dead in Aragón), which loses the reference to war in *frente* (the battlefront) as well as the idea that the poet is a friend of the subject (*joven* is more impersonal than *compañero*). Paz thought that his friend José Bosch had died in the fighting in 1937 and composed his "Elegía a un compañero muerto en el Frente de Aragón," only to discover that Bosch had not died. Garro describes the meeting with Bosch in *Memorias* (35). When some critics refer to the friend who inspired this poem, they fall into the same mistake that Garro committed; she called the young man "Juan Bosch" (a more familiar figure: Juan Bosch of the Dominican Republic) and not "José"—the ill-fated member of POUM and friend of Paz.

7. Estimates suggest that five hundred thousand people were killed, with union leaders, anarchists, and members of the Communist Party especially targeted for execution. In a book that is part of a series providing succinct introductions to important topics, Andy Durgan states that "during the first years of the Franco regime it is estimated that 200,000 people died of hunger" (126).

8. I use the term "outright autobiographical" because Garro's many fictional pieces are always linked to real events in her life, making so many of them romans à clef, especially according to readers such as Rhina Toruño and Patricia Rosas Lopátegui.

9. It is interesting to note that Hemingway was inspired in part by Azuela's iconic novel of the Mexican Revolution, *Los de abajo*. For a comparative reading, see Zivley.

10. Dos Passos returned to Mexico in 1930, 1931, 1932, and 1946 and wrote about his experiences during the 1926–1927 trip; in *The 42nd Parallel* he re-creates a fictionalized Mexico City. For further information, see Gallo's essay.

11. Toruño writes that their marriage occurred on May 25, 1937 (*Cita con la memoria*, 9).

12. See Melgar, "Octavio Paz y Helena Garro." Toruño cites Garro, who admits that "desde esa primera noche de bodas hubo problemas" (since the first night of the marriage there had been problems; *Cita con la memoria*, 9).

13. For information about the Contemporáneos, see Forster; Sheridan, *Los Contemporáneos ayer*; and Stanton, "Octavio Paz y los 'Contemporáneos.'"

14. Paz's penchant for revision has been studied carefully by a number of critics; for example, Aguilar Mora follows the changes in *Los hijos del limo*. Although Paz did not include "¡No pasarán!" (They Shall Not Pass!) in his subsequent anthologies, it is ironic that a number of websites, including *Britannica Online*, suggest that the poem is on an equal footing with "Piedra de sol" (Sunstone), one of his recognized masterpieces: "His major poetic publications included *¡No pasarán!* (1937; 'They Shall Not Pass!'), *Libertad bajo palabra* (1949; 'Freedom under Parole'), *¿Águila o sol?* (1951; *Eagle or Sun?*), and *Piedra de sol* (1957; *The Sun Stone*)" (http://www.britannica .com/eb/article-9058840). As Stanton reminds us, Paz's exclusion of this poem and subsequent critical disregard led to the poem's almost being erased from the Paz canon ("La poesía de Octavio Paz," 652).

15. During his *sexenio* (six-year term of office), Cárdenas decreed the end of the use of capital punishment (usually in the form of a firing squad). Capital punishment has been banned in Mexico since that time.

16. The Spanish Republican exiles of 1939, many of whom went to Mexico, hold a very special place in the history and collective memory of contemporary Spain and Mexico. The contributions of these Spanish exiles were enormous, as discussed by Naharro-Calderón and Cate-Arries, among others. The Colegio de México, founded by Spanish exiles, became one of the most important educational facilities in Latin America. For a more complete discussion of the Spanish exiles, see Naharro-Calderón.

17. "Era inútil que los obreros franceses organizaran manifestaciones para gritar: 'Des avions pour l'Espagne!' Nadie hacia caso de ellos. El Comité de No Intervención se oponía a enviar armas a los republicanos y Roosevelt era enemigo de la República Española" (133). Compare Garro's idea that Roosevelt was the enemy of Republican Spain with the view of Tom Conley, who comments that Roosevelt's support of the arms embargo to the Republicans was tantamount to supporting the fascist forces (quoted in Camino, 94). Moreover, these comments by Garro show that she was reading the newspapers of the time: her words are a direct reference to headlines in *L'Humanité* (Humanity), organ of the Communist Party of France: "GUNS! PLANES! END THE BLOCKADE WHICH IS KILLING OUR BROTHERS IN SPAIN" (September 5, 1936).

18. "En los años treinta la poesía en idioma español vive un momento de esplendor. En ese tiempo, además de los mexicanos, escriben los chilenos Gabriela Mistral, Pablo Neruda y Vicente Huidobro, el peruano César Vallejo, los argentinos Jorge Luis Borges y Oliverio Girondo, los cubanos Nicolás Guillén, Emilio Ballagas y José Lezama Lima, el ecuatoriano Jorge Carrera Andrade, el guatemalteco Luis Cardoza y Aragón, los nicaragüenses Salomón de la Selva y José Coronel Urtecho. Y en España se ha consolidado la Generación de 1927, que la guerra civil dispersará, no sin una breve etapa de la creación intensa de Federico García Lorca, Rafael Alberti, Vicente Aleixandre, Gerardo Diego, Luis Cernuda, Jorge Guillén, Pedro Salinas, Emilio Prados, Dámaso Alonso, León Felipe. Y anteriores a ellos también escriben Antonio Machado y Juan Ramón Jiménez" (Monsiváis, "Adonde yo soy tú somos nosotros" [*La Jornada Semanal*]).

19. "[L]a hermandad de los pueblos oprimidos y denunciando el abismo social entre los que tienen el poder y aquellos despojados completamente de él" (139).

20. Stephen Spender and John Lehmann edited *Poems for Spain* in 1939. My observation is not meant to discount the many *corridos* that were written on themes and figures of the Mexican Revolution; Boyd suggests that Zapata alone figures in over four hundred *corridos* (909).

21. "Neruda también tenía noticias de mi persona y años mas tarde, al referirse a mi presencia en el congreso, dijo que él 'me había descubierto.' En cierto modo era

cierto: en esos días yo le había enviado mi primer libro; él lo había leído, le había gustado, y hombre generoso, lo había dicho" (*Itinerario*, 58).

22. This is W. S. Merwin's translation.

23. "No cabe duda de que este 'primer libro' que recibe Neruda es *Raíz del hombre*, en cuyos versos habrá percibido ecos y resonancias de su propia poesía" (Stanton, "Poesía de Paz," 654).

24. "A Paz le resulta decisivo el encuentro en Europa con Pablo Neruda. 'La influencia de Neruda fue como una inundación que se extiende y cubre millas y millas—aguas confusas, poderosas, sonámbulas, informes.' Paz conoce a Neruda en París y lo re-encuentra en Valencia, en el Congreso Mundial de Escritores Antifascistas, y luego en México, donde es cónsul de Chile. Pero lo que Neruda aporta de genio poético y solicitud amistosa, lo rebaja con su sectarismo y su exigencia de vasallaje. Paz se pelea con él y se aleja en definitiva de un tipo de poesía y de 'compromiso.' Neruda detesta a los 'artepuristas,' a los cultivadores del 'arte por el arte.' Paz defiende el derecho a la libre expresión. Y se desentiende de una estética y de una ética fundadas en la utilidad política de la poesía, abocándose a la construcción (o mejor: el perfeccio-namiento) de su voz original" (Monsiváis, "Octavio Paz y la izquierda," 31).

25. "Su literatura está contaminada por la política, su política. . . . Es muy posible que el señor Neruda logre algún día escribir un buen poema con las noticias de la guerra, pero dudo mucho que ese poema influya en el curso de ésta. . . . lo que nos separa de su persona no son las convicciones políticas sino, simplemente, la vanidad . . . y el sueldo" (quoted by Poniatowska, *Octavio Paz*, 40).

26. "El conflicto entre poesía pura y poesía social marcó toda una época de la literatura hispánica. Cuando Paz empieza a escribir, a principios de la década de los 30, la balanza ya se inclinaba visiblemente a favor de los opositores de la pureza artística" (Stanton, "Octavio Paz y los 'Contemporáneos,'" 1004).

27. "Me impresionó mucho la miseria de los campesinos mayas atados al cultivo del henequén y a las vicisitudes del comercio mundial del sisal" ("Excéntrica—Escritor de la semana: Octavio Paz").

28. This poem went through many revisions; Paz comments in a *Letras Libres* version of the poem: "En 1976, al preparar la edición de mis obras poéticas, lo releí y per-cibí SUS insuficiencias, ingenuidades y torpezas. Sentí la tentación de desecharlo; después de mucho pensarlo, más por fidelidad al tema que a mí mismo, decidí re-hacer el texto enteramente. El resultado fue el poema que ahora presento—no sin dudas: tal vez habría sido mejor destruir un intento tantas veces fallido" (In 1976, as I prepared the edition of my poetic works, I reread it and realized ITS insuffi-ciencies, ingenuous qualities, and infelicities. I felt the temptation to throw it out; after thinking a great deal, more for fidelity to the theme than to myself, I decided to redo the text entirely. The result was the poem that I now present—not without doubts: perhaps it would have been better to destroy an attempt [that has been] consistently unsuccessful" ("Entre la piedra y la flor," 12).

29. As for so many of his poems, Paz worked on many versions of "Entre la piedra y la flor." The version quoted here can be found online at http://www.cuentosyfabulas .com.ar/2010/11/poema-entre-la-piedra-y-la-flor-octavio.html.

30. Stanton discusses these issues in detail in "La prehistoria estética."

31. "[H]a entregado al pueblo de México y al de España el medio más efectivo de comunión y entendimiento. Ha creado una autentica poesía de ilimitadas perspectivas" (quoted by Stanton, "La poesía de Octavio Paz," 652).

32. For a discussion of this debate and why *Los de abajo* was selected as an example of "virile literature," see Irwin, "*Los de abajo* y los debates." Irwin provides this summary of the Jiménez Rueda/Monterde exchange: "Jiménez Rueda buscaba una literatura nacional más viril, pero no la encontró. No obstante, pocos días después de que se publicara su articulo, Francisco Monterde lo contestó con las buenas noticias de que sí, 'Existe una literatura mexicana viril.' Monterde mencionó un sólo ejemplo: *Los de abajo* de Mariano Azuela" (Jiménez Rueda was searching for a national literature that was more virile, but he could not find it. Nevertheless, a few days after he published his article, Francisco Monterde answered him with the good news that yes, "A virile Mexican literature exists." Monterde mentioned only one example: *The Underdogs* of Mariano Azuela; 73).

33. The reasons for the contentiousness or "war" between Paz and Garro are discussed in Chapter 6.

34. "[E]s increíble la cantidad de 'escritores' que han levantado su prestigio denunciando como criminales a los homosexuales" (Sheridan, *Los Contemporáneos ayer*, 259).

35. On Paz's complex relationship to Marxism, see Grenier, "Octavio Paz: An Intellectual and His Critics," 263; and Van Delden and Grenier, *Gunshots at the Fiesta*, 120–124.

36. For the importance of communism in the United States during this period, see Lyons.

37. Paz says: "Don Ireneo, mi abuelo, es la figura masculina de mayor impacto en mi primera edad" ("Octavio Paz por él mismo 1914–1924").

38. Don Ireneo's changing political ideas are discussed in greater detail in Chapters 2 and 3. He had fought in the War of Intervention against the French and had been a supporter of the conservative politician and demagogue Porfirio Díaz but rejected Díaz's brand of politics and subsequently supported Madero's revolt against his former leader.

39. An article in the Spanish newspaper *ABC* online clearly discusses this point of León's relationship with Alberti and what it meant to her reputation: http://www.abc .es/hemeroteca/historico-17-03-2003/abc/Cultura/la-memoria-de-maria-teresa-leon-contra-viento-y-marea_168363.html.

40. For further readings on María Teresa León, see Ferrán; and Vosburg.

41. "Durante mi matrimonio, siempre tuve la impresión de estar en un internado de reglas estrictas y regaños cotidianos, que entre paréntesis, no me sirvieron de nada, ya que seguí siendo la misma" (150).

42. I suggest that purporting to have been born in 1920 allows Garro to continue the performance of the "naïf."
43. "Sus inocentes comentarios traen consigo las furias de Octavio Paz contra ella" (70).
44. "Yo nunca había oído hablar de Karl Marx" (5).
45. "¡[L]os griegos, a los romanos, a los franceses, a los románticos alemanes, a los clásicos españoles, a los mexicanos, pero a Marx, no!" (5).
46. "El grupo de los 'Contemporáneos' reinstaló la cultura en México después de la Revolución y de la sangrienta revolución cristera. Los Contemporáneos no eran políticos, sólo eran eruditos" (5).
47. When the Republican cause was lost and Franco's victory was secure, Modotti fled with other leftists to Mexico, where she had already lived in the twenties. In 1941 she was guaranteed asylum and reclaimed her real name. On January 5, 1942, she was found dead in a taxi. The details of her death have never been entirely clarified. See Rivera Villegas for a comparison of the two women.
48. "En México se daban de bofetadas en la calle los partidarios de uno y otro bando. Los mexicanos acudían a la embajada española para enrolarse en el ejército español. 'Sí sí, pero ¿en cuál bando?' preguntaban los funcionarios. 'En cualquiera, lo que quiero es ir a matar gachupines' contestaban" (7). Similar to "gringo" for North Americans, *gachupín* is a disrespectful word used in Mexico to refer to native Spaniards.
49. "Había algo que yo no entendía y le pregunté al chofer:
"—¿Por qué se visten igual los soldados franquistas y los soldados republicanos?
"Nadie pudo contestar. Hubo un silencio y de repente el chofer me dio la explicación:
"—Toma mira qué pregunta, ¿no ves que todos somos españoles?—dijo asombrado" (61).
50. José Vasconcelos (1882–1959) held many governmental posts during the postrevolutionary years and quarreled with some of the presidents—most notably Carranza and Plutarco Elías Calles. He is famous for his book *La raza cósmica* (The Cosmic Race), about the mestizo characteristics of the population of Mexico.
51. "Juan [de la Cabada] tenía 'una trayectoria revolucionaria impecable.' Había estado en la cárcel y había sido vecino de celda de Carlos Pellicer, que estaba detenido por vasconcelista, no por comunista, como Juan, lo que indicaba, según aprendí en España, que Juan era superior en la jerarquía revolucionaria. De manera que, cuando Juan protestaba, los 'oportunistas' callaban" (39).
52. See the explication of the poem earlier in this chapter.
53. "Ahora, con Juan Bosch escondido detrás de la cortina, sentí una ira inexplicable: ¿por qué los rusos o los comunistas perseguían a otros comunistas? ¿por qué Juan Bosch estaba en aquel estado infrahumano? ... En adelante la sombra de Juan Bosch nos siguió por Barcelona" (35).
54. The diminutive form of Elena's name is used as a sign of endearment and also perhaps as a reference to her naïve condition.

55. "'Es curioso, mano. Aquí en este jardín, nos podemos morir todos juntos,' le dijo a Paz para disculpar que yo hubiera hablado con un reaccionario" (47).

56. "Los mexicanos siempre compadecieron a Paz por haberse casado conmigo. Su elección fue fatídica. Me consuela saber que está vivo y goza de buena salud, reputación y gloria merecida, a pesar de su grave error de juventud" (48).

57. "Pensaba al revés de como pensaba yo" (88).

58. "[N]adie era condenable y Dios era el único que tenía poder para juzgarnos" (88); "todos éramos juzgables y cometíamos pecados ininteligibles" (88).

59. "Por ejemplo: me acababa de enterar de que había homosexuales. Era insólito, ¡pero cierto! . . . Y renglón seguido me explicaban que Shakespeare, Platón, Homero, Miguel Ángel, Byron, Shelley, Oscar Wilde, Marcel Proust, André Gide, Botticelli, Sófocles, y García Lorca también eran homosexuales. ¡Caramba! Como la burguesía odiaba a la cultura por eso asesinaba a los artistas" (88).

60. "[E]s bueno o es malo ser homosexual"; "No había bueno ni había malo" (88).

61. "¿Y entonces cómo podían condenar a alguien si no es bueno ni malo?" (88)

62. "[M]e irritaban y además eran antipáticos. Sus argumentos eran tan válidos o tan gratuitos como los míos" (91).

63. "Si la metralla era capaz de lastimar así la piedra, ¿qué haría con la piel humana? Me vi las manos. El hombre era demasiado frágil para tratarse con aquella brutalidad" (92).

64. For a discussion of homosexuality and homophobia as contexts for García Lorca's works, see Dawes, "On the Textualization of Sexuality."

65. "[M]e puse a llorar. Me sentí cansada y con ganas de estar en mi casa" (31).

66. "Cuando apareció el libro de Stephen Spender, nos dedicó una línea que Paz leyó triunfante: 'El guapo poeta Octavio Paz y su joven y bella mujer que en Minglanilla se puso histérica . . . ' Nunca le perdoné la frase. Spender olvidó que, durante el banquete, Nordal Grieg pidió que se regalaran al pueblo las viandas espléndidas que estaban en la mesa. Sin ningún éxito" (31).

67. "Años más tarde, cuando en París Aldous Huxley me encontró encantadora, no dije una palabra. Había aprendido la lección" (31).

68. See, for example, the comments of the character Conchita in *Recuerdos del porvenir* on the sad role of women, who are forced to be silent while men may speak: "¡qué dicha ser hombre y poder decir lo que se piensa, dijo con melancolía!" (what a blessing it is to be a man and be able to say what one thinks, she said with melancholy; 26).

69. "Paz era injusto al no defenderme" (99).

70. Paz met André Breton when he came to Mexico to visit Leon Trotsky in 1938. Many critics have studied the relationship between Paz and surrealism. See Quiroga; Rodríguez García; and Wilson.

71. As Dawes suggests ("Octavio Paz," 242–243), after the battles of his youth Paz concludes that democracy is an ideal principle that has no roots in modern history.

72. For some ideas about the experiences of the Spanish exiles in Mexico, see Cate-Arries; and Faber.

73. The memoirs of Helena Paz Garro describe how very different, and sometimes difficult, life was with two such creative, volatile beings as parents. She knew that they did not get along: "[M]e di cuenta que había un dolor perpetuo en mi casa, que no existía en los hogares de mis amigas, por eso era tan feliz fuera de mi casa" (I realized that there was a perpetual sadness in my house that didn't exist in the homes of my friends; for that reason I was so happy away from my home) (145).

74. See Pacheco's "Libertad bajo palabra cincuenta años después" for a description of the difficulties Paz encountered as he tried to publish this collection of poems.

75. Paz is said to have wanted to go to Europe to follow his lover, the Italian painter Bona Tibertelli de Pisis (see http://www.s9.com/Biography/Paz-Octavio). Garro's affair with Bioy Casares is alluded to in her novel *Testimonios sobre Mariana* and in José Bianco's *La pérdida del reino* and Bioy Casares's *El sueño de los héroes* (Ramírez, 36). References to the other men who were fascinated by Garro also exist (see Poniatowska, "Elena Garro y sus tormentas"; Melgar, "Octavio Paz y Elena Garro"; and Paz Garro, *Memorias*; and Rosas Lopátegui, *Testimonios sobre Elena Garro*). The many lovers of Paz do not seem to have been given much literary play, except in the *Memorias* of his daughter, Helena, who does refer to the existence of lovers in her father's life (151).

CHAPTER FIVE

1. To this day the exact number of students who were present has not been determined—the official record does not include an accurate account. See Doyle, "The Dead of Tlatelolco"; and Volpi on this point.

2. In 1536 Sebastián Ramírez de Fuenleal along with Fray Bernardino de Sahagún and others inaugurated the Colegio Imperial de Santa Cruz de Tlatelolco, which associated the name "Tlatelolco" with a school that brought together indigenous and Spanish scholars as a way to help preserve the remnants of indigenous culture that were almost all but destroyed in the Conquest. (See León-Portilla's comments in his interview with Krauze ["Entrevista"] after his award of the Premio Internacional Menéndez y Pelayo in the summer of 2001.) In 1967, just before the tragic events that occurred at the site, the Mexican government entered into an agreement called "Tratado de Tlatelolco: Tratado para la Proscripción de las Armas Nucleares en América Latina" (Treaty of Tlatelolco: Treaty for the Prohibition of Nuclear Weapons in Latin America). This treaty made Latin America the first nuclear-weapon-free zone in the world.

3. Miguel Leon-Portilla of Mexico served as his country's ambassador and permanent delegate to the United Nations Educational, Scientific and Cultural Organization (UNESCO). Professor emeritus at the Universidad Autónoma Nacional de México, he is the author of a number of books, articles, and papers on pre-Columbian cultures, which have been translated into several languages.

4. "Y allí ocurre un encuentro de dos mundos en su mejor versión. Por un lado están Olmos, Sahagún, Gaona; y del otro lado, una serie de sabios indígenas, médicos, conocedores de los códices, gente versada en la tradición prehispánica y jóvenes estudiantes indígenas. Pensemos que en 1536 han pasado sólo 15 años desde la caída de la ciudad" (Krause, "Entrevista con Miguel León-Portilla").

5. To date, there is still no definitive count of how many people were killed at that time. Mexican government records were kept sealed, and U.S. records were finally opened by the work of Kate Doyle ("Tlatelolco Massacre"); it is based on collaboration between *Proceso* magazine and the National Security Archive and launched on March 2, 2003).

6. See the Bibliography for listings of texts on these crucial demonstrations.

7. For more detailed discussion of the students' demands as they relate to the protest movement, see Volpi; see also Carey.

8. In his study "Tlatelolco, Tlatelolco," Leal also points out the historical parallels between the Porfirian excesses in celebrating Mexico's centenary of independence and the Gustavo Díaz Ordaz government's preparations for the Olympic Games.

9. The story circulated that Poniatowska's own brother had died in the Tlatelolco Massacre, largely because of the dedication she included in her novel *¡Hasta no verte, Jesús mío!*: "A Jan, mi hermano; a todos los muchachos que murieron en 1968: Año de Tlatelolco" (To Jan, my brother; to all the young people who died in 1968: Year of Tlatelolco). In an interview she said: "Still, it means something to see so many young people dying, though, of course, my brother didn't die in the Plaza de las Tres Culturas, nor did he die in a police roundup or in jail. But it means something because a young person has died, doesn't it?" (García Pinto, 164). As Kimberle López concludes: "Poniatowska's defensive attitude makes it clear that she has been accused of lying about her brother's death, and that this attempt to associate him metonymically with the student protests at Tlatelolco has not been perceived as justifiable" (37, n. 26).

10. The bibliography on Poniatowska in general and on *La noche de Tlatelolco* is enormous, but readers can begin by consulting Michael Schuessler's *Elena Poniatowska: An Intimate Biography* and Beth Jorgensen's many articles on Poniatowska. The bibliography on testimonials in general is also vast, but one way to begin is to consult Beverley; Prada Oropeza; and Sklodowska, among others.

11. *Y Matarazo no llamó* has been related to Garro's experiences during the events of 1968 by Cypess ("Elena Garro and Tlatelolco"), Melgar ("Silencio y represión"), Rosas Lopátegui (*Testimonios*), and Toruño (*Tiempo, destino y opresión*).

12. According to an email (July 27, 2004) from Pacheco, he wrote "La Lectura de los cantares mexicanos" shortly after the day of the massacre, and it first appeared in "La Cultura en México," the supplement to *Siempre!*, dated three weeks later. This text also was reprinted in his collection *No me preguntes cómo pasa el tiempo* (1969; translated as *Don't Ask Me How the Time Goes By*, 1978). It is the version from that

edition that Poniatowska cites in her 1971 *La noche de Tlatelolco*. At the tenth anniversary of the Tlatelolco Massacre, Pacheco published "Las voces de Tlatelolco" (The Voices of Tlatelolco) in *Proceso* (October 1978). In the third edition of *Tarde o temprano* (Late or Early, 2000), both poems are united under the title "Manuscrito de Tlatelolco" (67–71). Alastair Reid translated "Lectura de los Cantares Mexicanos" in *Don't Ask Me How the Time Goes By*, 23–25.

13. *Webster's*, http://www.merriam-webster.com/dictionary/lucidity.

14. In an essay about Castellanos and the impact of power and gender on her writings, Cynthia Steele adds this piece of information regarding the mysterious nature of Castellanos's death in Israel in 1974. A friend of Castellanos, Óscar Bonifaz, told Steele about the strange allusions in one of the last letters that Castellanos had written to him: "Un gato amarillo anda rondando mi casa. A ver si logro ponerle mordaz" (A yellow cat is prowling around my house. Let's see if I can manage to muzzle him). Bonifaz, says Steele, "reads this as an allusion to a stalker who went on to murder Castellanos. He points out the use of the term 'mordaz' and its resemblance to 'Díaz Ordaz,' the previous Mexican president, whom Castellanos presumably had angered in 1968 with her eloquent poem 'Memorial de Tlatelolco,' protesting the student massacre" (Steele, "Letters from Rosario," 71).

15. *Visión de los vencidos* (1959) was translated into English as *Broken Spears: The Aztec Account of the Conquest of Mexico* (1962).

16. The editors Mara García and Robert Anderson used the title *Baúl de recuerdos* for their anthology of essays about Garro because she had always referred to her manuscripts being hidden in her *baúl* (trunk). Garro explains that she had no home and had to keep her papers in a trunk (Rosas Lopátegui and Toruño).

17. Ironically, Paz's grandfather Don Ireneo had once been imprisoned in the Tlatelolco Convent. During his imprisonment, in 1871, he wrote *Los héroes del día siguiente* (Heroes of the Day After).

18. "[C]omenzó la matanza" (38).

19. "[E]l 2 de octubre de 1968 terminó el movimiento estudiantil. También terminó una época de la historia de México" (38).

20. "La matanza de Tlatelolco nos revela que un pasado que creíamos enterrado está vivo e irrumpe entre nosotros" (40).

21. "[S]in crítica, y, sobre todo, sin autocrítica, no hay posibilidad de cambio" (40).

22. "[L]a crítica no es el sueño pero ella nos enseña a soñar y a distinguir entre los espectros de las pesadillas y las verdaderas visiones" (155).

23. La Llorona (the Weeping Woman) is a mythical woman figure from the Hispanic oral tradition who has two main characteristics. She is supposed to cry for her lost children or, echoing the Medea myth, to have killed her children because of her love for a man. See Pérez, *There Was a Woman*.

24. "[A]ño del movimiento estudiantil y año de mi desgracia" (quoted in Poniatowska, *Las siete cabritas*, 112).

25. "[D]enuncia muy sostenida de la violencia en todos sus aspectos" (Muncy, "Encuentro," 70).

26. "[A]unque su relación matrimonial era muy mala, Octavio fue más amigo de la verdad literaria y puso todo su peso para que la obra se publicara" (quoted by Ramírez, 44).

27. In an interview with Lucía Melgar ("Conversaciones"), Elena Garro informed Melgar that she was in Paris at the time Jaramillo was assassinated. She had been forced to leave Mexico in 1959 by order of President Adolfo López Mateo; he had told Paz to send her away because she was a gadfly (245). When the news came that Jaramillo had been killed, Paz reminded her: "Por favor no digas nada. Esto es una cosa que no la mandó el Presidente. Es cosa de un sargento" (Please don't say anything. This is not something that the President ordered. It is a sergeant's doing; 245). Garro's response was not only to tell Paz that he was wrong, that the order must have come directly from the president, but to react decisively: "No dije nada, pero preparé el viaje para venir a México" (I didn't say anything, but I got ready to return to Mexico; 245).

28. Carlos Madrazo had become a friend of Garro's because of their mutual interest in the struggle for greater equality for Mexican peasants and for political reforms in the PRI itself. Madrazo's agenda of reform did not sit well with other key officials of the PRI. He died in an apparent plane accident at Pico del Fraile; Ramírez sets his death in 1969, six months after Tlatelolco; but Rosas Lopátegui and Toruño mention 1971 ("Entrevista," 70). As noted by these critics, some suggest that Madrazo's death was a planned murder, not an accident. Garro herself accuses Luis Echeverría of having assassinated Madrazo (see Melgar-Palacios and Mora, 298). For a more detailed biography, see Hernández Rodríguez, *El caso de Carlos A. Madrazo*.

29. Garro's character in *Y Matarazo no llamó* follows this trajectory from supporter to traitor, which led me to consider the novel another way for her to retell her experiences in the aftermath of Tlatelolco.

30. See Carey for a perspective on the effect of the testimony of Campos Lemus vis-à-vis the intellectuals he named as collaborators, including Garro (144–145). Campos Lemus also wrote his own version in *El otoño de la revolución (octubre)* (The Autumn of the Revolution [October]). For an account whose easy accessibility may influence readers, see http://en.wikipedia.org/wiki/Tlatelolco_massacre, which states that the Díaz Ordaz government "arranged" to have student leader Sócrates Campos Lemus accuse dissident PRI politicians such as Carlos Madrazo of funding and orchestrating the student movement.

31. "Oculta en una casa de huéspedes en compañía de su hija, Elena Garro aceptó en parte su participación en el movimiento estudiantil, pero dijo que solamente como mediadora, ya que está dispuesta a desenmascarar a todos los catedráticos e intelectuales que adoctrinaron a los estudiantes mexicanos para tratar de derrocar al gobierno" (50).

32. "[N]o son los jóvenes estudiantes los responsables. Son los catedráticos e intelectuales izquierdistas los que los embarcaron en la peligrosa empresa, y luego los traicionaron. Que den la cara ahora. No se atreven. Son unos cobardes, comentó entristecida" (Ramírez, 50).

33. "[C]ómplice y principal responsable de toda la conspiración que se encunó en la Ciudad Universitaria" (53).

34. Garro gave the names of about twenty intellectuals. She and her daughter even gave interviews in both French and English with foreign correspondents, castigating and "indiscriminately" blaming a group of Mexican intellectuals, according to sources (Toruño, *Tiempo, destino y opresión*, 23).

35. "La razón es que soy el más fuerte" (Volpi, 374).

36. "¡Andamos huyendo, Lola! Claro que no sabemos de quién huimos, Lola, ni por qué huimos, pero en este tiempo de los Derechos del Hombre y de los Decretos es necesario huir y huir sin tregua" (quoted by Ramírez, 55).

37. "La revolución comunista es la toma de poder por la pequeña burguesía y por el pequeño intelectual. Se trata de exterminar no sólo a los grandes burgueses sino a los grandes creadores y pensadores" (54).

38. "Hago muchas tonterías, pero nunca me arrepiento" (59).

39. "La fecha del manuscrito es 1960 anterior a los sucesos del 2 de octubre de 1968. Sin embargo por ciertos datos, parecería que Garro antes de darlo a la imprenta [1991] lo revisó y agregó nuevos datos relacionados a los sucesos del 68. Por ejemplo a raíz de los sucesos del 68 le llevaron a Garro un hombre muy mal herido, dejándolo abandonado en la puerta de su casa, tal como ella lo describe en la novela" (Toruño, *Tiempo, destino y opresión*, 83).

40. "Yo creo que la imaginación es un poder para llegar a la verdad, porque la mentira es muy aburrida, en cambio la imaginación es exacta y es lindísima" (Rosas Lopátegui and Toruño, 55).

41. "La gente cree con más facilidad una mentira que una verdad" (*Testimonios sobre Mariana*, 164).

42. See one of the first essays on this play: Cypess, "¿Quién ha oído hablar de ellas?"

43. While Garro changed some of the names of the historical characters, the title is an obvious clue to one of the more controversial figures, the student leader Sócrates Campos Lemus.

44. Teresa de Lauretis explains that "the personal is political because the political becomes personal by way of its subjective effects through the subject's experience" (115).

45. No women writers are included in the anthology compiled by Campos and Toledo. See Steele's observations on the absence of women writers in *Politics, Gender, and the Mexican Novel* (9).

46. "[M]iserable hoja seca arrebatada por el vendaval" (63).

47. For further reading on intertextuality and Tlatelolco texts, see Jorgensen.

48. "[S]e inflama de orgullo por andar en su compañía" (18).

49. "[N]uevo en la lucha"; "Sí, es decir, ni siquiera nuevo, digamos un espontáneo . . . confesó Eugenio súbitamente ruborizado" (18).

50. "'¡Imagínese, compañero! . . . Nos echaron encima a todas las fuerzas. ¡Qué tiroteo! Dicen que hay muchos muertos. . . . Y también muchos heridos'—gritó Ignacio exaltado, casi con alegría" (27).

51. "'Nos dispararon,' . . . dijo Tito como si fuera a echarse a llorar. Estaba conmocionado; no esperaba una reacción tan violenta de parte del gobierno, se sentía traicionado" (29).

52. "¿Y cómo podía saber él si eran bromistas o simplemente estaban encargados de espiar sus palabras?" (61)

53. "En una carta signada el 25 de septiembre de 1974, Elena Garro escribe a Gabriela Mora lo que probablemente pudiera considerarse una síntesis objetiva de su vida y obra: 'Querida Gabriela, si piensas que hace seis años que vivo sin hablar con nadie, como una apestada y con la angustia de no tener dinero, ni esperanzas de trabajo, tal vez me comprendas. No entiendo qué me ha sucedido. Me dices que escriba mi biografía personal: es muy fácil. Mi derrota no se debe a mi educación, ni a mi tendencia de depender de mi marido, ¡sino todo lo contrario!'"

54. "Iba huyendo sin saber adónde, ni por qué huía" (95).

55. The two men suffer the fate of the traditional "ley de fuga" (law of flight), which Garro had railed against in relation to the death of Madero (see Chapter 3 and her discussion of the death of Madero in *Revolucionarios mexicanos*).

56. "Yáñez era un justo" (132).

57. "Son los catedráticos e intelectuales izquierdistas los que los embarcaron en la peligrosa empresa, y luego los traicionaron" (quoted in Ramírez, *La ingobernable*, 52).

58. "'Escogieron a Yáñez porque lo vieron con nosotros y algo tenían que esconder . . . Vendidos,' . . . repitió Pedro en voz baja" (235).

CHAPTER SIX

1. Limon goes on to cite Harold Bloom's point that "feminism poses the first radical challenge to traditional literary history because it would establish a pedigree that does not descend from Homer" (184).

2. In 1976 *Plural*, which had been supported by the editor of *Excélsior*, was victim of the change in editorship of the newspaper. Julio Scherer García, then editor of *Excélsior*, was forced from his post by Mexican president Luis Echeverría, who was angry about the paper's attacks on his government. That same year Paz founded the literary and cultural monthly *Vuelta*, which soon acquired the same prestige that *Plural* had enjoyed. See King.

3. As noted earlier, Garro said that Paz sent her divorce papers from Ciudad Júarez in 1959 but that the Mexican government declared the divorce "illegal" (Muncy, "The Author Speaks . . . ," 35).

4. Both Toruño and Rosas Lopátegui discuss Garro's belief in the role that Paz played in keeping her from being published. Some critics agree with them, while others question this assertion. René Avilés Fabila writes in "En busca de Elena Garro" that Paz had something to do with his ex-wife's difficulties in publishing (http://recordan zas.blogspot.com/search?q=Paz&updated-max=2007–07–09T16%3A59%3A00–07%3A00&max-results=20). See both Earle and Melgar, *Writing Dark Times,* for sustained and reasoned presentations on this issue.

5. For a straightforward discussion of Paz's letters to Garro and Garro's description of their relationship, see the several studies by Melgar in the bibliography (analyses of the letters between Paz and Garro archived in the Princeton library) and also the essays in Melgar-Palacios and Mora.

6. Mora discusses the "antifeminism" of Garro and points out that she nevertheless expresses in her work solidarity with many of the goals of feminism. See "*Los perros y La mudanza.*"

7. Some of the texts that deal with masculinity issues in Latin America include Olcott, Vaughan, and Cano; Sigal; Guttmann; and Chant and Craske. While these four anthologies focus on different historical periods and geographical areas, they offer perspectives on various aspects of gender construction in Latin America.

8. Vega attributes the comparison of Garro's persecution with that of Sor Juana to José María Fernández Unsaín (100).

9. Interestingly, the short story is the basis for a children's picture book by Catherine Cowan, *My Life with the Wave* (New York: Lothrop, Lee and Shepard Books, 1997).

10. Arrangements can be made to consult the letters in the Princeton archive. Melgar has written detailed essays on the contents of the letters. See "Elena Garro en París (1947–1952)"; "¿La escritora que no quería serlo?"; and "Correspondencias literarias."

11. According to Garro, Paz did not let her return to her university studies after they were married; but others suggest that it was the birth of their daughter, Helena, in 1939 that prevented her from continuing her studies (Rosas Lopátegui, *Testimonios,* 141).

12. Orlando reminds us of the difficulties of speaking out for the women writers that she studies: "the act of speaking for women becomes a political act" (42).

13. See the essays that analyze that aspect of the novel *Balún-Canán,* including Cypess, "Balún-Canáan"; Lagos, "'Balún-Canán'"; and others.

14. In *Testimonios,* Augusto often tells Mariana to be quiet: "Cállate—ordenó Augusto" ("Quiet," ordered Augusto; 10); "Te prohibo que hables—le ordenó su marido" ("I forbid you to speak," her husband commanded her; 129).

15. A number of critics have become associated with portraying Garro as the victim of Paz; see the many texts of Rosas Lopátegui and Toruño. Melgar and Mora discuss the kind of criticism that portrays Garro as victim and offer various essays that explore these different portrayals. Mora was the recipient of many letters from Garro,

which she was able to republish in *Elena Garro: Correspondencia* (Letters), in which Garro claims that she was being persecuted.

16. Helena Paz openly states in *Memorias* (Memoirs) that the two women were afraid of being murdered in the post-1968 environment; Garro portrays their fears in *Socrates y los gatos*; see also the interview with the journalist Ramírez (*La ingobernable*).

17. In "Exposing Silence as Cultural Censorship: A Brazilian Case" (*American Anthropologist* 102.1 [March 2000]: 114–132), Robin E. Sheriff analyzes "cultural censorship."

18. Melgar writes: "[L]os textos garrianos amplían la gama de silencios y muestran no sólo que la 'mudez' de los grupos subordinados es producto de un proceso sociohistórico en gran medida institucionalizado, sino también que el silencio de grupos o individuos 'mudos' puede ser de hecho un silencio elegido, una opción expresiva" ("Violencia y silencio," 13).

19. Many rumors surround Garro, including that she was a spy for the government in the 1960s but also that the government spied on her, contradictory tales which would discredit her "credentials" as an intellectual and opponent of the official discourse in Mexico. These rumors circulated in several newspaper articles. For Rosas Lopátegui, the gossip arose as a way to deflect opinion from serious issues during the 2006 presidential campaign. She also suggests that it was Garro's particular association with Carlos Madrazo, himself a severe critic of the PRI, that provoked the bitterness of the PRI against Garro and caused her to become the object of false accounts.

20. Garro continues to depict a negative image of the mother-in-law in *Mi hermanita Magdalena*. Garro's description of her treatment by Paz and his mother was similar to a "guerra entre titanes" (war among Titans; Vega, 118). Paz supposedly prevented Garro from returning to her university studies after they came back from Spain; similarly, he and his mother supposedly blocked her every attempt at self-expression.

21. "Eres un genio . . . Eres mejor escritora que yo" (80).

22. "[M]i padre se ponía feliz" (81).

23. See Poniatowska's own comments in her prologue to the polemical book *El asesinato de Elena Garro* by Rosas Lopátegui and the review by Domínguez Michael.

24. In accordance with the suggestion of my scientist husband, I also checked how many entries there are for another woman of the same era, Rosario Castellanos: 294 entries for Castellanos in 2009. Evidently, Garro has just a few more than Castellanos, but Paz clearly is a greater draw than either of the women. Fuentes, interestingly, has 1,098. These figures suggest that more attention is paid to male writers than to female writers.

25. The German translator Verónica Beucker notes that as late as 1997 Garro was practically unknown in the German-speaking world (38).

26. "[C]uando te compara con las demás mujeres (todas, sin excepción), las encuentra aburridas, banales, vanidosas, ininteligentes" (quoted in Melgar, "Correspondencias literarias," 426).

27. The letters between Bioy Casares and Garro have been published; for a reaction from the Argentine literary community, see Beltrán del Río.

28. "Elena era una mujer guapa, pero cuando hablaba se transfiguraba y algo la hacía ser la mujer más hermosa, más inteligente, más etérea, la que decía las últimas palabras de una reunión. Juntos, Paz y Garro, el talento estaba de lado de Garro" (Ramírez, 43).

29. See Melgar, *Writing Dark Times*, for a carefully developed essay about Garro's involvement with Madrazo and other aspects of her political life. See also Biron, "The Eccentric Elena Garro."

30. See Rosas Lopátegui, *El asesinato de Elena Garro*, for texts of these articles.

31. See Mora, *Elena Garro*; Melgar also elaborates on the confluence of events that led to Garro's ostracism from the Mexican literary world in *Writing Dark Times*, 2.

32. Vega also emphasizes this point: Augusto "no es una copia fiel del poeta, ni de la relación entre Garro y Paz" (is not a faithful copy of the poet, nor of the relationship between Garro and Paz; 100). According to Toruño, "En general en la obra de Garro hay una relación estrecha entre la ficción y su vida personal: sus personajes principales . . . son mujeres perseguidas y con una hija" (In general in Garro's work there is a close relationship between the fiction and her personal life; her principal characters . . . are persecuted women who have a child; "Protesta contra la opresión," 94). Moreover, Meyer explains that the protagonists appear to represent aspects of Garro's own experience, but without being strictly autobiographical ("Alienation and Escape in Elena Garro's *La semana de colores*," 153).

33. "Tú dices que persigo a Paz. Seguramente te lo dijo él. ¿Podrías decirme cómo lo persigo? ¿Escribiendo? La novela [*Testimonios sobre Mariana*] no es un pleito privado, es ¡una novela! Te diré algo: ¿recuerdas que Mariana lleva a Vicente a visitar a una bailarina en Nueva York? Pues era una amiga rusa, bailarina del Ballet de Montecarlo, que se casó con un monstruo, que la perseguía y la destruyó. . . . Yo ignoro la vida y milagros de Octavio Paz. Si los ignoraba cuando estuve casada con él, pues ahora mucho más, entre él y sus amigos lo cubren con un espeso velo de misterio imposible de penetrar" (Ponce). Garro is also quoted by Carballo as denying that *Testimonios sobre Mariana* is pure autobiography, "una simple calca de mi vida al papel" (a simple copy of my life on paper; Carballo, 514). She does say enigmatically: "Creo que todas las novelas son *romans a clef* o no son novelas" (I believe that all novels are romans à clef or they aren't novels; Carballo, 514).

34. Garro's reference to her trunk of manuscripts is so well known that Robert Anderson and Mara García make use of the allusion in the title of their anthology *Baúl de recuerdos: Homenaje a Elena Garro*.

35. Ibsen notes that "Vicente's description of Mariana [in *Testimonios*] bears many similarities to André Breton's *Nadja*" (96).

36. A number of critics have written about Sor Juana's parody of Calderón de la Barca's play, including Cypess, "Los géneros re/velados"; Rabell; and Weimer.

37. Garro probably chose Ascona as a setting because at the start of the twentieth century it had the reputation of being home to a colorful colony of artists living alternative lifestyles and of revolutionaries, anarchists, philosophers, writers, vegetarians, poets, dancers, and painters from all over the world. The psychoanalyst Carl Gustav Jung, the writer Hermann Hesse, and the artists Alexej von Jawlensky and Marianne von Werefkin are just some of the well-known personalities who lived in Ascona.

38. "Dolor de viuda mucho duele y poco dura" (14).

39. See Freud and Breuer; Gilbert and Gubar, *The Madwoman in the Attic*; and further feminist responses to this, especially the special issue *Psychoanalysis and La Femme* (January 2010): http://www.womenwriters.net/january10/klement.html.

40. As Orlando reminds us, "So often the socialization of women in patriarchal societies has led to hysteria and sickness, creating women-mutants out of pain and stifling access to subjectivity" (44).

41. "Me casé para poder tomar café" (I got married in order to be able to drink coffee; http://redescolar.ilce.edu.mx/redescolar/publicaciones/publi_quepaso/elena_garro.htm).

42. "No soy feminista. Nada de eso. ¿Por qué? Las mujeres manejamos sólo ideas que han descubierto los hombres. El día que manejemos ideas propias entonces seré feminista. No hay mujer que haya tenido una idea" ("Los recuerdos son mi manera de vivir," Beucker, 42).

43. While no writer is willing to admit to this chilling effect, it is certainly a rumor among the critics who work with Elena Garro's texts. Some suggest that Garro was nominated twice for the Premio Nacional de Literatura but that other members of the jury refused to accept her name because of Paz. See Melgar, *Writing Dark Times*, 12.

44. One of Melgar's essays relating to Garro's role in the student uprisings of 1968 ("IFAI vs. Garro, ¿Información o difamación?") has yet to be published. I want to thank Melgar for giving me a copy of the essay and for sharing her wealth of knowledge about Garro and Mexican sociocultural history.

45. "Quiero que sepas de una vez: . . . que yo vivo contra él . . . , estudié contra él, hablé contra él, tuve amantes contra él, escribí contra él y defendí a los indios contra él, escribí de política contra él, en fin *todo, todo, todo* lo que soy es contra él. Por eso persigue a mis amigos y familiares" (Mora, "Elena cuenta su historia," 296).

46. "El Laureado no quiso, no quiere, ni querrá que trabajemos. Es la manera de anularnos, esclavizarnos y volvernos esquizofrénicas" (Mora, "Elena cuenta su historia," 296).

47. Fernández Unsáin likened their interactions to a war (quoted in Vega, 102).

48. Rosas Lopátegui expects to publish a collection of Garro's poetry just as she has done with the theater pieces and the journalistic essays.

49. "[E]lla puede convertirlo en oro en su literatura" (Carballo and Batis, 65).

BIBLIOGRAPHY

PRIMARY SOURCES

Garro, Elena. "A mí me ha ocurrido todo al revés." *Cuadernos Hispanoamericanos* 346 (April 1979), 38–51.

———. *Andamos huyendo Lola.* Mexico City: Joaquín Mortiz, 1980.

———. "Andarse por las ramas." In *Un hogar sólido y otras piezas*, 65–78. Xalapa: Universidad Veracruzana, 1983.

———. "Benito Fernández." In *Un hogar sólido y otras piezas*, 271–309. Xalapa: Universidad Veracruzana, 1983.

———. *Busca mi esquela & Primer amor.* Monterrey, Nuevo León: Ediciones Castillo, 1996.

———. *La casa junto al río.* Mexico City: Grijalbo, 1983.

———. "La culpa es de los tlaxcaltecas." In *La semana de colores*, 9–33. Xalapa: Editorial Veracruzana, 1964.

———. "The Dogs." Trans. Beth Miller. In *A Different Reality*, ed. Anita K. Stoll, 68–79. Lewisburg: Bucknell UP, 1990.

———. "El encanto, tendajón mixto." In *Un hogar sólido y otras piezas*, 129–149. Xalapa: Universidad Veracruzana, 1983.

———. "Era Mercurio." In *La semana de colores*, 155–164. Mexico City: Editorial Grijalbo, 1989.

———. *Felipe Ángeles.* Mexico City: Universidad Nacional Autónoma de México, 1979.

———. *First Love & Look for My Obituary: Two Novellas*. Trans. David Unger. Willimantic, CT: Curbstone P, 1997.

———. *Un hogar sólido*. Xalapa, Mexico: Universidad Veracruzana, 1958.

———. *Inés*. Mexico City: Grijalbo, 1995.

———. "The Lady on Her Balcony." Trans. Beth Miller. In *A Different Reality*, ed. Anita K. Stoll, 59–68. Lewisburg: Bucknell UP, 1990.

———. *Memorias de España 1937*. Mexico City: Siglo XXI, 1992.

———. *Mi hermanita Magdalena*. Monterrey, Mexico: Ediciones Castillo, 1998.

———. "La mudanza." *La Palabra y el Hombre* 10 (April–June 1959): 263–274. Reprinted in *Un hogar sólido y otras piezas*, 311–332. Xalapa: Universidad Veracruzana, 1983.

———. "Nuestras vidas son los ríos." In *La semana de colores*, 165–174. Mexico City: Editorial Grijalbo, 1989.

———. "Los perros." *Revista de la Universidad de México* 19.7 (1965): 20–23.

———. "Los pilares de doña Blanca." In *Un hogar sólido y otras piezas*, 29–41. Xalapa: Universidad Veracruzana, 1958.

———. *Recollections of Things to Come*. Trans. Ruth L. C. Simms. Austin: U of Texas P, 1969.

———. *Los recuerdos del porvenir*. Mexico City: Joaquín Mortiz, 1963.

———. *Reencuentro de personajes*. Mexico City: Grijalbo, 1982.

———. *Revolucionarios mexicanos*. Mexico City: Seix Barral, 1997.

———. *La semana de colores*. Xalapa: Universidad Veracruzana, 1964.

———. "La señora en su balcón." In *Teatro breve hispanoamericano contemporáneo*, 344–358. Madrid: Aguilar, 1970.

———. *Sócrates y los gatos*. Mexico City: Océano, 2003.

———. "A Solid Home." Trans. Francesca Colecchia and Julio Matas. In *Selected Latin American One Act Plays*, 35–52. Pittsburgh: U of Pittsburgh P, 1973.

———. *Testimonios sobre Mariana*. Mexico City: Grijalbo, 1981.

———. *Un traje rojo para un duelo*. Monterrey, Mexico: Ediciones Castillo 1996.

———. *Y Matarazo no llamó*. Mexico City: Grijalbo, 1991.

Paz, Ireneo. *Amor y suplicio* (1873). Mexico City: Impr. y Litografía de I. Paz, 1881.

———. *Doña Marina*. Mexico City: Impr. y Litografía de I. Paz, 1883.

Paz, Octavio. *¿Águila o sol?* Mexico City: Tezontle, 1951.

———. *Águila o sol/Eagle or Sun*. Trans. Eliot Weinberger. New York: New Directions, 1970.

———. *Alternating Current*. Trans. Helen R. Lane. New York, Viking Press, 1973.

———. "André Bretón: La niebla y el relámpago." *Vuelta* 20.232 (1996): 20–21.

———. *El arco y la lira*. Mexico City: Fondo de Cultura Económica, 1956.

———. *Children of the Mire*. Trans. Rachel Phillips. Cambridge, MA: Harvard UP, 1974.

———. *The Collected Poems of Octavio Paz, 1957–1987*. Trans. Eliot Weinberger. New York: New Directions Publishing, 1991.

———. *Conjunctions and Disjunctions*. New York, Viking Press, 1974.

———. "Contemporáneos." In *Generaciones y semblanzas: Obras completas 4*, 69–93. Mexico City: Fondo de Cultura Económica, 1991.

———. "Conversación con Claude Fell: Vuelta a *El laberinto de la soledad*." In *El ogro filantrópico*, 17–37. Mexico City: Joaquín Mortiz, 1979. Reprinted in *The Labyrinth of Solitude; The Other Mexico; Return to the Labyrinth of Solitude; Mexico and the United States; The Philanthropic Ogre*, 329–353. Trans. Lysander Kemp, Yara Milos, and Rachel Phillips Belash. New York: Grove P, 1985.

———. *Corriente alterna*. Mexico City: Siglo Veintiuno, 1969.

———. *The Double Flame: Love and Eroticism*. Trans. Helen K. Lane. New York: Grove P, 1995.

———. "Entre la piedra y la flor." http://www.cuentosyfabulas.com.ar/2010/11/poema -entre-la-piedra-y-la-flor-octavio.html.

———. "Entre la piedra y la flor." *Letras Libres* (August 1977): 12–13.

———. *Los hijos del limo: Del romanticismo a la vanguardia*. Barcelona: Seix Barral, 1974.

———. *Hombres en su siglo y otros ensayos*. Barcelona: Seix Barral, 1989.

———. "Homenaje a Sor Juana Inés de la Cruz en su tercer centenario (1651–1695)." *Sur* 206 (1951): 29–40.

———. *In Light of India*. Trans. Eliot Weinberger. New York: Harcourt Brace, 1997.

———. "Interview." Roberto González Echevarría; Emir Rodríguez Monegal. Trans. Rolena Adorno. *Diacritics* 2.3 (1972): 35–40.

———. *Itinerario*. Mexico City: Fondo de Cultura Económica, 1993.

———. *Itinerary*. Trans. Jason Wilson. London: Menard P, 1999.

———. *El laberinto de la soledad* (1950). Mexico City: Fondo de Cultura Económica, 1983.

———. *The Labyrinth of Solitude; The Other Mexico; Return to the Labyrinth of Solitude; Mexico and the United States; The Philanthropic Ogre*. Trans. by Lysander Kemp, Yara Milos, and Rachel Phillips Belash. New York: Grove P, 1985.

———. *La llama doble, amor y erotismo*. Barcelona: Seix Barral, 1993.

———. "México, después del seis de julio: Una encuesta." *Vuelta* (July 1997): 17–19.

———. *México en la obra de Octavio Paz, 2: Generaciones y semblanzas*. Escritores y Letras de México. Mexico City: Fondo de Cultura Económica, 1987.

———. "México: Olimpiada de 1968." In *La Cultura en México*, October 30, 1968, 3.

———. *The Monkey Grammarian*. Trans. Helen R. Lane. New York: Arcade, 1990.

———. *El mono gramático*. Barcelona: Seix Barral, 1974.

———. "Novela y provincia: Agustín Yañez." In *Puertas al campo*, 142–150. Mexico City: Universidad Nacional Autónoma de México, 1966.

———. *Obras completas de Octavio Paz*. Mexico City: Fondo de Cultura Económica, 1994.

———. *Obras completas: Vol. 13*. Mexico City: Fondo de Cultura Económica, 1994.

———. "Octavio Paz por él mismo 1914–1924." Guillermo Sheridan and Gustavo Jiménez Aguirre, eds., *Reforma*, April 6, 1994, 12D and 13D. http://www.horizonte.unam .mx/cuadernos/paz/pazz.html.

———. *El ogro filantrópico: Historia y política 1971–1978.* Mexico City, Joaquín Mortiz, 1979.

———. *The Other Mexico: Critique of the Pyramid.* New York: Grove P, 1972.

———. "Pablo Neruda en el corazón." In *Primeras letras (1931–1943),* ed. Enrico Mario Santí, 143–152. Mexico City: Vuelta, 1988.

———. *El peregrino en su patria.* Mexico City: Fondo de Cultura Económica, 1994.

———. "Piedra de sol." In *Libertad bajo palabra: Obra poética (1935–1958).* Mexico City: Fondo de Cultura Económica, 1960.

———. "La poesía de Carlos Pellicer." In *Las peras del olmo,* 75–83. Barcelona: Seix Barral, 1971.

———. *Posdata.* Mexico City: Siglo XXI, 1970.

———. *Raíz del hombre.* Mexico City: Simbad, 1937.

———. "The Shame of the Olympics." Trans. Mark Strand. *New York Review of Books* 11.8 (November 7, 1968), 4.

———. *Sor Juana Inés de la Cruz o las trampas de la fe.* Barcelona: Seix Barral, 1982.

———. *Sor Juana or the Traps of Faith.* Trans. Margaret Sayers Peden. Boston: Harvard UP, 1988.

———. "Twilight of Revolution." *Dissent* 21.1 (January 1974): 56–62.

———. *Vislumbres de la India.* Barcelona: Seix Barral, 1995.

———. "Vuelta a *El laberinto de la soledad* (Conversación con Claude Fell)." In *El laberinto de la soledad; Posdata; Vuelta a El laberinto de la soledad,* 303–329. 3rd ed. Mexico City: Fondo de Cultura Económica, 1999.

———. "Who Won the Spanish Civil War?: The Barricades and Beyond." *New Republic* 197.19 (November 9, 1987): 26–30.

———. *Xavier Villaurrutia en persona y en obra.* Mexico City: Fondo de Cultura Económica, 1978.

Paz Garro, Helena. *Memorias.* Mexico City: Océano, 2003.

SECONDARY SOURCES

Adorno, Rolena. "The Warrior and the War Community: Constructions of the Civil Order in Mexican Conquest History." *Dispositio* 14.36–38 (1989): 225–246.

Aguilar Camín, Héctor, and Lorenzo Meyer. *In the Shadow of the Mexican Revolution: Contemporary Mexican History, 1919–1989.* Trans. Luis Alberto Fierro. Austin: U of Texas P, 1996.

Aguilar Mora, Jorge. "Diálogo con *Los hijos del limo* de Octavio Paz." In *Octavio Paz: La dimensión estética del ensayo,* 187–211. Mexico City: Siglo Veintiuno, 2004.

———. *La divina pareja, historia y mito: Valoración e interpretación de la obra ensayística de Octavio Paz* (1978). Mexico City: Ediciones Era, 1991.

———. *Una muerte sencilla, justa, eterna: Vultura y guerra durante la Revolución Mexicana.* Mexico City: Ediciones Era, 1990.

———. "Prólogo: El silencio de Nellie Campobello." In *Cartucho,* 9–42. Mexico City: Era, 2000.

Alarcón, Norma. "Chicana's Feminist Literature: A Re-Vision through Malintzin: Putting Flesh Back on the Object." In *This Bridge Called My Back*, ed. Cherríe Moraga and Gloria Anzaldúa, 182–190. New York: Kitchen Table Press, 1983.

———. "Traddutora, Traditora: A Paradigmatic Figure of Chicana Feminism." *Cultural Critique* 13 (1989): 57–87.

Alegría, Juana Armanda. *Psicología de las mexicanas*. Mexico City: Samo, 1975.

Álvarez Lobato, Carmen. "Perspectiva crítica de la cristiada en *Los recuerdos del porvenir*, de Elena Garro, y *José Trigo*, de Fernando del Paso." *Revista de Literatura Mexicana Contemporánea* 10.22 (2004): xxviii–xl.

Ancona, Eligio. *Los mártires de Anáhuac: La novela del México colonial* (1870). Vol. 1. Ed. Antonio Castro Leal. Mexico City: Aguilar, 1964.

Anderson, Robert K. "El ahogado más hermoso del mundo y Felipe Hurtado: Dos agentes de metamorfosis." *Selecta: Journal of the Pacific Northwest Council on Foreign Languages* 9 (1988): 102–106.

———. "La cuentística mágico-realista de Elena Garro." *Selecta: Journal of the Pacific Northwest Council on Foreign Languages* 3 (1982): 117–121.

———. "Myth and Archetype in *Recollections of Things to Come*." *Studies in Twentieth Century Literature* 9.2 (1985): 213–227.

———. "*La señora en su balcón* y *Los recuerdos del porvenir*: Paralelismos temáticos." In *Baúl de recuerdos: Homenaje a Elena Garro*, ed. Robert K. Anderson and Mara García, 133–143. Tlaxcala, Mexico: Universidad Autónoma de Tlaxcala, 1999.

Anderson, Robert K., and Mara García, eds. *Baúl de recuerdos: Homenaje a Elena Garro*. Tlaxala, Mexico: Universidad Autónoma de Tlaxcala, 1999.

Anzaldúa, Gloria. *Borderlands/La frontera: The New Mestiza*. San Francisco: Aunt Lute, 1987.

Aparicio, Frances R. "On Sub-versive Signifiers: U.S. Latina/o Writers Tropicalize English." *American Literature* 66.4 (1994): 795–801.

Arrizón, Alicia. "Soldaderas and the Staging of the Mexican Revolution." *TDR: The Drama Review—A Journal of Performance Studies* 42.1 (Spring 1998): 90–112.

Ashby, Joe C. *Organized Labor and the Mexican Revolution under Lázaro Cárdenas*. Chapel Hill: U of North Carolina P, 1967.

Assmann, Jan. "Collective Memory and Cultural Identity." *New German Critique* 65 (1995): 125–133.

Azuela, Mariano. *Los de abajo* (1915). 6th ed. Mexico City: Fondo de Cultura Económica, 1967.

———. *The Underdogs: Pictures and Scenes from the Present Revolution: A Translation of Mariano Azuela's "Los de abajo" with Related Texts*. Trans. Gustavo Pellón. Indianapolis: Hackett Publishing Company, 2006.

Balam, Gilberto. *Tlatelolco: Reflexiones de un testigo 1969*. Mexico City: Talleres Lenasas, 1969.

Balderston, Daniel. "The New Historical Novel: History and Fantasy in *Los recuerdos del porvenir*." *Bulletin of Hispanic Studies* 66 (1989): 41–46.

Bartra, Roger. "A la chingada." In *La jaula de la melancolía*, 205–224. Mexico City: Editorial Grijalbo, 1987.

Baudot, Georges. "Malintzin, imagen y discurso de mujer en el primer Mexico virreinal." In *La Malinche, sus padres y sus hijos*, ed. Margo Glantz, 55–89. Mexico City: UNAM P, 1995.

Beckjord, Sarah H. "'Con sal y ají y tomates': Las redes textuales de Bernal Díaz en el caso de Cholula." *Revista Iberoamericana* 61.170–171 (1995): 147–160.

Beltrán del Río, Pascal. "Cartas de Adolfo Bioy Casares a Elena Garro." *Suplemento Literario La Nación (Buenos Aires)* (November 30, 1997): 1–2.

Benjamin, Thomas. *La Revolución: Mexico's Great Revolution as Memory, Myth, and History*. Austin: U of Texas P, 2000.

Benjamin, Thomas, and Marcial Ocasio-Meléndez. "Organizing the Memory of Modern Mexico: Porfirian Historiography in Perspective, 1880's–1980's." *Hispanic American Historical Review* 64.2 (1984): 323–364.

Berler, Beatrice. "The Mexican Revolution as Reflected in the Novel." *Hispania* 42 (1964): 41–46.

Berman, Sabina. *Entre Villa y una mujer desnuda*. Mexico City: Milagro, 1994.

Bermúdez, Sari. *Voces que cuentan*. Mexico City: Plaza y Janes 2002.

Bertrand de Muñoz, Maryse. "Les poètes hispano-américains et la guerre civile espagnole." In *Actas del Simposio Internacional de Estudios Hispánicos*, 265–276. Budapest: Maison d'Édition de l'Académie des Sciences de Hongrie, 1976.

Beucker, Verónica. "Encuentro con Elena Garro." In *Lectura múltiple de una personalidad compleja*, ed. Lucía Melgar-Palacios and Gabriela Mora, 37–52. Puebla, Mexico: Benemérita Universidad Autónoma de Puebla, 2002.

Beverley, John. *Testimonio: On the Politics of Truth*. Minneapolis: U of Minnesota P, 2004.

Bianco, José. *La pérdida del reino*. Buenos Aires: Siglo XXI, 1972.

Bidault de la Calle, Sophie. *Una escritura salida del cuerpo*. Mexico City: CONACULTA-INBA/CENIDI DANZA, 2003.

Bioy Casares, Adolfo. *El sueño de los héroes*. Buenos Aires: Emecé, 1954.

Biron, Rebecca. "The Eccentric Elena Garro: Critical Confrontations in the 1960s." *Torre de Papel* 10.2 (2000): 102–117.

———. "Un hogar insólito: Elena Garro and Mexican Literary Culture." In *The Effects of the Nation: Mexican Art in an Age of Globalization*, 138–159. Philadelphia: Temple UP, 2001.

———. "No se trata de la influencia, sino de la injerencia: Armonía Somers y Octavio Paz en diálogo con los modernistas ingleses y europeos." *Palabra y el Hombre: Revista de la Universidad Veracruzana* 121 (2002): 83–90.

———. "*Testimonios sobre Mariana*: Representación y la otra mujer." In *Sin imágenes falsas, sin falsos espejos: Narrados mexicanas del siglo XX*, 161–183. Mexico City: El Colegio de México, 1995.

———. "El tiempo femenino y los colonizados en Elena Garro y Rosario Castellanos." In *Pensamiento y crítica: Los discursos de la cultura hoy*, 301–314. East Lansing: Michigan State U/U of Louisville/Centro de Cultura Casa Lamm, 2000.

Blanco Moheno, Roberto. *Tlatelolco: Historia de una infamia*. Mexico City: Editorial Diana, 1969.

Bloom, Harold, ed. *Octavio Paz*. Philadelphia: Chelsea House, 2002.

Boschetto, Sandra. "Romancing the Stone in Elena Garro's *Los recuerdos del porvenir*." *Journal of the Midwest Modern Language Association* 22.2 (1989): 1–11.

Bowskill, Sarah E. L. "Women, Violence, and the Mexican Cristero Wars in Elena Garro's *Los recuerdos del porvenir* and Dolores Castro's *La ciudad y el viento*." *Modern Language Review* 104, no. 2 (April 2009): 438–452.

Boyd, Lola E. "Zapata in the Literature of the Mexican Revolution." *Hispania* 52.4 (1969): 903–910.

Brenan, Gerald. *The Spanish Labyrinth: An Account of the Social and Political Background of the Spanish Civil War*. Cambridge: Cambridge University Press, 1943.

Brewster, Claire. *Responding to Crisis in Contemporary Mexico: The Political Writings of Paz, Fuentes, Monsiváis, and Poniatowska*. Tucson: U of Arizona P, 2005.

Bruce Novoa, Juan. "La novela de la Revolución Mexicana: La topología del final." *Hispania* 74.1 (1991): 36–44.

Bryan, Anthony. *The Politics of the Porfiriato: A Research Review*. Bloomington: Latin American Studies Program, Indiana University, 1973.

Buck, Sarah A. "Constructing a Historiography of Mexican Women and Gender." *Gender & History* 20.1 (2008): 152–160.

Bunk, Brian D. *Revolutionary Warrior and Gendered Icon: Aida Lafuente and the Spanish Revolution of 1934*. Baltimore: Johns Hopkins UP, 2003.

Butler, Judith. *Gender Trouble: Feminism and the Subversion of Identity*. New York: Routledge, 1990.

Cabrera Rafael. "'Cuando decidimos traer a Elena Garro a México para apoyarla, fue un error': René Avilés Fabila." *Alba de América* 23.43–44 (2004): 615–624.

Camino, Mercedes M. "War, Wounds and Women: The Spanish Civil War in Victor Erice's *El espíritu de la colmena* and David Trueba's *Soldados de Salamina*." *International Journal of Iberian Studies* 20.2 (2007): 91–104.

Campbell, Joseph. *The Hero with a Thousand Faces*. Princeton: Princeton UP, 1968.

Campobello, Nellie. *Apuntes sobre la vida militar de Francisco Villa*. Mexico City: Edición y Distribución Ibero-Americana de Publicaciones, 1940.

———. *Cartucho and My Mother's Hands*. Trans. Doris Meyer and Irene Matthews. Austin: U of Texas P, 1988.

———. *Cartucho: Relatos de la lucha en el norte de México* (1931). Ed. Jorge Aguilar Mora. Mexico City: Ediciones Era, 2000.

Campos, Marco A., and Alejandro Toledo. *Narraciones sobre el movimiento estudiantil de 1968*. Xalapa, Mexico: Universidad Veracruzana, 1986.

Campos Lemus, Sócrates. *El otoño de la revolución (octubre).* Mexico City: B. Costa-Amic, 1974.

Candelaria, Cordelia. "La Malinche, Feminist Prototype." *Frontiers* 5 (1980): 1–6.

Cantú Hernández, Arturo. "Octavio Paz: Una mala interpretación de Tlatelolco." *Armas y Letras* 2 (1970): 22–28.

Carballo, Emmanuel. *Diecinueve protagonistas de la literatura mexicana del siglo XX,* 408–515. Mexico City: Empresas Editoriales, S.A., 1965.

Carballo, Emmanuel, and Huberto Batis. "Los cazamemorias: ¿Perseguidos o perseguidores? Conversación radiofónica sobre Elena Garro." In *Elena Garro: Lectura múltiple de una personalidad compleja,* ed. Lucía Melgar-Palacios and Gabriela Mora, 53–66. Puebla, Mexico: Benemérita Universidad Autónoma de Puebla, 2002.

Cárdenas Fernández, Blanca. "Discurso y poder en 'La culpa es de los tlaxcaltecas,' de Elena Garro." In *El indio Malanga: Écrire la domination en Amérique Latin: Rosario Castellanos, "Balún-Canán," 1957; José María Arguedas, "Los ríos profundos," 1958; Jorge Icaza, "El Chulla Romero y Flores," 1958,* 265–280. Perpignan, France: Presses Universitaires de Perpignan, 2006.

Carey, Elaine. *Plaza of Sacrifices: Gender, Power, and Terror in 1968 Mexico.* Albuquerque: U of New Mexico P, 2005.

Carpenter, Victoria. "Dream-Sex and Time Travel: The Meaning of 'Piedra de Sol' by Octavio Paz." *Bulletin of Hispanic Studies* 78.4 (October 2001): 493–513.

Carrasco, David. *Quetzalcoatl and the Irony of Empire.* Chicago: U of Chicago P, 1982.

Castellanos, Rosario. *Balún-Canán.* Mexico City: Fondo de Cultura Económica, 1957.

———. *El eterno femenino.* Mexico City: Fondo de Cultura Económica, 1975.

———. "In Memory of Tlatelolco." In *Massacre in Mexico,* ed. Elena Poniatowska, trans. Helen R. Lane, 171–172. New York: Viking Press, 1975.

———. *The Nine Guardians.* Trans. Irene Nicholson. New York: Vanguard, 1960.

Castillo, Debra. *Easy Women: Sex and Gender in Modern Mexican Fiction.* Minneapolis: U of Minnesota P, 1998.

———. *Talking Back: Toward a Latin American Feminist Literary Criticism.* Ithaca: Cornell University Press, 1992.

Castro-Gómez, Santiago. "Traditional vs. Critical Cultural Theory." Trans. Francisco González and Andre Moskowitz. *Cultural Critique* 49.0 (2001): 139–154.

Castro Leal, Antonio, and Berta Gamboa. *La novela de la revolución mexicana.* Mexico City: Aguilar, 1964.

Cate-Arries, Francie. "Re-imagining the Cultural Legacy of a Sixteenth-Century Empire: Spanish Exiles in 1940s Mexico." *Hispanic Research Journal: Iberian and Latin American Studies* 6.2 (2005): 117–130.

Chant, Sylvia, and Nikki Craske, eds. *Gender in Latin America.* New Brunswick: Rutgers UP.

Chariomonte, Nicola. *The Paradox of History: Stendhal, Tolstoy, Pasternak, and Others.* Philadelphia: U of Pennsylvania P, 1985.

Chavarría, Jesús. "A Brief Inquiry into Octavio Paz' *Laberinto* of *Mexicanidad*." *Americas* 27.4 (1971): 381–388.

Chiles, Frances. *Octavio Paz: The Mythic Dimension*. New York: Peter Lang, 1986.

Cohn, Carol. "Wars, Wimps and Women: Talking Gender and Thinking War." In *Gendering War Talk*, ed. Miriam Cooke and Angela Woollacott, 227–246. Princeton, NJ: Princeton UP, 1993.

Cohn, Deborah. "The Mexican Intelligentsia, 1950–1968: Cosmopolitanism, National Identity, and the State." *Mexican Studies/Estudios Mexicanos* 21.1 (2005): 141–182.

Collier, George, with Elizabeth Lowery Quaratiello. *Basta: Land and the Zapatista Rebellion in Chiapas*. Oakland, CA: Institute for Food and Development Policy, 1994.

Conley, Tom. "Broken Blockage: Notas sobre la Guerra civil española en el cine de Hollywood (1937–1944)." *Revista de Occidente* 53 (1985): 47–59.

Conteris, Hiber. "Octavio Paz: Crítica de la revolución." *Siglo XX/20th Century* 10.1–2 (1992): 143–163.

Cooke, Miriam, and Angela Woollacott. *Gendering War Talk*. Princeton: Princeton UP, 1993.

Cortés, Eladio. "Felipe Ángeles, Theater of Heroes." In *A Different Reality: Studies on the Work of Elena Garro*, ed. Anita K. Stoll, 80–89. Lewisburg: Bucknell UP, 1990.

———. "*Memorias de España: Obra inédita* de Elena Garro." In *De literatura hispánica*, 65–77. Mexico City: Editores Mexicanos Unidos, 1989.

Cortés, Hernán. *Letters from Mexico*. Trans. and ed. Anthony Pagden. New Haven: Yale UP, 1986.

Cypess, Sandra Messinger. "*Balún-Canán*: A Model Demonstration of Discourse as Power." *Revista de Estudios Hispánicos* 19.3 (1985): 1–15.

———. "The Cultural Memory of Malinche in Mexico City: Stories by Elena Garro and Cristina Pacheco." In *Unfolding the City: Women Write the City in Latin America*, ed. Anne Lambright and Elisabeth Guerrero, 147–166. Minneapolis: U of Minnesota P, 2007.

———. "Del corpus dramático al corpus político." In *Baúl de recuerdos: Homenaje a Elena Garro*, ed. Robert K. Anderson and Mara García, 85–97. Tlaxcala, Mexico: Universidad Autónoma de Tlaxcala, 1999.

———. "Dramaturgia femenina y transposición histórica." *Alba de América: Revista Literaria* 7.12–13 (July 1989): 283–304.

———. "Elena Garro and Tlatelolco: A Mexican Writer and the Student Massacre of 1968." *Latin American Studies Center News* 13.1 (Fall 2002): 3.

———. "The Figure of La Malinche in the Texts of Elena Garro." In *A Different Reality: Studies in the Works of Elena Garro*, ed. Anita Stoll, 117–135. Lewisberg, PA: Bucknell UP, 1990.

———. "Los géneros re/velados en 'Los empeños de una casa de Sor Juana Inés de la Cruz.'" *Hispamérica: Revista de Literatura* 22.64–65 (1993): 177–185.

———. *La Malinche in Mexican Literature: From History to Myth*. Austin: U of Texas P, 1991.

———. "'Mother' Malinche and Allegories of Gender, Ethnicity and National Identity in Mexico." In *Feminism, Nation, and Myth: La Malinche*, ed. Rolando Romero and Amanda Nolacea Harris, 14–27. Houston: Arte Público P, 2005.

———. "¿Quién ha oído hablar de ellas? Una revisión de las dramaturgas mexicanas." *Texto Crítico* (Xalapa, Mexico) 10 (1978): 55–64.

———. "Titles as Signs in the Translation of Dramatic Texts." In *Translation Perspectives II: Selected Papers, 1984–1985*, 95-104. Binghamton: Translation Research and Instruction Program, State U of New York at Binghamton, 1985.

———. "Tlatelolco: From Ruins to Poetry." In *Telling Ruins in Contemporary Latin America*, ed. Michael Lazzara and Vicky Unruh, 163–173. New York: Palgrave/Macmillan, 2009.

Darrow, Margaret H. *French Women and the First World War*. New York: Berg Press, 2000.

Dauster, Frank. "Elena Garro y sus *Recuerdos del porvenir*." *Journal of Spanish Studies: Twentieth Century* 8.1–2 (1980): 57–65.

Dawes, Greg. "Octavio Paz: El camino hacia la desilusión." In *Octavio Paz: La dimensión estética del ensayo*, ed. Héctor Jaimes, 233–248. Mexico City: Siglo xxi Editores, 2004.

———. "On the Textualization of Sexuality and History in Hispanism." *Cultural Logic: An Electronic Journal*. http://clogic.eserver.org/1-1/dawes.html.

———. "Realism, Surrealism, Socialist Realism and Neruda's 'Guided Spontaneity.'" http://clogic.eserver.org/2003/dawes.html.

de Lauretis, Teresa. "Eccentric Subjects." *Feminist Studies* 16. 1 (1990): 115–150.

Del Castillo, Adelaida R. "Malintzín Tenepal: A Preliminary Look into a New Perspective." *Encuentro Femenil* 1.2 (1974): 58–77. Reprinted in *Essays on La Mujer*, ed. Rosaura Sánchez and Rosa Martínez Cruz, 124–149. Los Angeles: Chicano Studies Center, 1977.

del Paso, Fernando. *José Trigo*. Mexico City: Siglo XXI Editores, 1966.

Del Río, Marcela. *Perfil del Teatro de la Revolución Mexicana*. New York: Peter Lang, 1993.

Díaz del Castillo, Bernal. *The Conquest of New Spain* (Penguin Classics). Trans. John M. Cohen. Hammondsworth, Middlesex, England: Penguin Books, 1963. Rpt. 1978.

———. *La historia verdadera de la conquista de la Nueva España* (1632). 6th ed. Madrid: Espasa-Calpe, 1984.

Domínguez Michael, Christopher. "*El asesinato de Elena Garro*, de Patricia Rosas Lopátegui." *Letras Libres* (October 2006). http://www.letraslibres.com/index.php ?art=11552.

Domínguez Miguela, Antonia. "Language Tropicalization in Latino/a Literature." *US Latino/a Literature*. http://www.uhu.es/antonia.dominguez/latinas/growing.pdf.

Doremus, Anne. "Indigenism, Mestizaje, and National Identity in Mexico during the 1940s and the 1950s." *Mexican Studies/Estudios Mexicanos* 17.2 (2001): 375–402.

Dove, Patrick. "Reflections on the Origin: Transculturation and Tragedy in Pedro Páramo." *Angelaki* 6.1 (2001): 91–110.

Doyle, Kate. "The Dead of Tlatelolco." National Security Archive Electronic Briefing Book No. 201. October 1, 2006. http://www.gwu.edu/~nsarchiv/NSAEBB/NSAEBB 201/index.htm#article.

———. "Tlatelolco Massacre: Declassified U.S. Documents on Mexico and the Events of 1968." *The National Security Archive Electronic Briefing Books.* 2003. http://www.gwu .edu/~nsarchiv/NSAEBB/.

Duncan, Cynthia. "'La culpa es de los tlaxcaltecas': A Reevaluation of Mexico's Past through Myth." *Crítica Hispánica* 7.2 (1985): 105–120.

———. "Time and Memory as Structural Unifiers in Elena Garro's *Los recuerdos del porvenir.*" *Journal of Interdisciplinary Studies* 4.1–2 (1992): 31–53.

Duncan, J. Ann. *Voices, Visions, and a New Reality: Mexican Fiction since 1970.* Pittsburgh: U of Pittsburgh P, 1986.

Durgan, Andy. *The Spanish Civil War.* New York: Palgrave, 2007.

Earle, Peter G. "Octavio Paz y Elena Garro: Una incompatibilidad creativa." *Revista Iberoamericana* 76.232–233 (July 2010): 877–897.

Eliot, T. S. "Hamlet and His Problems" (1920). In *The Sacred Wood: Essays on Poetry and Criticism,* 95–103. London: Methuen and Company, 1921.

Elshtain, Jean Bethke. *Women and War.* Chicago: U of Chicago P, 1987.

Elu de Leñero, María del Carmen. *¿Hacia dónde va la mujer mexicana? Proyecciones a partir de los datos de una encuesta nacional.* Mexico City: Instituto Mexicano de Estudios Sociales, 1969.

Enloe, Cynthia. *The Morning After: Sexual Politics at the End of the Cold War.* Berkeley: U of California P, 1993.

Erll, Astrid, and Ann Rigney. "Literature and the Production of Cultural Memory." *European Journal of English Studies* 10.2 (2006): 111–212.

Espinosa, Fernando. "Ideology in the Works of Octavio Paz and José Carlos Mariátegui: The Pre-Columbian Case." *Atisbos Journal of Chicano Research* (1976–1977): 71–96.

Espinosa, Gabriela. "La revolución mexicana: Imaginar la revolución: Escritura revolucionaria." *Alba de América: Revista Literaria* 17.32 (1999): 117–128.

Esquivel, Laura. *Como agua para chocolate.* Mexico City: Planeta, 1989.

———. *Malinche.* Mexico City: Suma de Letras, 2006.

Evangelista, Matthew. "Culture, Identity, and Conflict: The Influence of Gender." In *Conflict and Reconstruction in Multiethnic Societies,* 81–85. Washington, DC: National Academies Press, 2003.

Excéntrica—Escritor de la semana: Octavio Paz. http://www.excentricaonline.com/li bros/escritores_more.php?id=6231_0_8_0_M.

Faber, Sebastiaan. "Between Cernuda's Paradise and Buñuel's Hell: Mexico through Spanish Exiles' Eyes." *Bulletin of Spanish Studies* 80.2 (2003): 219–239.

Feito, Francisco E., and Juan Chabas. "Notas a una crítica olvidada sobre Vallejo, Neruda y Paz." *Texto Crítico* 9 (1978): 184–204.

Felman, Shoshana. *What Does a Woman Want?: Reading and Sexual Difference.* Baltimore: Johns Hopkins University Press, 1993.

Fernández Retamar, Roberto, John Beverley, and Miguel Llinás. "Martí in His (Third) World." *Boundary 2: An International Journal of Literature and Culture* 36.1 (2009): 61–94.

Ferrán, Ofelia. "*Memoria de la melancolía* by María Teresa León: The Performativity and Disidentification of Exilic Memories." *Journal of Spanish Cultural Studies* 6.1 (2005): 59–78.

Figueroa Torres, Jesús. *Doña Marina: Una india ejemplar*. Mexico City: Costa-Amic, 1957.

Finoglio-Limón, Irene. "Reading Mexico 1968: Literature, Memory and Politics." In *Memories of 1968: International Perspectives*, ed. Ingo Cornils and Sarah Walters, 299–319. Oxford/New York: Peter Lang, 2010.

Fisher, Lillian Estelle. "The Influence of the Present Mexican Revolution upon the Status of Women." *Hispanic American Historical Review* 23.1 (1942): 211–228.

Fitts, Alexandra. "Sandra Cisneros's Modern Malinche: A Reconsideration of Feminine Archetypes in *Woman Hollering Creek*." *International Fiction Review* 29.1 and 2 (2002): 11–22.

Florescano, Enrique. *National Narratives in Mexico: A History*. Trans. Nancy T. Hancock. Norman: U of Oklahoma P, 2006.

Forster, Merlin H. *Las vanguardias literarias en México y la América Central: Bibliografía y antología crítica*. Madrid: Vervuert, 2001.

Franco, Jean. *The Modern Culture of Latin America: Society and the Artist*. New York: F. A. Praeger, 1967.

———. *Plotting Women*. New York: Columbia UP, 1989.

———. "Vallejo and the Crisis of the Thirties." *Hispania* 72.1 (1989): 42–48.

Frazier, Lessie Jo, and Deborah Cohen. "Defining the Space of Mexico '68: Heroic Masculinity in the Prison and 'Women' in the Streets." *Hispanic American Historical Review* 83.4 (2003): 617–660.

Freud, Sigmund, and Joseph Breuer. *Studies in Hysteria*. Trans. Nicola Luckhurst. London: Penguin, 2004.

Fuentes, Carlos. *The Death of Artemio Cruz*. Trans. Sam Hileman. New York: Farrar, Straus and Giroux, 1964.

———. "Las dos Elenas." In *Cantar de ciegos* (1964), 9–24. Mexico City: Joaquín Mortiz, 1970.

———. *La muerte de Artemio Cruz* (1962). Mexico City: Fondo de Cultura Económica, 1970.

———. *El naranjo, o los círculos del tiempo*. Mexico City: Alfaguara, 1993.

———. *Tiempo mexicano*. Mexico City: Editorial J. Moritz 1971.

———. *Todos los gatos son pardos*. Mexico City: Siglo Veintiuno, 1970.

Fuss, Diana. *Essentially Speaking: Feminism, Nature & Difference*. New York: Routledge, 1989.

Gallo, Rubén. "John Dos Passos in Mexico." *Modernism/Modernity* 14.2 (2007): 329–345.

Galván, Delia V. "Felipe Ángeles de Elena Garro: Sacrificio heroico." *Latin American Theatre Review* 20.2 (1987): 29–35.

———. "Feminism in Elena Garro's Recent Works." In *A Different Reality: Studies on the Work of Elena Garro*, ed. Anita K. Stoll, 136–146. Lewisburg: Bucknell UP, 1990.

———. "Multiplicidad de testigos *en Testimonios sobre Mariana* de Elena Garro." *Deslinde* (Monterrey, Mexico) 11.35–36 (1992): 88–92.

Galván, Felipe, ed. *Antología Teatro del 68.* Puebla: Tablado Iberoamericano, 1999.

García-Barragán, Guadalupe. "El tema del cacique y la cuestión religiosa en Bramadero y *Los recuerdos del porvenir.*" In *Proceedings: Pacific Northwest Conference on Foreign Languages*, 310–316. Corvallis: Oregon State U, 1973.

García Pinto, Magdalena. *Women Writers of Latin America: Intimate Histories.* Austin: U of Texas P, 1991.

Garner, Shirley Nelson. "Breaking Silence: *The Woman Warrior.*" In *The Intimate Critique: Autobiographical Literary Criticism*, ed. Diane P. Freedman, Olivia Frey, and Frances Murphy Zauhar, 117–125. Durham and London: Duke UP, 1993.

Gilbert, Dennis. "Emiliano Zapata: Textbook Hero." *Mexican Studies/Estudios Mexicanos* 19.1 (2003): 127–159.

Gilbert, Sandra, and Susan Gubar. *The Madwoman in the Attic: The Woman Writer and the Nineteenth-Century Literary Imagination.* New Haven: Yale UP, 1979.

———. *No Man's Land: The Place of the Woman Writer in the Twentieth Century, I: The War of the Words.* New Haven: Yale UP, 1988.

Gladhart, Amalia. "Present Absence: Memory and Narrative in *Los recuerdos del porvenir.*" *Hispanic Review* 73.1 (2005): 91–111.

Glantz, Margo. "Criadas, malinches, ¿esclavas?: Algunas modalidades de escritura en la reciente narrativa mexicana." In *América Latina: Palabra, Literatura e Cultura*, vol. 3, ed. Ana Pizarro, 603–620. São Paulo: Fundação Memorial da América Latina, 1995.

———. "Los enemigos de Elena Garro." In *Los colores de la memoria*, ed. Alicia V. Ramírez, Patricia Rosas Lopátegui, and Alejandro Palma Castro, 41–57. Puebla, Mexico: Benemérita Universidad Autónoma, 2007.

———. "Octavio Paz and Sor Juana Inés de La Cruz's Posthumous Fame." *Pacific Coast Philology* 28.2 (1993): 129–137.

———. *Sor Juana: La comparación y la hipérbole.* Mexico City: Conaculta, 2000.

———. "Vigencia de Nellie Campobello." FULGOR: *Flinders University Languages Group Online Review* 3.1 (December 2006): 37–50.

Gobineau, Count Joseph-Arthur. *Essay on the Inequality of Human Races* (1915). Trans. Adrian Collins. New York: H. Fertig, 1967.

Gómez de Orozco, Federico. *Doña Marina: La dama de la conquista.* Mexico City: Ediciones Xochitl, 1942.

González, Aníbal. "La Cuarentona and Slave Society in Cuba and Puerto Rico." *Latin American Literary Review* 8 (1980): 47–54.

González, Eduardo G. "Octavio Paz and the Critique of the Pyramid." *Diacritics: A Review of Contemporary Criticism* 2.3 (1972): 30–34.

González Casanova, Pablo. *La democracia en México.* Mexico City: Ediciones Era, 1965.

Grenier, Yvon. "Octavio Paz and the Changing Role of Intellectuals in Mexico." *Discourse: Journal for Theoretical Studies in Media and Culture* 23.2 (2001): 124–143.

———. "Octavio Paz: An Intellectual and His Critics." *Mexican Studies/Estudios Mexicanos*, 21.1 (2005): 251–268.

———. "The Romantic Liberalism of Octavio Paz." *Mexican Studies/Estudios Mexicanos* 17.1 (2001): 171–191.

———. "Socialism in One Person: Specter of Marxism in Octavio Paz's Political Thought." In *Octavio Paz: Humanism and Critique*, ed. Oliver Kozlarek, 47–64. New Brunswick: Transaction Publishers, 2009.

Gutiérrez de Velasco, Luzelena. "Violencia constante más allá del amor en *Mi hermanita Magdalena* de Elena Garro." In *Repensando la violencia y el patriarcado frente al nuevo milenio: Nuevas perspectivas en el mundo hispánico y germánico/Rethinking Violence and Patriarchy for the New Millenium: A German and Hispanic Perspective*, 137–144. Ottawa, Ontario: U of Ottawa P, 2002.

Guttmann, Matthew. *Changing Men and Masculinities in Latin America*. Durham, NC: Duke UP, 2003.

Gyurko, Lanin A. "The Literary Response to Nonoalco-Tlatelolco." In *Contemporary Latin American Culture: Unity and Diversity*, ed. C. Gail Guntermann, 45–78. Tempe: Center for Latin American Studies, Arizona State U, 1984.

———. "The Vindication of La Malinche in Fuentes' 'Todos los gatos son pardos.'" *Ibero-Amerikanisches Archiv* 3 (1977): 233–266.

Halperin, Maurice. "Pablo Neruda in Mexico." *Books Abroad* 25 (1941): 164–168.

———. "The Social Background of Contemporary Mexican Literature." *PMLA: Publications of the Modern Language Association of America* 55.3 (September 1940): 875–880.

Harris, Amanda Nolacea. "Imperial and Postcolonial Desires: Sonata de Estío and the Malinche Paradigm." *Discourse: Journal for Theoretical Studies in Media and Culture* 26.1–2 (2004): 235–257.

Harvey, Neil. "Rebellion in Chiapas: Rural Reforms, Campesino Radicalism, and the Limits to Salinismo." In *Transformation of Rural Mexico, No. 5*. La Jolla: Center for U.S.-Mexican Studies, U of California, San Diego, 1994.

Hennessy, Alistair. "Artists, Intellectuals, and Revolution: Recent Books on Mexico." *Journal of Latin American Studies* 3.1 (1971): 71–88.

Herlinghaus, Hermann, Jr., and Svend Plesch, "España en la pluma: Sobre el impacto de la Guerra Española en las obras de Pablo Neruda y Alejo Carpentier." *Islas* 89 (1988): 135–153.

Hernández-Rodríguez, Rafael. "Whose Sweaty Men Are They? Avant-Garde and Revolution in Mexico." *Ciberletras* 8 (December 2002). http://www.lehman.cuny.edu /ciberletras/vo8/hernandez.html.

Hernández Rodríguez, Rogelio. *El caso de Carlos A. Madrazo*. Mexico City: Colegio de México, Centro de Estudios Sociológicos, 1991.

Higonnet, Margaret R., Jane Jenson, Sonya Michel, and Margaret C. Wetz, eds. *Behind the Lines: Gender and the Two World Wars*. New Haven: Yale UP, 1987.

Hirsch, Edward. "Bookend; Octavio Paz: In Defense of Poetry." *New York Times Book Review* (June 7, 1998): 39.

Hirsch, Marianne, and Valerie Smith. "Feminism and Cultural Memory: An Introduction." *Signs: Journal of Women in Culture & Society* 28.1 (2002): 1–19.

Hopkinson, Amanda. "*Malinche*, by Laura Esquivel, trans. Ernesto Mestre-Reed." *Independent*, August 18, 2006. http://www.independent.co.uk/arts-entertainment/books/reviews/malinche-by-laura-esquivel-trans-ernesto-mestrereed-412291.html.

Howe, Irving, and Lewis Coser. *The American Communist Party: A Critical History: 1919–1957.* Boston: Beacon P, 1957.

Hurley, Teresa. *Mothers and Daughters in Post-Revolutionary Mexican Literature.* Woodbridge, England: Tamesis, 2003.

Hutson Mihaly, Deanna. "Gendering the Narrator of *Los recuerdos del porvenir.*" *RLA: Romance Languages Annual* 11 (1999): 556–561.

Ibsen, Kristine. "Self-Representation, Silence, and the Discourse of Madness in *Testimonios sobre Mariana.*" *Confluencia: Revista Hispánica de Cultura y Literatura* 14.2 (1999): 93–102.

Irwin, Robert McKee. "The Famous 41: The Scandalous Birth of Modern Mexican Homosexuality." *GLQ: A Journal of Lesbian and Gay Studies* 6.3 (2000): 353–376.

———. "*Los de abajo* y los debates sobre la identidad masculina nacional." In *La otredad: Los discursos de la cultura hoy, 1995,* 71–81. Mexico City: Universidad Autónoma Metropolitana-A., 1997.

———. *Mexican Masculinities.* Minneapolis: U of Minnesota P, 2003.

———. "La pedo embotellado: Sexual Roles and Play in Salvador Novo's *La estatua de sal.*" *Studies in the Literary Imagination* 33.1 (2000): 125–132.

Jaquette, Jane S. "Women in Revolutionary Movements in Latin America." *Journal of Marriage & Family* 35.2 (May 1973): 344–354.

Jiménez Rueda, Julio. "El afeminamiento en la literatura mexicana." *El Universal,* December 21, 1924.

Johnson, David E. "Excavating Spirit on the American Border: Hegel, Paz, la Crítica, and the Pachuco." *Siglo XX/20th Century: Critique and Cultural Discourse* 10.1–2 (1992): 49–80.

———. "Marking (Out) Ethics, in Other Words: On a Single Line in Kant and Juan García Ponce." *Interdisciplinary Literary Studies: A Journal of Criticism and Theory* 5.2 (2004): 50–72.

———. "Woman, Translation, Nationalism: La Malinche and the Example of Juan García Ponce." *Arizona Quarterly: A Journal of American Literature, Culture, and Theory* 47.3 (Autumn 1991): 93–116.

———. "'Writing in the Dark': The Political Fictions of American Travel Writing." *American Literary History* 7.1 (Spring 1995): 1–27.

Jones, Julie. "Text and Authority in Elena Garro's *Reencuentro de personajes.*" *Canadian Review of Comparative Literature/Revue Canadienne de Littérature Comparée* 18.1 (March 1991): 41–50.

Jorgensen, Beth E. "La intertextualidad en *La noche de Tlatelolco* de Elena Poniatowska." *Hispanic Journal* 10.2 (1989): 81–93.

Josef, Bella. "La poética de Octavio Paz, entre el ensayo y la lírica." *La Nueva Literatura Hispánica* 2 (1998): 45–56.

Kaminsky, Amy. "Autobiographical Criticism." *Intertexts* 10.1 (2006): 87–103.

——. *Reading the Body Politic: Feminist Criticism and Latin American Women.* Minneapolis: U Minnesota P, 1992.

——. "Residual Authority and Gendered Resistance." In *Critical Theory, Cultural Politics, and Latin American Narrative,* ed. Steven Bell, Albert H. Le May, and Leonard Orr, 103–121. Notre Dame: U of Notre Dame P, 1993.

Karttunen, Frances. "Rethinking Malinche." In *Indian Women of Early Mexico,* ed. Susan Schroeder et al., 291–312. Norman: U of Oklahoma P, 1997.

——. "To the Valley of Mexico: Doña Marina, La Malinche (ca 1500–1527)." In *Between Worlds: Interpreters, Guides, and Survivors,* 11–22. New Brunswick: Rutgers UP, 1994.

Katra, William H. "Ideology and Society in *El laberinto de la soledad,* by Octavio Paz." *Chasqui: Revista de Literatura Latinoamericana* 15.2–3 (1986): 3–13.

King, John. *The Role of Mexico's "Plural" in Latin American Literary and Political Culture: From Tlatelolco to the "Philanthropic Ogre."* New York: Palgrave Macmillan, 2007.

Knight, Alan. *The Mexican Revolution.* 2 vols. Cambridge: Cambridge UP, 1986.

——. "The Myth of the Mexican Revolution." *Past & Present* 209.1 (November 2010): 223–273.

Kolodny, Annette. *The Lay of the Land: Metaphor as Experience and History in American Life and Letters.* Chapel Hill: U of North Carolina P, 1975.

Kranz, Travis Barton. "Sixteenth-Century Tlaxcalan Pictorial Documents on the Conquest of Mexico." http://whp.uoregon.edu/Lockhart/Kranz.pdf.

Krauze, Enrique. "Entrevista con Miguel León-Portilla." *El País* (Madrid), June 30, 2001. http://www.elhistoriador.com.ar/entrevistas/l/leon_portilla.php.

——. *Mexico, Biography of Power: A History of Modern Mexico, 1810–1996.* Trans. Hank Heifetz. New York: Harper-Collins, 1997.

——. "Octavio Paz." In *The Company They Kept,* ed. Robert B. Silvers and Barbara Epstein, 227–236. New York: New York Review of Books, 2006.

——. "The Sun of Octavio Paz." *Voices of Mexico* 44 (1998): 98–99.

Kuhnheim, Jill. "Verbal Society: Poetry and Poets at the End of the Twentieth Century." *Latin American Research Review* 38.3 (2003): 200–209.

Lagos, María Inés. "'Balún Canán': Una novela de formación de protagonista femenina." *Revista Hispánica Moderna* 50.1 (1997): 159–179.

Lambie, George. "Poetry and Politics: The Spanish Civil War Poetry of César Vallejo." *Bulletin of Hispanic Studies* 69 (1992): 153–170.

——. "Vallejo and the End of History." *Romance Quarterly* 49.2 (Spring 2002): 126–143.

Lanyon, Anna. *Malinche's Conquest.* New South Wales: Allen and Unwin, 1999.

Larson, Catherine. "El juego de la historia en Felipe Ángeles." In *Baúl de recuerdos: Homenaje a Elena Garro*, ed. Robert K. Anderson and Mara García, 73–84. Tlaxcala, Mexico: Universidad Autónoma de Tlaxcala, 1999.

———. "Recollection of Plays to Come: Time in the Theater of Elena Garro." *Latin American Theatre Review* 22.2 (1989): 5–17.

Larson, Ross. *Fantasy and Imagination in the Mexican Narrative*. Tempe: Arizona State U, 1977.

Leal, Luis. "Female Archetypes in Mexican Literature." In *Women in Hispanic Literature: Icons and Fallen Idols*, ed. Beth Miller, 227–242. Berkeley: U of California P, 1983.

———. "Introduction." In *Jicoténcal*, vii–xxxvi. Houston: Arte Público P, 1995.

———. "Jicoténcal, primera novela histórica en castellano." *Revista Iberoamericana* 25 (1960): 9–31.

———. "Octavio Paz." In *Dictionary of Literary Biography Year Book. 1998*, 310–317. A Bruccoli Clark Layman Book. Detroit: Gale Research, 1999.

———. "Octavio Paz and the Chicano." *Latin American Literary Review* 5.10 (1977): 115–123.

———. "Octavio Paz y la literatura nacional: Afinidades y oposiciones." *Revista Iberoamericana* 37.74 (1971): 239–250.

———. "Sin fronteras: (Des)mitificación en las letras norteamericanas y mexicanas." *Mexican Studies/Estudios Mexicanos* 9.1 (Winter 1993): 95–118.

———. "Tlatelolco, Tlatelolco." *Denver Quarterly* 14.1 (1979): 3–13.

Leal, Luis, and Ilan Stavans. *A Luis Leal Reader*. Evanston, IL: Northwestern UP, 2007.

León, María Teresa. *Contra viento y marea*. Buenos Aires: Ediciones Aiape, 1941.

———. *Juego limpio*. Buenos Aires: Goyanarte, 1959.

———. *Memoria de la melancolía*. Bueno Aires: Losada, 1970.

León-Portilla, Miguel. *Broken Spears: The Aztec Account of the Conquest of Mexico*. Trans. Lysander Kemp. Boston: Beacon P, 1962.

———. *Visión de los vencidos: Relaciones indígenas de la conquista*. Mexico City: UNAM, 1959.

Limon, John. *Writing after War*. Oxford and New York: Oxford UP, 1994.

Lines, Lisa. "Female Combatants in the Spanish Civil War: Milicianas on the Front Lines and in the Rearguard." *Journal of International Women's Studies* 10.4 (2009): 168–187.

———. Review of Martin Baumeister and Stefanie Schüler-Springorum, *"If You Tolerate This . . . ": The Spanish Civil War in the Age of Total War*. H-Net Reviews in the Humanities & Social Sciences (2009): 1 http://www.h-net.org/reviews/showrev.php ?id=244812. H-Soz-u-Kult, H-Net Reviews. March 2009. http://www.h-net.org/re views/showrev.php?id=24481.

Linhard, Tabea Alexa. *Fearless Women in the Mexican Revolution and the Spanish Civil War*. Columbia and London: U of Missouri P, 2005.

———. "A Perpetual Trace of Violence: Gendered Narratives of Revolution and War." *Discourse* 25:3 (2003): 30–47.

Lomnitz, Claudio. "Times of Crisis: Historicity, Sacrifice, and the Spectacle of Debacle in Mexico City." *Public Culture* 15.1 (2003): 127–147.

López, Kimberle S. "Internal Colonialism in the Testimonial Process: Elena Poniatowska's *Hasta no verte, Jesús mío*." *Symposium: A Quarterly Journal in Modern Literatures* 52.1 (1998): 21–39.

López de Gómara, Francisco. *Historia de la conquista de México*. Caracas: Biblioteca Ayacucho, 1979.

López de Gómara, Francisco, and Lesley Byrd Simpson. *Cortés: The Life of the Conqueror by His Secretary*. Berkeley: University of California Press, 1964.

Ludmer, Josefina. "Tretas del débil." In *La sartén por el mango: Encuentro de escritoras latinoamericanas*, 47–54. Río Piedras, Puerto Rico: Huracán, 1984.

Lyons, Eugene. *The Red Decade: The Stalinist Penetration of America*. Indianapolis: Bobbs-Merrill, 1941.

Mackey, Theresa M. "Giving a Damn: An Interdisciplinary Reconsideration of English Writers' Involvement in the Spanish Civil War." *Clio* 27.1 (1997): 89–108.

MacLachlan, Colin M., and William H. Beezley. *El Gran Pueblo: A History of Greater Mexico*. New York: Prentice Hall, 2003.

Maier, Linda S., and Isabel Dulfano. *Woman as Witness: Essays on Testimonial Literature by Latin American Women*. New York: P. Lang, 2004.

Mancall, Mark. "Revolution in the Counter-Revolution: A Paradigm." *Journal of Interdisciplinary History* 1.2 (1971): 338–348.

Mandrell, James. "The Prophetic Voice in Garro, Morante, and Allende." *Comparative Literature* 42.3 (1990): 227–246.

Mangini González, Shirley. *Memories of Resistance: Women's Voices from the Spanish Civil War*. New Haven, CT: Yale UP, 1995.

Manzoni, Celina. "Heterodoxa y subjetiva: *Las Memorias de España* de Elena Garro." *Torre de Papel* 10.2 (2000): 142–160.

Marcos, Sylvia. "Twenty-five Years of Mexican Feminisms." *Women's Studies International Forum* 22.4: 431–433. http://www.sciencedirect.com/science/article/pii/S0277539599000369.

María y Campos, Armando de. *La Revolución mexicana a través de los corridos populares*. Mexico City: Biblioteca INEHRM, 1962.

Martín del Campo, Marisol. *Amor y conquista*. Mexico City: Editorial Planeta/Joaquín Mortiz, 1999.

Martínez. José Luis. "Los caciques culturales." *Letras Libres* 7.1 (July 1999): 29. http://www.letraslibres.com/index.php?art=5878.

———. *Hernán Cortés: Semblanza*. Mexico City: Fondo de Cultura Económica, 1990.

———. "El momento literario de los contemporáneos." *Letras Libres* 2.15 (March 2000): 60–62. http://www.letraslibres.com/index.php?art=6242.

Mastretta, Ángeles. *Arráncame la vida*. Mexico City: Océano, 1985.

———. *Lovesick*. Trans. Margaret Sayers Peden. New York: Riverhead Books, 1997.

———. *Mal de amores*. Mexico City: Alfaguara, 1996.

―――. *Tear This Heart Out.* Trans. Margaret Sayers Peden. New York: Riverhead Books, 1997.

Mata, Oscar. "La revolución mexicana escrita con mirada de niña." EL ARCHIVO *de Tiempo y Escritura, 2001.* http://www.azc.uam.mx/publicaciones/tye/larevolucionmex icana.htm.

McCaa, Robert. "Missing Millions: The Demographic Cost of the Mexican Revolution." University of Minnesota Population Center. *Mexican Studies/Estudios Mexicanos* 19.2 (2003): 367–400.

McLynn, Frank. *Villa and Zapata: A History of the Mexican Revolution.* New York: Carroll and Graf, 2001.

Medina, Rubén. *Autor, autoridad, autorización: Escritura y poética de Octavio Paz.* Mexico City: El Colegio de México, 1999.

Meléndez, Priscilla. "Co(s)mic Conquest in Sabina Berman's *Águila o sol.*" *Bucknell Review: A Scholarly Journal of Letters, Arts and Sciences* 40.2 (1996): 19–36.

―――. "Genealogía y escritura en *Balún-Canán* de Rosario Castellanos." *Modern Language Notes* 113.2 (1998): 339–363.

―――. "Marx, Villa, Calles, Guzmán . . . : Fantasmas y modernidad en *Entre Villa y una mujer desnuda* de Sabina Berman." *Hispanic Review* 72.4 (2004): 523–546.

Melgar, Lucía. "Conversaciones con Elena Garro (Cuernavaca, México, 1997)." In *Elena Garro: Lectura múltiple de una personalidad compleja,* 237–277. Puebla, Mexico: Benemérita Universidad Autónoma de Puebla, 2002.

―――. "Correspondencias literarias: Bianco, Garro y *La pérdida del reino.*" In *Actas del* XIV *Congreso de la Asociación Internacional de Hispanistas, IV: Literatura hispanoamericana,* 425–430. Newark, DE: Cuesta, 2004.

―――. "Elena Garro en París (1947–1952): Una lectura de sus cartas a José Bianco y Ninfa Santos." In *Elena Garro: Lectura múltiple de una personalidad compleja,* ed. Lucía Melgar-Palacios and Gabriela Mora, 149–172. Puebla, Mexico: Benemérita Universidad Autónoma de Puebla, 2002.

―――. "¿La escritora que no quería serlo? Hacia un perfil de Elena Garro a través de su correspondencia (1947–1968)." *Torre de Papel* 10.2 (2000): 76–101.

―――. "IFAI vs. Garro, ¿Información o difamación?" Unpublished MS.

―――. "Octavio Paz y Helena Garro a través de las palabras del poeta (1935, 1937, 1944, 1945)." *Literatura Mexicana* 13.1 (2002): 173–196.

―――. "Relectura desde la piedra: Ambigüedad, violencia y género en *Los recuerdos del porvenir* de Elena Garro." In *Pensamiento y crítica: Los discursos de la cultura hoy,* 58–74. East Lansing: Michigan State U/U of Louisville/Centro de Cultura Casa Lamm, 2000.

―――. "Silencios enmascarados: Hacia una interpretación del silencio en textos de Paz, Rulfo y Garro." In *Visiones alternativas: Los discursos de la cultura hoy,* 76–83. N.p.: U of Louisville/Michigan State U/Centro de Cultura Casa Lamm/Universidad Autónoma Metropolitana, 2001.

———. "Silencios expresivos: Gamas y matices del silencio en la obra de Elena Garro." *Monographic Review/Revista Monográfica* 16 (2000): 357–367.

———. "Silencio y represión en *Y Matarazo no llamó*." Special issue: "Vida y ficción en la obra de Elena Garro." *Letras Femeninas* 29.1 (Summer 2003): 139–159.

———. "Violencia y silencio en obras selectas de Elena Garro." Ph.D. dissertation. University of Chicago, 1996.

———. *Writing Dark Times: Elena Garro, Writing and Politics.* Program in Latin American Studies: Working Papers 5. Princeton, NJ: Princeton UP, 2000.

Melgar-Palacios, Lucía, and Gabriela Mora, eds. *Elena Garro: Lectura múltiple de una personalidad compleja.* Puebla, Mexico: Benemérita Universidad Autónoma, 2002.

Méndes Rodenas, Adriana. "Magia y pasión: Huellas del deseo femenino en Elena Garro." *Torre de Papel* 10.2 (2000): 18–35.

———. "Tiempo femenino, tiempo ficticio: *Los recuerdos del porvenir* de Elena Garro." *Revista Iberoamericana* 51.132–133 (1985): 843–851.

Mendieta Alatorre, Ángeles. *La mujer en la revolución mexicana.* Mexico City: INEHRM, 1961.

Merrim, Stephanie, ed. *Feminist Perspectives on Sor Juana Inés de la Cruz.* Detroit: Wayne State UP, 1999.

Meyer, Doris. "Alienation and Escape in Elena Garro's *La semana de colores*." *Hispanic Review* 55.2 (1987): 153–164.

Meyer, Jean. *The Cristero Rebellion: The Mexican People between Church and State, 1926–1929.* Trans. Richard Southern. New York: Cambridge UP, 1976.

Meyer, Michael, William L. Sherman, and Susan M. Deeds, eds. *The Course of Mexican History.* 8th ed. New York: Oxford UP, 2007.

Miller, Richard B. "The Moral and Political Burdens of Memory." *Journal of Religious Ethics* 37.3 (2009): 533–564.

Minardi, Giovanna. "La Revolución Mexicana en la obra de Elena Garro." *Rassegna Iberistica* 79 (February 2004): 79–81.

Minh-ha, Trinh T. *Woman, Native, Other: Writing Postcoloniality and Feminism.* Bloomington: Indiana UP, 1989.

Moi, Toril. *Sexual/Textual Politics: Feminist Literary Theory.* London: Routledge, 2002.

Monsiváis, Carlos. "Adonde yo soy tú somos nosotros." *La Jornada Semanal*, April 26, 1998. www.jornada.unam.mx/1998/04/26/sem-monsi.html.

———. *Adonde yo soy tú somos nosotros: Octavio Paz, crónica de vida y obra.* Mexico City: Hoja Casa Editorial, 2000.

———. "'Adonde yo soy tú somos nosotros': Octavio Paz, el poeta de la otredad." http://www.excentricaonline.com/libros/escritores_more.php?id=6231_0_8_0_M.

———. *Días de guarder.* Mexico City: Era, 1970.

———. "Octavio Paz y la izquierda." *Letras Libres* (April 1999): 30–35.

Montes de Oca Navas, Elvira. *Protagonistas de la Revolución Mexicana.* Toluca: Instituto Mexiquense de Cultura, 1996.

Mora, Gabriela. "Elena cuenta su historia: Fragmentos de cartas a Gabriela Mora." In *Elena Garro: Lectura múltiple de una personalidad compleja*, ed. Lucía Melgar-Palacios and Gabriela Mora, 281–299. Puebla, Mexico: Benemérita Universidad Autónoma de Puebla, 2002.

———, ed. *Elena Garro: Correspondencia con Gabriela Mora (1974–1980)*. Puebla, Mexico: Benémerita Universidad Autónoma de Puebla, 2007.

———. "*Los perros* y *La mudanza* de Elena Garro: Designio social y virtualidad feminista." *Latin American Theatre Review* 8.2 (1975): 5–14.

———. "A Thematic Exploration of Elena Garro." In *Latin American Women Writers: Yesterday and Today*, ed. Yvette E. Miller and Charles M. Tatum, 91–97. Pittsburgh: Latin American Literary Review, 1977.

Moraga, Cherríe. "A Long Line of Vendidas." In *Loving in the War Years*, 90–142. Boston: South End P, 1983.

Morton, Adam D. "The Social Function of Carlos Fuentes: A Critical Intellectual or in the 'Shadow of the State'?" *Bulletin of Latin American Research* 22.1 (2003): 27–51.

Müller-Bergh, Klaus. "La poesía de Octavio Paz en los años treinta." *Revista Iberoamericana* 37.74 (1971): 117–133.

Muncy, Michelle. "The Author Speaks . . . " In *A Different Reality: Studies on the Works of Elena Garro*, ed. Anita K. Stoll, 23–37. Lewisburg: Bucknell UP, 1990.

———. "Encuentro con Elena Garro." *Hispanic Journal* 7.2 (1986): 65–71.

Naharro-Calderón, José María. "Los exilios de las Españas de 1939." *Nueva Literatura Hispánica* 3: 87–254.

Nash, Mary. *Defying Male Civilization: Women in the Spanish Civil War*. Denver, CO: Arden Press, 1995.

Neruda, Pablo. *Confieso que he vivido: Memorias*. Barcelona: Seix Barral, 1974.

———. "Poema XV: Me gustas cuando calles"/"I Like for You to Be Still." In *Twenty Love Poems and a Song of Despair*, trans. W. S. Merwin, 38–39. London: Cape, 1969.

Nickel, Catherine. "Nellie Campobello." In *Spanish American Women Writers: A Bio-Bibliographical Source Book*, ed. Diane E. Marting, 117–126. Westport, CT: Greenwood Press, 1990.

Nolasco, Margarita. "REGION CHOLULA." *Etnografia Polska* 14.2 (1970): 39–53.

Ochoa, Debra J. "Memory and Exile in Maria Teresa León's *Las peregrinaciones de Teresa* (1950)." *Letras Hispanas: Revista de Literatura y Cultura* 4.2 (2007). http://letrashispanas.unlv.edu/Index_files/vol4iss2.html.

Olcott, Jocelyn, Mary Kay Vaughan, and Gabriela Cano, eds. *Sex in Revolution: Gender, Politics and Power in Modern Mexico*. With a foreword by Carlos Monsiváis. Durham, NC: Duke UP, 2006.

Ontiveros, José Luis. "Rubén Salazar Mallén: Proscrito de los Contemporáneos." *La Palabra y el Hombre* 53–54 (1985): 97–100.

Orlando, Valérie. "Writing New H(er)stories for Francophone Women of Africa and the Caribbean." *World Literature Today* 75.1 (2001): 40–50.

Oviedo, José Miguel. "The Modern Essay in Spanish America." In *The Cambridge History of Latin American Literature*, vol. 2: *The Twentieth Century*, ed. Roberto González Echevarría and Enrique Pupo-Walker, 365–424. Cambridge and New York: Cambridge UP, 1996.

Pacheco, José Emilio. *Don't Ask Me How the Time Goes By: Poems*. Trans. Alastair Reid. New York: Columbia UP, 1978.

———. "*Libertad bajo palabra* cincuenta años después." *Letras Libres* 1.4 (April 1999): 22–24.

———. *Tarde o temprano*. 3rd ed. Mexico City: Fondo de Cultura Económica, 2000.

Pankhurst, Donna. "The 'Sex War' and Other Wars: Towards a Feminist Approach to Peace Building." *Development in Practice* 13.2/3 (May 2003): 154–177.

Parra, Max. *Writing Pancho Villa's Revolution: Rebels in the Literary Imagination of Mexico*. Austin: U of Texas P, 2005.

Pastén, J. Agustín. *Octavio Paz: Crítico practicante en busca de una poética*. Madrid, Spain: Pliegos, 1999.

"Paz, Octavio." In *Encyclopaedia Britannica* (2007). Encyclopaedia Britannica Online, December 25, 2007. http://www.britannica.com/eb/article-9058840.

Peña Doria, Olga Martha. "Elena Garro y la dramaturgia de la Revolución Mexicana." In *Baúl de recuerdos: Homenaje a Elena Garro*, ed. Robert K. Anderson and Mara García, 47–54. Tlaxcala, Mexico: Universidad Autónoma de Tlaxcala, 1999.

Perales, Jaime. "Review of 'A treinta años de *Plural*, revista fundada y dirigida por Octavio Paz.'" *Americas* 54.2 (March 2002). 63.

Peralta, Jaime. "España en tres poetas hispanoamericanos: Neruda, Guillén y Vallejo." *Atenea* 45.170 (1968): 37–49.

Perelmuter, Rosa. "Female Voices in the Poetry of Sor Juana Inés de la Cruz." In *Estudios sobre escritoras hispánicas en honor de Georgina Sabat-Rivers*, ed. Lou Charnon-Deutsch, 246–253. Madrid: Editorial Castalia, 1992.

Pérez, Domino Renee. *There Was a Woman: Cultural Readings of La Llorona from Folklore to Popular Culture*. Austin: U of Texas P, 2008.

Pérez, Janet. "Behind the Lines: The Spanish Civil War and Women Writers." In *The Spanish Civil War in Literature*, 161–174. Lubbock: Texas Tech UP, 1990.

Pertusa, Inmaculada. "Una aproximación a las realidades mágicas propuestas en el teatro de Elena Garro." *Explicación de Textos Literarios* 25.1 (1996): 105–115.

Phillips, Rachel. "Marina/Malinche: Masks and Shadows." In *Women in Hispanic Literature: Icons and Fallen Idols*, ed. Beth Miller, 97–114. Berkeley: U of California P, 1983.

"A Poet Passes." *New Republic* 218. 19 (May 11, 1998): 10.

Ponce, Armando. Review of *Testimonios sobre Mariana*. In *Proceso* online. http://www.lopategui.com/ProcessoPonceGarro.htm.

Poniatowska, Elena. "Elena Garro y sus tormentas." In *Baúl de recuerdos: Homenaje a Elena Garro*, 5–15. Tlaxcala, Mexico: Universidad Autónoma de Tlaxcala, 1999.

———. *¡Hasta no verte, Jesús mío!* Mexico City: Ediciones Era, 1969.

———. *Massacre in Mexico*. Trans. Helen R. Lane. New York: Viking Press, 1975.

———. *Nada, nadie: Las voces del temblor*. Mexico City: Era, 1988.

———. *La noche de Tlatelolco*. Mexico City: Biblioteca Era, 1971.

———. *Octavio Paz: Las palabras del árbol*. Mexico City: Plaza Janés, 1998.

———. *Las siete cabritas*. Mexico City: Biblioteca Era, 2000.

———. *Tinísima*. Mexico City: Ediciones Era, 1992.

Prada Oropeza, Renato. *El discurso-testimonio y otros ensayos: Textos de difusión cultural*. Mexico City: Coordinación de Difusión Cultural, Dirección de Literatura, UNAM, 2001.

Pratt, Mary Louise. "Mi cigarro, mi Singer, y la revolución mexicana: La danza ciudadana de Nellie Campobello." *Revista Iberoamericana* 70.206 (2004): 253–273.

Presley, James. "Langston Hughes, War Correspondent." *Journal of Modern Literature* 5.3 (September 1976): 481–491.

Quiroga, José. *Understanding Octavio Paz*. Columbia: U of South Carolina P, 1999.

Rabell, Carmen Rita. "Los empeños de una casa: Una re-escritura femenina de la comedia de enredo del Siglo de Oro español." *Revista de Estudios Hispánicos* 20 (1993): 11–25.

Rader, Pamela J. "Boys to Men: Redefining Masculinities in Woman Hollering Creek and Other Stories." In *Sandra Cisneros's "Woman Hollering Creek,"* ed. Cecilia Donohue and M. Meyer, 131–149. Amsterdam, Netherlands: Rodopi, 2010.

Ramírez, Luis Enrique. *La ingobernable: Encuentros y desencuentros con Elena Garro*. Mexico City: Raya en el Agua, 2000.

———. *La muela del juicio*. Mexico City: Consejo Nacional para la Cultura y las Artes, 1994.

Reséndez Fuentes, Andrés. "Battleground Women: Soldaderas and Female Soldiers in the Mexican Revolution." *Americas* 51.4 (1995): 525–553.

Riboldi, Liliana E. "Octavio Paz's *Entre la piedra y la flor*: De la contemplación a la filosofía." *Utah Foreign Language Review* 1 (1991): 109–115.

Rivera Villegas, Carmen, "Otras miradas sobre la Guerra Civil Española: Tina Modotti y Elena Garro." *Bulletin of Hispanic Studies* 81.3 (2004): 347–359.

Rodríguez, Antoine. "El papel de los héroes en la dramaturgia mexicana contemporánea: El caso de la Revolución Mexicana." *Revista Iberoamericana* 71.213 (2005): 1149–1165.

Rodríguez, Victoria E. *Women in Contemporary Mexican Politics*. Austin: U of Texas P, 2003.

Rodríguez García, José María. "Surrealismo, vorticismo e historia en Octavio Paz." *Bulletin Hispanique* 108.2 (December 2006): 517–554.

Romero, Rolando, and Amanda Nolacea Harris. *Feminism, Nation and Myth: La Malinche*. Houston: Arte Público P, 2005.

Rosas Lopátegui, Patricia. *El asesinato de Elena Garro*. Mexico City: Editorial Porrúa, 2005.

———. "Autobiografía y literatura en *Testimonios sobre Mariana*: Escenas de un matrimonio llamado Elena Garro y Octavio Paz." *Alba de América* 26.49–50 (2007): 219–231.

———. "El exilio y el baúl en *Testimonios sobre Mariana*: Una perspectiva psicoanalítica." *Alba de América: Revista Literaria* 9.16–17 (1991): 121–140.

———. *Testimonios sobre Elena Garro: Biografía exclusiva y autorizada de Elena Garro.* Monterrey, Mexico: Ediciones Castillo, 2002.

———. *Yo sólo soy memoria.* Mexico City: Ediciones Castillo, 2000.

Rosas Lopátegui, Patricia, and James Casey Reed. "El baúl receptáculo de la vida subconsciente y vehículo de la emancipación femenina en *Testimonios sobre Mariana*." In *La nueva mujer en la escritura de autoras hispánicas: Ensayos críticos*, 67–78. Montevideo, Uruguay: Instituto Literario y Cultural Hispánico, 1995.

Rosas Lopátegui, Patricia, and Rhina Toruño. "Entrevista: Elena Garro." *Hispamérica* 20.60 (1991): 55–71.

Rubin, Gayle. "On the Traffic of Women: Notes on the 'Political Economy' of Sex." In *Toward an Anthropology of Women*, ed. Rayna Reiter, 157–210. New York: Monthly Review Press, 1975.

Rulfo, Juan. *The Burning Plain and Other Stories.* Trans. George D. Schade. Austin: U of Texas P 1967.

———. *El llano en llamas y otros cuentos.* Mexico City: Fondo de Cultura Económica, 1953.

———. *Pedro Páramo.* Mexico City: Fondo de Cultura Económica, 1955.

Sabat de Rivers, Georgina. "Biografías: Sor Juana vista por Dorothy Schons y Octavio Paz." *Revista Iberoamericana* 51.132–133 (1985): 927–937.

———. "Octavio Paz ante Sor Juana Inés de la Cruz." *MLN: Modern Language Notes* 100.2 (1985): 417–423.

Salas, Elizabeth. *Soldaderas in the Mexican Military: Myth and History.* Austin: U of Texas P, 1990.

Salaün, Serge. *La poesía de la guerra de España.* Madrid: Castalia, 1985.

Sánchez, Marta Ester. *"Shakin' Up" Race and Gender: Intercultural Connections in Puerto Rican, African American, and Chicano Narratives and Culture (1965–1995).* Austin: U of Texas P, 2005

Sánchez-Prado, Ignacio M. "La destrucción de la escritura viril y el ingreso de la mujer al discurso literario: *El libro vacio* y *Los recuerdos del porvenir*." *Revista de Crítica Literaria Latinoamericana* 32.63–64 (2006): 149–167.

Santí, Enrico Mario. *El acto de las palabras.* Mexico City: Fondo de Cultura Económica, 1998.

———. *Ciphers of History: Latin American Readings for a Cultural Age.* New York: Palgrave Macmillan, 2005.

———. "Diez claves para *El laberinto de la soledad*." *Antipodas: Journal of Hispanic Studies of the University of Auckland and La Trobe University* 4 (1992): 177–194.

———. "Octavio Paz: The Family Romance." *Taller de Letras* 24 (November 1996): 51–77.

———. "Los pininos de un chamaco: Los primeros escritos de Octavio Paz." In *Octavio Paz: La dimensión estética del ensayo*, 17–24. Mexico City: Siglo XXI, 2004.

———. "Primeras palabras sobre Primeras letras: Diálogo con Octavio Paz." *Insula: Revista de Letras y Ciencias Humanas* 46. 532–533 (1991): 5–8.

———. "Sor Juana, Octavio Paz and the Poetics of Restitution." *Indiana Journal of Hispanic Literatures* 1.2 (1993): 101–139.

———. "Ten Keys to *The Labyrinth of Solitude*." *Review: Literature and Arts of the Americas* 38.1, no. 70 (2005): 17–30.

Saville, John. "Valentine Cunningham and the Poetry of the Spanish Civil War." *Social Register* 270–83. http://socialistregister.com/index.php/srv/article/view/5470.

Sawhney, Minni. "The Unreachable Other: The Myth of the Mestizo in the Novels of Carlos Fuentes." *Central Institute of English and Foreign Languages Bulletin* 7 (June–December 1995): 168–185.

Schneider, Luis Mario. *Segundo congreso internacional de escritores antifascistas (1937), Vol. I: Inteligencia y guerra civil en España.* Barcelona: Editorial Laia, 1978.

Schons, Dorothy. "Some Obscure Points in the Life of Sor Juana Inés de la Cruz." *Modern Philology: A Journal Devoted to Research in Medieval and Modern Literature* 24.2 (1926): 141–162.

Schuessler, Michael. *Elena Poniatowska: An Intimate Biography.* Tucson: U of Arizona P, 2007.

Schwartz, Stephen. "Mexico Loses a Modern Revolutionary Thinker." *Wall Street Journal* (Eastern Edition), April 24, 1998, A15.

Schwartz, Stuart B. *Victors and Vanquished: Spanish and Nahua Views of the Conquest of Mexico.* Boston: Bedford/St. Martin's, 2000.

Sela Obarrio, Alejandro. "La Malinche y Octavio Paz." Doctoral dissertation. State U of New York, Albany, 1996.

Serrano, Francisco. "Los caracteres del estrago." *Vuelta* 22.259 (1998): 77–79.

Seydel, Ute. *Narrar historia(s): La ficcionalización de temas históricos por las escritoras mexicanas Elena Garro, Rosa Beltrán y Carmen Boullosa.* Madrid: Iberoamericana, 2007.

Sheridan, Guillermo. *Los Contemporáneos ayer.* Mexico City: Fondo de Cultura Económica, 1985.

———. "Octavio Paz en Yucatán." *Letras Libres* (January 2001): 14–20.

———. *Poeta con paisaje: Ensayos sobre la vida de Octavio Paz.* Mexico City: Ediciones Era, 2004.

Shirk, David A. *Mexico's New Politics: The PAN and Democratic Change.* Boulder, CO: Lynne Rienner Publishers, 2005.

Sigal, Pete, ed. *Infamous Desire: Male Homosexuality in Colonial Latin America.* Chicago: U of Chicago P, 2003.

Skinner, Lee. "Martyrs of Miscegenation: Racial and National Identities in Nineteenth-Century Mexico." *Hispanófila* 132 (2001): 25–42.

Sklodowska, Elzbieta. "Hacia una bibliografía sobre el testimonio hispanoamericano." *Chasqui* 20.1 (1991): 108–116.

Slattery, Matthew T. *Felipe Ángeles and the Mexican Revolution.* Dublin, IN: Privately printed, 1982.

Smith, Eric. "The Communist Party, Cooptation, and Spanish Republican Aid." *American Communist History* 8.2 (December 2009): 137–165.

Sommer, Doris. *Foundational Fictions: The National Romances of Latin America.* Berkeley/ Los Angeles: U of California P, 1991.

Sorensen, Diana. "Tlatelolco 1968: Paz and Poniatowska on Law and Violence." *Mexican Studies/Estudios Mexicanos* 18.2 (2002): 297–321.

Soto, Shirlene. *Emergence of the Modern Mexican Woman: Her Participation in Revolution and Struggle for Equality 1910–1940.* Denver: Arden Press, 1990.

Spender, Stephen, and John Lehmann, eds. *Poems for Spain.* London: Hogarth P, 1939.

Stabb, Martin. "The New Essay of Mexico: Text and Context." *Hispania* 70.1 (1987): 47–61.

Stanton, Anthony. "Models of Discourse and Hermeneutics in Octavio Paz's *El Laberinto de la Soledad.*" *Bulletin of Latin American Research* 20.2 (2001): 210–232.

———. "Octavio Paz, Alfonso Reyes y el análisis del fenómeno poético." *Hispanic Review* 3 (1963): 363–378.

———. "Octavio Paz y los contemporáneos: La historia de una relación." In *Actas del X Congreso de la Asociación de Hispanistas, I–IV,* 1003–1010. Barcelona: Promociones y Pubs. Universitarias, 1992.

———. "La poesía de Octavio Paz durante la Guerra Civil de España." In *Actas del XIV Congreso de la Asociación Internacional de Hispanistas, IV: Literatura hispanoamericana,* ed. Isaías Lerner, Robert Nival, and Alejandro Alonso, 649–657. Newark, DE: Cuesta, 2004.

———. "La prehistoria estética de Octavio Paz: Los escritos en prosa (1931–1943)." *Literatura Mexicana* 2 (1991): 23–55.

———. *Las primeras voces del poeta Octavio Paz (1931–1938).* Mexico City: CONACULTA, 2001.

Steele, Cynthia. "Letters from Rosario: On Power, Gender, and Canon Formation in Mexico." *Studies in 20th Century Literature* 20 (1996): 65–100.

———. *Politics, Gender, and the Mexican Novel, 1968–1988: Beyond the Pyramid.* Texas Pan American series. Austin: U of Texas P, 1992.

Tafoya, Jesús L. "Ruptura y continuidad del discurso hegemónico en *Cómo mataron a mi abuelo español* de Beatriz Espejo." *Revista de Literatura Mexicana Contemporánea* 5.11 (1999): 65–69.

———. "Voces contextuales: El discurso femenino ante la patriarcalidad discursiva revolucionaria." *Lamar Journal of the Humanities* 30.1 (2005): 17–26.

Taibo, Paco Ignacio. *Pancho Villa: Una biografía narrativa.* Mexico City: Planeta, 2007.

Terrazas, Ana Cecilia. "Anecdotario de Henestrosa, Martínez y Soriano." *Letras Libres* (July 1999). http://www.letraslibres.com/index.php?art=5885.

Thomas, Hugh. *The Spanish Civil War.* 4th ed. London: Penguin, 2003.

Thornton, Niamh, and Ciaran Cosgrove. *Women and the War Story in Mexico: La novela de la Revolución.* Lewiston, NY: Mellen, 2006.

Torres Fierro, Danubio. *Octavio Paz en España, 1937*. Mexico City: Fondo de Cultura Económica, 2007.

Toruño, Rhina. *Cita con la memoria: Elena Garro cuenta su vida a Rhina Toruño*. Buenos Aires: Prueba de Galera, 2004.

———. "Protesta contra la opresión: Categorías medulares en la obra narrativa y dramática de Elena Garro." *Deslinde* 11.35–36 (1992): 93–95.

———. *Tiempo, destino y opresión en la obra de Elena Garro*. Lewiston, NY: Mellen, 1996.

———. "Y Matarazo no llamó . . . : Novela política y la última escrita por Elena Garro." *Boletín Letras Informa* 2.6 (1994) 9–14.

Trexler, Richard C. *Sex and Conquest: Gendered Violence, Political Order, and the European Conquest of the Americas*. New York: Cornell UP, 1995.

Trigo, Benigno. *Remembering Maternal Bodies: Melancholy in Latina and Latin American Women's Writing*. New York: Palgrave Macmillan, 2006.

Tuck, Jim. "Democrat to Autocrat: The Transformation of Porfirio Díaz." *Mexconnect*. http://www.mexconnect.com/mex_/history/jtuck/jtporfdiaz.html.

———. *The Holy War in Los Altos: A Regional Analysis of Mexico's Cristero Rebellion*. Tucson: U of Arizona P, 1982.

———. "Octavio Paz: Nobel Winner and Noble Man." *Mexconnect*. http://www.mexconnect.com/articles/265-octavio-paz-nobel-winner-and-noble-man-1914%E2%80%931998.

Turner, Victor. *Dramas, Fields, and Metaphors: Symbolic Action in Human Society*. Ithaca/London: Cornell UP, 1974.

Unger, Roni. *Poesía en Voz Alta in the Theatre of Mexico*. Columbia: U of Missouri P, 1981.

Unruh, Vicky. *Performing Women and Modern Literary Culture in Latin America: Intervening Acts*. Austin: U of Texas P, 2006.

Valdés, María Elena de. *The Shattered Mirror: Representations of Women in Mexican Literature*. Austin: U of Texas P, 1998.

Van Delden, Maarten. "Polemical Paz." *Literal* 7 (Winter 2006–2007): 16–18.

Van Delden, Maarten, and Yvon Grenier. *Gunshots at the Fiesta: Literature and Politics in Latin America*. Nashville, TN: Vanderbilt UP, 2009.

Vankelevich, Pablo. "Gachupines rigurosamente vigilados: La excepcionalidad del gobierno de Lázaro Cárdenas en la política de expulsión de españoles indeseables." *Historias* 59.1 (2004): 45–62.

Vaughan, Mary Kay. "Introduction." In *Sex in Revolution: Gender, Politics and Power in Modern Mexico*, ed. Jocelyn Olcott, Mary Kay Vaughan, and Gabriela Cano, with a foreword by Carlos Monsiváis, 21–32. Durham, NC: Duke UP, 2006.

Vega, Patricia. "Elena Garro o la abolición del tiempo." In *Elena Garro: Lectura múltiple de una personalidad compleja*, ed. Lucía Melgar-Palacios and Gabriela Mora, 93–148. Puebla, Mexico: Benemérita Universidad Autónoma de Puebla, 2002.

Velázquez, Mario. "*Múltiples caras de Elena Garro*: Review of *Elena Garro: Lectura múltiple de una personalidad compleja*." *La crónica de hoy*, March 16, 2003. http://webcache

.googleusercontent.com/search?q=cache:faqASmWtMeUJ:www.cronica.com.mx
/nota.php%3Fid_nota%3D54461+M%C3%BAltiples+caras+de+Elena+Garro+%5D
&cd=1&hl=en&ct=clnk&gl=us&source=www.google.com.

Vidal, Gore. *The Selected Essays of Gore Vidal.* Ed. Jay Parini. New York: Doubleday, 2008.

Vollendorf, Lisa, ed. and introduction. *Recovering Spain's Feminist Tradition.* New York: Modern Language Association of America, 2001.

Volpi, Jorge. *La imaginación y el poder: Una historia intelectual de 1968.* Mexico City: Era, 1998.

Vosburg, Nancy. "The Tapestry of a Feminist Life: María Teresa León (1903–88)." In *Recovering Spain's Feminist Tradition,* 260–277. New York: Modern Language Association of America, 2001.

Wake, Eleanor. "Codex Tlaxcala: New Insights and New Questions." *Estudios de Cultura Náhuatl* 33 (2002): 91–140. http://www.ejournal.unam.mx.

Warner, Robin. "Persona as Propaganda: Neruda and the Spanish Civil War." In *European Socialist Realism,* 113–127. Oxford: Berg, 1988.

Weimer, Christopher Brian. "Sor Juana as Feminist Playwright: The Gracioso's Satiric Function in *Los empeños de una casa.*" *Latin American Theatre Review* 26.1 (1992): 91–98.

Williams, Susan. "Cultural Memory: How We See Ourselves as a People and Nation." April 25, 2003. http://www.iu.edu/~ocmhp/042503/text/memorywar.html.

Wilson, Jason. *Octavio Paz: A Study of His Poetics.* Cambridge: Cambridge UP, 1979.

Wing, George G. "Octavio Paz, or the Revolution in Search of an Actor." *Books Abroad* 47 (1973): 41–48.

Winkler, Julie A. "Elena Garro ante la Revolución Mexicana." In *Baúl de recuerdos: Homenaje a Elena Garro,* ed. Robert K. Anderson and Mara García, 35–46. Tlaxcala, Mexico: Universidad Autónoma de Tlaxcala, 1999.

———. "Insiders, Outsiders, and the Slippery Center: Marginality in *Los recuerdos del porvenir.*" *Indiana Journal of Hispanic Literatures* 8 (Spring 1996): 177–195.

———. *Light into Shadow: Marginality and Alienation in the Work of Elena Garro.* New York/Vienna: Peter Lang, 2001.

Womack, John. *Zapata and the Mexican Revolution.* New York: Knopf, 1969.

"Women in the Culture of Belief." July 6, 2005. World Humanist Congress 2005. http://www.iheu.org/node/1737.

Wood, Andrew Grant. "Death of a Political Prisoner: Revisiting the Case of Ricardo Flores Magón." *Contracorriente: A Journal of Social History and Literature in Latin America* 3.1 (2005): 38–66.

Woolf, Virginia. *A Room of One's Own* (1929). New York: Harcourt Brace and Company, 1989.

Wucker, Michele. "Distant Neighbor." *New York Times,* March 28, 2004. http://www.nytimes.com/2004/03/28/books/distant-neighbor.html?scp=1&sq=March%20 28,%202004%20fuentes&st=cse.

Yamamoto, Traise. "Different Silences." In *The Intimate Critique: Autobiographical Literary Criticism*, ed. Diane P. Freedman, Olivia Frey, and Frances Murphy Zauhar, 127–134. Durham, NC: Duke University Press, 1993.

Young, Dolly J. "Mexican Literary Reactions to Tlatelolco 1968." *Latin American Research Review* 20.2 (1985): 71–85.

Zaid, Gabriel. "Recuento de Octavio Paz." *Letras Libres* (April 2003): 48–50.

Zama, Patricia. "El robo intelectual." *El Buho* 4.38 (February 2003). http://www.renea vilesfabila.com.mx/universodeelbuho/38/38zama.htm.

Zamora, Lois Parkinson. *The Usable Past: The Imagination of History in Recent Fiction of the Americas*. Cambridge: Cambridge UP, 1997.

Zivley, Sherry Lutz. "The Conclusion of Azuela's *The Underdogs* and Hemingway's *For Whom the Bell Tolls*." *Hemingway Review* 17.2 (1998): 118–123.

INDEX

Bergamín, José, 83, 84, 86

Berman, Sabina, 18

Beucker, Verónica, 174, 204n25, 206n42

Bianco, José, 3, 163, 180n4

Bioy Casares, Adolfo, 3, 163, 167, 175, 180n4, 197n75, 205n27

Biron, Rebecca, 153, 179n2, 205n29

Bishop, Elizabeth, 4

Blackburn, Paul, 4

Bloom, Harold, 16–17

Bombal, María Luisa, 151

Borges, Jorge Luis, 88

Bosch, José, 95, 103–104, 111, 191n6

Boullosa, Carmen, 180n9

Bracho, Julio, 101

Breton, André, 113, 196n70

Buck, Sarah, 8

Burns, Archibald, 131, 163, 175

Butler, Judith, 39

Cabrera, Luis, 60

Calderón de la Barca, Pedro, 74, 155, 170

Callado, María, 135

Calleja, Father Diego, 155

Campbell, Joseph, 127

Campbell, Roy, 83

Campesino, Pilar, 137

Campobello, Nellie, 8, 51–52, 61, 75, 97, 176, 180n12, 186n6, 188n29. See also *Cartucho*

Campos Lemus, Sócrates Amado, 132, 134, 135, 200n30, 201n43

Candelaria, Cordelia, 31

canon, 47, 51, 66, 69, 72, 80, 83, 94, 97, 155, 162, 169, 186n6; Garro and, xi, 66–67, 75, 162; Paz and, 6, 14, 58, 76, 162, 191n14

Capa, Robert, 102

Carballido, Emilio, 3, 164

Carballo, Emanuel, 130, 131, 163–164, 166–167, 178

Cárdenas, Cuauhtémoc, 187n17

Cárdenas, Lázaro, 60, 87, 98, 187n17, 192n15

Cardoza y Aragón, Luis, 88

Carpentier, Alejo, 84, 88, 96, 101

Carranza, Venustiano, 51, 60, 65, 67, 195n50

Carrera Andrade, Jorge, 88

Carrington, Leonora, 133

Cartucho (Campobello), 8, 51, 75, 180n12, 186n6, 188n29

Castellanos, Rosario, x, 4, 13, 18, 121, 133, 134, 139, 159, 177, 180n9, 190n51, 204n24; and "Memorial de Tlatelolco," 120, 121, 122, 123, 124, 125, 127, 199n14

Castillo, Debra, 154

Castro, Fidel, 97

Castro-Gómez, Santiago, 6

Catholic Church, 68, 81, 155, 156, 184n44

Ceceña, José Luis, 133, 134

Cervantes, Miguel de, 108

Chamson, André, 84

Chávez Morado, José, 102

Chicanas, 18, 19, 30–31

Chile, 149

La Chingada, 27, 28, 29, 32, 33, 37, 59. See also La Malinche

chingadas, 1–2, 19, 27–28, 36, 47, 181n10

chingar, 28, 29, 30, 183n36

chingones, 19, 27, 46, 181n10, 184n40

Cohen, Deborah, 119, 126

Cohn, Carol, 107, 109

Colegio Imperial de Santa Cruz de Tlatelolco, 116, 197n2

Communists/communism, 86, 94, 102, 109, 110, 192n17; Garro's attitude toward, 101, 103, 104, 106, 135–136; Paz's attitude toward, 80, 97–98, 100, 111, 156; in the Spanish Civil War, 79, 191n7

Confederación Nacional del Trabajo (CNT; National Labor Confederation), 82

Conquest period in Mexico, 9, 13–48, 58, 69, 72, 116, 129, 138, 154, 176; in Ireneo Paz's *Amor y suplicio*, 98; and parallels with contemporary Mexico, 140

conquistadors. *See* Conquest period in Mexico

Consejo Nacional de Huelga (CNH; National Strike Council), 133, 142–143
Contemporáneos, 86, 92, 93, 96, 101, 105, 106, 195n46
Conteris, Hiber, 55–56, 57
Convention of Aguascalientes, 65
Coronel Urtecho, José, 88
Cortés, Eladio, 100
Cortés, Hernán, 9, 14, 15, 17, 19, 22–33, 36–38, 43–44, 46, 48, 51, 69, 75, 138, 183n27, 190n48
Cortés, Martín, 31–32, 181n3, 184n39
Cortés Tamayo, Ricardo, 85
Cowley, Malcolm, 84
Cristero Rebellion, 34, 35, 68, 71, 101, 138, 184n44
Cuauhtémoc, 23, 33, 116
Cuesta, Jorge, 86
Cuevas, José Luis, 132, 133
cultural memory, ix, x, 6–8, 11, 13–16, 34, 39–41, 66, 69, 94, 138, 177; Garro and, 66, 69, 80; La Malinche and the Conquest's influence on, 14, 41, 43, 44, 45, 69; the Mexican Revolution's influence on, 8–9, 51
Cypess, Sandra Messinger, 26, 35, 37, 42, 45, 124, 138, 175

Dauster, Frank, 68
Dawes, Greg, 111
de la Cabada, Juan, 102, 103, 105, 195n51
de la Selva, Salomón, 88
de Lauretis, Teresa, 171
Del Castillo, Adelaida, 19, 31, 183n29
del Paso, Fernando, 8, 120, 137
del Río, Marcela, 66
Díaz, Félix, 185n2
Díaz, Porfirio, 21, 49–50, 51, 52, 62, 63, 64, 194n38
Díaz del Castillo, Bernal, 13, 15, 17, 18, 20, 24, 25, 32, 34, 44
Díaz Ordaz, Gustavo, 118, 122, 131, 140, 198n8, 199n14, 200n30

Diego, Gerardo, 88
Domínguez, Christopher, 3, 165
Doña Marina. See La Malinche
Donini, Ambroglio, 84
Doremus, Anne, 9
Dos Passos, John, 83, 191n10
Dove, Patrick, 76
Doyle, Kate, 117, 198n5

Echeverría, Luis, 129, 164, 200n28, 202n2
Ehrenburg, Ilya, 84
Ejército Zapatista de Liberación Nacional (EZLN; Zapatista Army of National Liberation), 51, 60
Eliot, T. S., 145
Enloe, Cynthia, 107
Espinosa, Fernando, 56
Esquivel, Laura, 13, 16, 17, 180n12
Eve. See Adam and Eve paradigm
Excélsior, 129, 130, 133, 152, 202n2

Falangists (in the Spanish Civil War), 79, 81, 99, 103, 107, 108, 111
fascism/fascists, 79, 81, 107, 108, 111, 190–191n5
Felipe, León, 84, 88
Fell, Claude, 54, 56–57, 58
feminism/feminists, xi, 4, 7, 18, 46, 126, 154, 155, 156, 202n1, 203n6
Ferrocarriles Nacionales de México (National Railways of Mexico), 87
Feuchtwanger, Leon, 84
Figueroa Torres, Jesús, 26
First International Congress of Antifascist Writers for the Defense of Culture, 83, 90
Fischer, Louis, 84
Florescano, Enrique, 54
Flores Magón, Enrique, 63, 187n18
Flores Magón, Ricardo, 62, 63, 187n18
Fondo de Cultura Económica, 96, 131
Forster, E. M., 83
France, 62, 113

Franco, Francisco, 81, 87, 195n47
Franco, Jean, 72, 161
Frank, Waldo, 83
Franquistas/Francoists, 110, 119, 126
Frazier, Lessie Jo, 119, 126
Freud, Sigmund, 56
Fuentes, Carlos, 2, 8, 13, 30, 52, 70, 73, 119, 120, 140, 180n4, 183n36, 189n43, 204n24; and *The Death of Artemio Cruz*, 8, 30, 52, 73, 158, 183n36
Fuentes, Vilma, 137
Fuss, Diane, 39

Galván, Felipe, 137
Gambaro, Griselda, 4
Gamboa, Berta, 186n6
Gamboa, Fernando, 102
García Lorca, Federico, 86, 88, 89, 107
García Márquez, Gabriel, 68, 189n41
garden of Eden. *See* Adam and Eve paradigm
Garibay, Ángel María, 124
Garner, Shirley Nelson, 159
Garro, Elena: autobiographical elements in work of, xi, 11, 82, 135, 136, 137, 158, 160, 165, 166–167, 169, 170, 172–173, 191n8, 205n32; awards for, 152, 206n43; birth of, 52, 186n7; daughter Helena Paz's similarities to, 134; and daughter Helena's birth, 203n11; death of, x; divorce of, 5, 130, 152, 179n3, 202n3; exile of, from Mexico, x, 3, 129, 134–135, 138, 144, 146, 153, 159, 164–165, 178; fascination with, for other writers, 180n4; and gender roles and attitudes, 10–11, 72–73, 153, 158–162, 165–176, 203n6; influence of the Mexican Revolution on, 9, 61–76; influence of the Spanish Civil War on, 10, 82, 98–109, 178; life of, in Spain, 80, 98–108, 158; love affairs of, 163–164, 167, 175, 197n75; on the Malinche paradigm, 9, 35–48; marriage and subsequent

relationship of, to Paz, 3–4, 5, 79, 84, 158, 162, 176; Paz accused of victimizing, 203–204n15, 204n20; personality and behavior of, 5, 100, 135, 153, 158, 163, 165, 173; politics of, 100–101, 109, 113–114, 125, 130–132, 152, 162–163, 164, 177, 187–188n23; publishing silence of, 153, 165, 179n2, 203n4; on the topic of death, 74–75; on the topic of time, 71–72; on the topic of war, 109; translations of work of, xi, 4–5, 180n8; and the traumatic events following the Tlatelolco Massacre, 10, 129–136, 178, 201n34; trunk of manuscripts belonging to, 113, 126, 168, 199n16, 205n34; writings of that allude to Tlatelolco, 135–149, 187n19, 200n29
Garro, Elena, works by:
—*Andamos huyendo Lola* (We Are Fleeing Lola), 135, 146, 152, 160
—*Andarse por las ramas* (Beat about the Bush), 113, 159, 165, 166, 173, 180n5
—*La casa junto al río* (The House by the River), 10, 82, 169, 174
—"La culpa es de los tlaxcaltecas" (It's the Fault of the Tlaxcaltecas), ix, x, 1, 5, 9, 14, 17, 34, 35, 39, 40, 45, 70, 144
—"Decena Trágica" (Ten Tragic Days), 63
—*El encanto, tendajón mixto* (Enchantment: Five and Dime), 170
—*Felipe Ángeles*, 9, 50, 64, 65, 187n20
—*First Love & Look for My Obituary: Two Novellas*, 5, 153, 180n8
—*Un hogar sólido* (A Solid Home), x, 113, 130, 180n5
—*Inés*, 157, 159, 169
—*Memorias de España 1937* (Memories of Spain 1937), 5, 10, 82, 98, 103, 109, 110, 112, 158, 175, 190n1, 191n6
—*Mi hermanita Magdalena*, xi, 11, 144, 157, 158, 169, 170, 172, 174
—*La mudanza* (The Move), 159, 165
—"Nuestras vidas son los ríos" (Our Lives Are the Rivers), 73–75

Ibsen, Kristine, 173
India, 3, 56, 113, 122, 127, 134, 152, 156, 184n42
Indians. *See* indigenous peoples
indigenous peoples, 98, 185nn54,58; during the Conquest, 9, 43–47, 58, 116; Garro's views on the treatment of, 3, 71, 114, 130, 153, 162–163, 164, 165, 175, 177; and the Mexican Revolution, 59; Paz gives assistance to, 85
Iturbide, Agustín de, 49

Jaquette, Jane, 8
Jaramillo, Juan, 24, 25, 38, 39, 200n27
Jaramillo, Rubén, 130, 152, 162, 164
Jiménez, Juan Ramón, 88
Jiménez Rueda, Julio, 96
Johnson, David, 27
Josef, Bella, 56
Juana Inés de la Cruz, Sor, x, 33, 153–157, 163, 165, 170, 175, 176, 184n45

Kafka, Franz, 138, 142
Kaminsky, Amy, 41, 173
Katra, William, 32
Kemp, Lysander, 19, 55, 186n12
Kennedy, Robert, 115
Kent State shootings, 117
King, Martin Luther, Jr., 115
Kingston, Maxine Hong, 159
Kisch, Egon Erwin, 84
Koltsov, Mikhail, 84
Krauze, Enrique, 2, 52

Lagerlöf, Selma, 83
Lambie, George, 104
land redistribution. *See* agrarian reform
Lanyon, Anna, 31
Larson, Ross, 69
League of Nations, 87
Leal, Luis, 1–2, 31–32, 33, 119, 120, 121, 124, 186n10, 198n8
León, María Teresa, 83, 84, 98–99

León de la Barra, Francisco, 62–63
León-Portilla, Miguel, 116, 124, 197n3
lesbianism, 153, 171
Lévi-Strauss, Claude, 56
Lewis, Sinclair, 83
"ley de fuga" (law of flight), 64, 202n55
Lezama Lima, José, 88
Liberal Party (Mexico), 57, 63
Liga de Escritores y Artistas Revolucionarios de México (LEAR; League of Revolutionary Writers and Artists), 89, 102
Limon, John, 7, 151
La Llorona, 129, 199n23
López de Gómara, Francisco, 24
López Mateos, Adolfo, 163, 200n27
Lorde Audre, 159
Loyalists. *See* Republicans (in the Spanish Civil War)
Lozano de Paz, Josefina, 53, 98
Ludmer, Josefina, 161, 175

Machado, Antonio, 84, 88
machismo, x–xi, 5, 19, 32, 154, 190n51
Madero, Francisco I., 50, 51, 52, 54, 60, 62, 63, 64, 67, 77, 185n2, 185–186n4, 187nn18,21, 188n24, 194n38, 202n55
Madrazo, Carlos A., 73, 131, 132, 133, 135, 141, 144, 152, 163, 164, 200nn28,30, 204n19
magical realism, 41, 42, 68
La Malinche, ix, 1, 6, 13–48, 51, 55, 58, 59, 138, 154, 176, 184n46, 190n48; the Malinche paradigm, 9, 11, 14, 17, 18, 22, 34, 35, 37, 39, 40, 41, 47, 69, 177
malinchismo/malinchista, 17, 20, 22, 28, 156, 183n32
Malraux, André, 83, 84, 101, 109
Mancisidor, José, 84, 101
Mandrell, James, 70, 71
Mann, Heinrich, 83
Mann, Thomas, 83
Manrique, Jorge, 74
Manzoni, Celina, 100

Partido de la Revolución Mexicana (PRM; Party of the Mexican Revolution), 87. *See also* Partido Revolucionario Institucionalizado

Partido Obrero de Unificación Marxista (POUM; Workers' Party of Marxist Unification), 82, 111, 191n6

Partido Revolucionario Institucionalizado (PRI; Institutional Revolutionary Party), 55, 59, 60, 62, 73, 118, 127, 128, 131, 132, 141, 148, 152, 156, 164, 200nn28,30, 204n19

"La Pasionaria." *See* Ibárruri Gómez, Dolores

Pasternak, Boris, 83

Patria Nueva (New Homeland; political party), 164

patriarchy, x–xi, 106, 127, 173, 174; Garro's critiques of, 5, 11, 34, 35, 46, 77, 80, 82, 158, 166, 171, 175; Paz as a member of, 154, 173, 177. *See also* machismo

Paz, Ireneo, 14–15, 18, 50, 52, 53, 64, 85, 194nn37,38, 199n17; gender relations in, 22, 46; on La Malinche, 9, 20–26, 31, 32, 33–34, 35, 38–39, 41, 43, 44, 46, 47, 48. See also *Amor y suplicio*

Paz, Josefa de, 144, 174, 175, 204n20

Paz, Octavio: autobiographical works of, 66, 85; awards and recognition for, x, 1–2, 16, 152; birth and early life of, 52–53; death of, x; as a delegate to the Second International Congress of Antifascist Writers, 5, 80, 85–86, 89, 90; as a diplomat, 3, 113; divorce of, 130, 152, 179n3, 202n3; essays of, 4; exile of, from Mexico, 129; influence of the Mexican Revolution on, 9, 52–61, 76–77, 80, 178, 187n16; influence of the Spanish Civil War on, 10, 82, 92–98, 110–112, 178; on the Malinche paradigm, 9, 13–15, 16–18, 26–33, 36, 38, 39, 44, 47, 48; marriage of, to Garro, 3–4, 79, 84, 158, 162; and Neruda, 89–92; poetry of, 4, 82, 85–86, 87, 88–98, 121–122,

193n28; politics of, 100, 109–110, 111, 156, 178; renunciation of government position by, 3, 56, 127, 134; second marriage of, 3, 113, 127, 152, 176; silence of, on women's issues, 153–154, 162, 177; and Sor Juana, 11, 153–157, 175; on the topic of time, 71; on the Tlatelolco Massacre, 10, 121–122, 125–129, 178, 187n19; and *Vuelta*, 2, 30, 97, 129, 152, 202n2

Paz, Octavio, works by:
—*¿Águila o sol?* (Eagle or Sun?), 4, 191n14
—*El arco y la lira* (The Bow and the Lyre), 4
—*Bajo tu clara sombra* (Under Your Clear Shadow), 157
—*Barandal* (Balustrade), 86
—"Blanco," 122
—*The Collected Poems of Octavio Paz*, 4
—*Conjunctions and Disjunctions*, 54
—*Corriente alterna* (Alternating Current), 4, 54
—"El desarrollo y otros espejismos" (Development and Other Mirages), 127
—"Elegía a un joven muerto en Aragón" (Elegy to a Young Man Dead in Aragón), 82, 85, 98, 104, 191n6
—"Los hijos de la Malinche" (The Sons of Malinche), ix, 2, 9, 13, 14, 47, 184n40
—*Los hijos del limo: Del romanticismo a la vanguardia* (Children of the Mire), ix, 4
—"Homenaje a Sor Juana Inés de la Cruz en su tercer centenario" (Homage to Sor Juana on the Third Centenary of Her Birth), 154
—*Itinerario* (Itinerary), 10, 53, 85, 160
—*El laberinto de la soledad* (The Labyrinth of Solitude), 11, 16, 56, 59, 63, 113, 127, 128, 154–155, 157, 160, 168, 177, 183n28; on history, 54, 56, 66; importance of, 4, 19, 53, 55; on La Malinche, 2, 14, 17, 26, 27, 29, 35, 36, 48, 154; on the Mexican Revolution, 50, 54, 56–58, 59